With all my love
Happy B'day L.
11/92

FOUR VOYAGES TO THE NEW WORLD

This is an exact reprint, unaltered and unabridged of the famous selection of letters of Christopher Columbus with other original documents relating to his discoveries that was originally published in 1847, by the Hakluyt Society, translated and edited by R. H. Major. Only Mr. Major's Preface and Introduction have been omitted and a new Introduction by Professor Fagg has been added. A facsimile of the original title page appears facing the new title page.

SELECT

LETTERS

OF

CHRISTOPHER COLUMBUS,

WITH OTHER ORIGINAL DOCUMENTS,

RELATING TO HIS

FOUR VOYAGES

TO

THE NEW WORLD.

TRANSLATED AND EDITED BY

R. H. MAJOR, Esq.

OF THE BRITISH MUSEUM.

———

"Tu spiegherai, Colombo, a un novo polo
Lontane sì le fortunate antenne,
Ch'a pena seguirà con gli occhi il volo
La Fama c'ha mille occhi e mille penne.
Canti ella Alcide e Bacco, e di te solo
Basti ai posteri tuoi ch'alquanto accenne ;
Chè quel poco darà lunga memoria
Di poema degnissima e d'istoria.
Tasso.—Gerusalemme Liberata

LONDON:
PRINTED FOR THE HAKLUYT SOCIETY.

M.DCCC.XLVII.

CHRISTOPHER COLUMBUS

Four Voyages to the New World

LETTERS and SELECTED DOCUMENTS

Bi-lingual Edition

Translated and Edited by R. H. Major

Introduction by John E. Fagg

A CITADEL PRESS BOOK
Published by Carol Publishing Group

First Carol Publishing Group edition 1992

Copyright © 1961 by Corinth Books Inc.

A Citadel Press Book
Published by Carol Publishing Group
Citadel Press is a registered trademark of Carol Communications, Inc.

Editorial offices: 600 Madison Avenue, New York, N.Y. 10022
Sales & Distribution Offices: 120 Enterprise Avenue, Secaucus, N.J. 07094

In Canada: Canadian Manda Group
P.O. Box 920, Station U
Toronto, Ontario M8Z 5P9

All rights reserved. No part of this book may be reproduced
in any form, except by a newspaper or magazine reviewer
who wishes to quote brief passages in connection with a review.

Queries regarding rights and permissions
should be addressed to Carol Publishing Group
600 Madison Avenue, New York, N.Y. 10022

Manufactured in the United States of America
ISBN 0-8065-1337-3

10 9 8 7 6 5 4 3 2 1

Carol Publishing Group books are available at special discounts
for bulk purchases, for sales promotions, fund raising, or
educational purposes. Special editions can be created to
specifications. For details contact: Special Sales Department,
Carol Publishing Group, 120 Enterprise Avenue, Secaucus, N.J. 07094

Cataloging data for this title is available from
the Library of Congress.

INTRODUCTION

The discovery of the American continents by western European sailors would likely have taken place around the beginning of the sixteenth century even had Christopher Columbus not undertaken his epochal voyage of 1492. Europe's need for a better route to the Far East, the increased nautical activities of the Atlantic kingdoms, and the improved techniques for deep-water sailing made it inevitable that the land mass of the New World would sooner or later have been encountered. Already the Vikings had landed in North America about the year 1000. For several generations there had been visits and even settlements by these barbarians until contact was lost without significant results. Many Portuguese fervently maintain today that seamen of their nationality landed in the western hemisphere prior to 1492. Reasonable as this contention is, it is supported by no proof whatever. Other claims of previous discoveries by Africans, Asians, or various Europeans must be discounted for the same reason. Columbus cannot be robbed of his title of the Discoverer of America. Since his first voyage Europe and the Americans have been constantly linked, with consequences so large they defy measurement. Nothing to parallel this event may be known until human beings make a round trip to another planet. Moreover, the historical accident that Columbus sailed for Castile opened an astonishing period of imperialism that would stamp the special character of Spain, together with its language, religion, and culture, on a major portion of the Americas. And many of the institu-

tions of the long-lived Spanish empire had their origins in the experiences of the Discoverer in his role as colonizer.

As men have always been impressed by the splendor of Columbus' achievement, so have they been fascinated by his career: the rise from obscurity, his mystical attachment to an idea that was both wrong and right, his defeat in victory. Because he made numerous misleading statements about his early life Columbus has often been regarded as a man of mystery. He was probably born in Genoa in 1451 of a humble family. He went to sea and developed the skills that made him a great navigator and commander. In 1476 he was stranded in Portugal after a sea fight. Although he was a foreigner, presumably poor and ill-educated, he soon married into the lower Portuguese nobility and became a prosperous merchant and shipmaster, making voyages down the western coast of Africa and perhaps to Iceland. Columbus must have been highly intelligent and very impressive, and at this stage fortune favored him.

During his years in Portugal he became obsessed with the idea of sailing west from Lisbon to the Far East, a possibility that had occurred to other imaginative men. After buttressing this theory with prophecies from many writers, most of them ancient, he presented his project to the king of Portugal in 1484. That monarch seriously considered the enterprise but finally rejected it on the correct grounds that Asia was more than twice as distant as Columbus had represented it to be. More than ever convinced he had an inspired mission, the Genoese went to Spain in 1485, where for almost seven years he pressed his project on Ferdinand and Isabella. After many fluctuations his cause seemed lost early in 1492 with a definite refusal. Then the queen changed her mind, and with the acquiesence of the king, recalled Columbus. The royal pair signed an agreement to support an expedition across the Atlantic. If he succeeded, Columbus was to become an admiral and viceroy and governor of the newly discovered lands. Also, he and his heirs were to enjoy one-tenth of

the profits derived from such territories. While the pact did not name Asia as his destination, his passport mentioned India and he carried a letter to the (non-existent) Grand Khan. On August 3, 1492, the fleet of three caravels, the *Santa María, Pinta,* and *Niña,* and ninety men sailed from Palos.

The famous Letter on the First Voyage reproduced herein was probably written in the Azores in February 1493 and sent from Lisbon in March. It is Columbus' first report to the world of his achievement. Not, as it would appear, addressed to Sanchez, who must have had it reproduced by command of the monarchs, this letter was apparently enclosed with another that has been lost, one dispatched by Columbus to Ferdinand and Isabella. The original of our letter has also disappeared, though eight early copies are extant. In 1847, when R. H. Major edited this selection of documents for the Hakluyt Society, he relied on Martín Fernández de Navarrete's invaluable collection.* Much later, the Hakluyt Society issued a similar publication but, in the case of the Letter on the First Voyage, was able to use a more accurate text based on a folio unknown to Major.†

Columbus offers only a brief summary of the historic voyage that took him to the Bahamas, Cuba, and Hispaniola. He affirms that he has been in the waters of India and refers to the proximity of Cathay. His reticence on nautical and geographical data stems from a wise determination not to enlighten foreigners. His descriptions of the natives as generous, timid, and willing to be converted may be said to have inspired both the myth of

* *Colección de los Viages y Descubrimientos que hicieron por mar los Españoles desde fines de siglo XV.* Madrid, 1825 (3 vols.)

† Cecil Jane, tr. and ed. *Select documents illustrating the Four Voyages of Columbus, including those contained in R. H. Major's Select Letters of Christopher Columbus.* The Hakluyt Society, London, 1930-32 (2 vols.)

the noble savage and the extensive missionary program that brought Christianity into the New World. Columbus is vague, even deceptive, about the ship and men he left in Haiti, omitting to state that the *Santa María* was wrecked. His reports of the gold, cotton, spices, and other riches would soon prove absurdly extravagant. Yet his letter accomplished its purpose. He received a hero's welcome in Spain and won the attention of educated men abroad. Ferdinand and Isabella received him with effusive cordiality, confirmed his titles, and lavishly supported his next expedition.

Columbus remained in Spain only six months, probably the most gratifying period of his life. Few doubted his claim to have reached the Indies. On September 25, 1493, he left Cadiz with seventeen vessels and twelve hundred or more men to establish a permanent settlement. Our accounts come from the fleet's physician, Dr. Diego Alvarez Chanca, and from a memorandum of January 30, 1494 by Columbus to the Catholic Kings carried by Antonio de Torres. These documents cover only the first months of the Second Voyage, when the Admiral led his expedition with marvelous skill to Dominica, after which he discovered other islands of the Lesser Antilles, the Virgin Islands, and Puerto Rico before returning to the harbor in northern Haiti where he had left the wreckage and crew of the *Santa María* a year before. In their first landings the Spaniards encountered the cannibalistic Caribs, natives who were very different from the gentle Arawakans on Cuba and Hispaniola.

Dr. Chanca conveys the dismay and confusion of the party when it was learned that the men who stayed behind had all been massacred by the Indians. A new settlement had to be established, Isabela, on the northern coast of the present Dominican Republic. The problems that would plague the colonists in the near future—native hostility, sickness, food shortages, and ungovernable Spaniards—appear in these accounts in their preliminary form.

Again, Columbus misrepresents the wealth of the region while apologizing for the small treasure he sends back with this memorandum. Necessarily, our documents do not treat the disappointments of the remainder of the Second Voyage. Columbus explored the coast of Cuba and discovered Jamaica but failed to locate the Far Eastern potentates he supposed to be near. Both Spaniards and Indians died off at a fearful rate. No great riches appeared. A native rebellion failed and led to dreadful oppressions. Columbus started the slave trade mentioned in the Torres memorial, much to the indignation of Queen Isabella. On June 11, he returned to Cadiz, having failed to create a profitable or even an orderly colony.

Our documents on the Third Voyage cover the beginning and the end of that disastrous affair. With his small fleet and crew of convicts the Admiral sailed on May 30, 1498, far to the south and then across the Atlantic to South America, which he discovered. His letter is repetitious and wandering, unconsciously supporting his complaints of sickness and mental depression. The effusions about the terrestrial paradise aroused neither interest nor credence. Columbus' inability to locate the sources of the pearls he mentions was an omission others would exploit. His letter throws no light on the most urgent problem, the rebellion of the Spanish settlers in Hispaniola. The next communication does, however. Written toward the end of 1500, after he had been relieved of his post and placed in chains for return to Spain, his letter to Doña Juana de la Torre, a sympathetic lady of the court, is a model of Christian resignation in the face of injustice. The fallen viceroy describes some of his difficulties in ruling the colony and the brutal manner in which a royal official ousted him. At length the Catholic Kings consoled Columbus, almost apologized to him, but they declined to restore him to his posts.

The Letter on the Fourth Voyage, written in Jamaica in July 1503, is also pathetic though dignified. In the only

known writing by the Admiral of this odyssey of suffering, which began on May 9, 1502 and ended on November 7, 1504, he tells of the hurricane at Santo Domingo that killed some of his worst persecutors, the fruitless explorations of the Central American coasts, and his marooning in Jamaica. Columbus tragically failed to pursue hints of Maya civilization and rumors of the vast ocean on the other side of the isthmus. Instead, he persisted in his delusions about the nearness of the Ganges, Cathay, and King Solomon's mines. Further details of this final voyage are supplied by Diego Méndez in his testament of June 26, 1536. It was Méndez who saw to it that Columbus was rescued after months of pain and danger in Jamaica. The Discoverer eventually returned to Spain, broken in health and defeated, wealthy but discredited. He died on May 20, 1506.

John E. Fagg
New York University

SELECT LETTERS

OF

CHRISTOPHER COLUMBUS.

ETC.

EDITOR'S PREFACE.

Should the reader of the following highly interesting letters meet with some passages deficient in that ease of expression, or that connectedness of construction to which his ear and his taste are accustomed, he is requested to bear in mind that the originals are the compositions of men, who, though intelligent observers of the facts they describe, and strongly actuated by the feelings to which they give expression, were yet far from being accomplished masters of the use of the pen.

The Spanish scholar will readily perceive that the inaccuracies of the original, both in spelling and grammar, the frequent use of obsolete words, and the disjointed character of the sentences, must have rendered it a matter of no inconsiderable difficulty to avoid a certain harshness of style, in the endeavour to give a correct version of the author's meaning. In the execution of his task, however, the Editor has

never hesitated to sacrifice ease to accuracy, where the two were incompatible with each other.

Since writing the following introduction to these letters, the Editor has seen those passages in *Kosmos* which refer to Columbus and to the antecedent voyages to the New World, and is happy to find the remarks of the illustrious Humboldt in this latter work in no way contradictory to the statements in the *Géographie du nouveau Continent*, to which the Editor has been indebted in the progress of the following pages.

R. H. M.

FIRST VOYAGE OF COLUMBUS.

*A Letter addressed to the noble Lord Raphael Sanchez,
Treasurer to their most invincible Majesties, Ferdinand
and Isabella, King and Queen of Spain, by Christopher
Columbus, to whom our age is greatly indebted, treating
of the islands of India recently discovered beyond the
Ganges, to explore which he had been sent eight months
before under the auspices and at the expense of their said
Majesties.*

KNOWING that it will afford you pleasure to learn that I have
brought my undertaking to a successful termination, I have
decided upon writing you this letter to acquaint you with all
the events which have occurred in my voyage, and the discoveries which have resulted from it.   Thirty-three days after

---

EPISTOLA CHRISTOFORI COLOM.

*Cui ætas nostra multum debet, de Insulis Indiæ supra Gangem nuper
inventis, ad quas perquirendas, octavo antea mense, auspiciis et
ære invictissimorum Ferdinandi ac Elizabeth Hispaniarum Regum, missus fuerat: ad magnificum Dominum Raphaelem
Sanxis, eorumdem Serenissimorum Regum Thesaurarium, missa:
quam generosus ac litteratus vir Leander de Cosco ab hispano
idiomate in latinum convertit: tertio Kalendas Maii,* MCCCCXCIII, *
Pontificatus Alex.* VI, *anno* I.

QUONIAM susceptæ provinciæ rem perfectam me consecutum fuisse
gratum tibi fore scio, has constitui exarare, quæ te uniuscujusque
rei in hoc nostro itinere gestæ inventæque admoneant.   Tricesimo
tertio die postquam Gadibus discessi, in mare indicum perveni, ubi

my departure from Cadiz[1] I reached the Indian sea, where I discovered many islands, thickly peopled, of which I took possession without resistance in the name of our most illustrious Monarch, by public proclamation and with unfurled banners. To the first of these islands, which is called by the Indians Guanahani, I gave the name of the blessed Saviour (San Salvador), relying upon whose protection I had reached this as well as the other islands; to each of these I also gave a name, ordering that one should be called Santa Maria de la Concepcion,[2] another Fernandina,[3] the third Isabella,[4] the fourth Juana,[5] and so with all the rest respectively. As soon as we arrived at that, which as I have said was named Juana, I

———————

plurimas insulas innumeris habitatas hominibus reperi, quarum omnium pro felicissimo Rege nostro, præconio celebrato, et vexillis extensis, contradicente nemine, possessionem accepi : primæque earum Divi Salvatoris nomen imposui, cujus fretus auxilio tam ad hanc quam ad ceteras alias pervenimus ; eam vero Indi Guanahanyn vocant.   Aliarum etiam unamquamque novo nomine nuncupavi : quippe aliam insulam Sanctæ Mariæ Conceptionis, aliam Fernandinam, aliam Isabelam, aliam Joannam, et sic de reliquis appellari jussi. Quamprimum in eam insulam (quam dudum Joannam vocari

[1] A strange mistake has crept into the Latin versions of this letter; in all the editions of which it is stated that Cadiz was the point from which Columbus sailed on his first voyage.   In the journal of that voyage, published by Mr. Navarrete, as well as in the accounts given by Don Fernando Columbus, and all other historians, it is distinctly said that he sailed from *Palos*, on the third of August.   The question is important, not simply as affecting the correctness of the letter, but also the length of time in which the voyage was accomplished ; for as Columbus reached the island of St. Salvador, or Guanahani, on the morning of the twelfth of October, it is apparent, that more than twice the number of days here mentioned, transpired between his leaving Spain and arriving at the West Indies.   The mistake evidently consists in the word " Gadibus" having been by some circumstance, at which we can only guess, carelessly exchanged for Gomera, whence Columbus started, according to the journal, on the eighth of September, which leaves an interval exactly coinciding with the thirty-three days here mentioned.

[2] North Caico.   [3] Little Inagua.   [4] Great Inagua.   [5] Cuba.

proceeded along its coast a short distance westward, and found
it to be so large and apparently without termination, that I
could not suppose it to be an island, but the continental province of Cathay. Seeing, however, no towns or populous places
on the sea coast, but only a few detached houses and cottages,
with whose inhabitants I was unable to communicate, because
they fled as soon as they saw us, I went further on, thinking
that in my progress I should certainly find some city or village. At length, after proceeding a great way and finding that
nothing new presented itself, and that the line of coast was
leading us northwards (which I wished to avoid, because it
was winter, and it was my intention to move southwards; and
because moreover the winds were contrary), I resolved not
to attempt any further progress, but rather to turn back and
retrace my course to a certain bay that I had observed, and
from which I afterwards dispatched two of our men to ascertain whether there were a king or any cities in that province.
These men reconnoitred the country for three days, and found
a most numerous population, and great numbers of houses,
though small, and built without any regard to order : with

---

dixi) appulimus ; juxta ejus litus occidentem versus aliquantulum
processi, tamque eam magnam nullo reperto fine inveni, ut non
insulam sed continentem Cathai provinciam esse crediderim ; nulla
tamen videns oppida, municipiave in maritimis sita confinibus,
præter aliquos vicos et prædia rustica, cum quorum incolis loqui
nequibam ; quare simul ac nos videbant, surripiebant fugam. Pro-
grediebar ultra, existimans aliquam me urbem villasve inventurum:
denique videns quod longe admodum progressis nihil novi emerge-
bat, et hujusmodi via nos ad septentrionem deferebat (quod ipse
fugere exoptabam, terris etenim regnabat bruma), ad austrumque
erat in voto contendere, nec minus venti flagitantibus succedebant;
constitui alios non operiri successus : et sic retrocedens, ad portum
quemdam, quem signaveram, sum reversus ; unde duos homines ex
nostros in terram missi, qui investigarent, esset ne Rex in ea provincia, urbesve aliquæ. Hi per tres dies ambularunt, invenerunt-
que innumeros populos et habitationes, parvas tamen et absque ullo

which information they returned to us.   In the mean time
I had learned from some Indians whom I had seized, that that
country was certainly an island: and therefore I sailed towards
the east, coasting to the distance of three hundred and twenty-
two miles, which brought us to the extremity of it; from this
point I saw lying eastwards another island, fifty-four miles distant from Juana, to which I gave the name of Española:[6] I went
thither, and steered my course eastward as I had done at
Juana, even to the distance of five hundred and sixty-four
miles along the north coast.[7]   This said island of Juana is
exceedingly fertile, as indeed are all the others; it is surrounded with many bays, spacious, very secure, and surpass-
ing any that I have ever seen; numerous large and healthful

---

regimine ; quapropter redierunt.   Interea ego jam intellexeram à
quibusdam Indis, quos ibidem susceperam, quod hujusmodi provincia insula quidem erat : et sic perrexi orientem versus, ejus semper
stringens litora, usque ad milliaria cccxxii, ubi ipsius insulæ sunt
extrema.   Hinc aliam insulam ad orientem prospexi, distantem ab
hac Joanna milliar.   liv, quam protinus Hispanam dixi, in eamque
concessi, et direxi iter quasi per septentrionem, quemadmodum in
Joanna ad orientem, milliaria dlxiv.   Quæ dicta Joanna et aliæ
ibidem insulæ quam fertilissimæ exsistunt.   Hæc multis atque
tutissimis et latis, nec aliis quos unquam viderim comparandis por-
tibus est circumdata : multi maximi et salubres hanc interfluunt

[6] Hispaniola, or San Domingo.

[7] Naverrete, the learned and industrious compiler of these original letters, in his translation of this first letter from the Latin into the Spanish
language, has mistakenly attributed to the preposition "per" the sense of
the Spanish word "hacia" (towards), a meaning which can under no circumstances be given to the word, but in this case renders the passage
unintelligible.   The editor has translated "per septentrionem" "along the
north coast" of the island, such a rendering of the preposition being per-
fectly grammatical, while it gives to the whole sentence a meaning con-
sistent with the course which Columbus in reality took.   There are,
moreover, two sentences in the immediate context of the original, where,
when the sense of "towards" is intended to be expressed, it is unmistake-
ably given by the words "versus" and "ad".

rivers intersect it, and it also contains many very lofty mountains. All these islands are very beautiful, and distinguished by a diversity of scenery; they are filled with a great variety of trees of immense height, and which I believe to retain their foliage in all seasons; for when I saw them they were as verdant and luxuriant as they usually are in Spain in the month of May,—some of them were blossoming, some bearing fruit, and all flourishing in the greatest perfection, according to their respective stages of growth, and the nature and quality of each : yet the islands are not so thickly wooded as to be impassable. The nightingale and various birds were singing in countless numbers, and that in November, the month in which I arrived there. There are besides in the same island of Juana seven or eight kinds of palm trees, which, like all the other trees, herbs, and fruits, considerably surpass ours in height and beauty. The pines also are very handsome, and there are very extensive fields and meadows, a variety of birds, different kinds of honey, and many sorts of metals, but no iron. In that island also which I have before said we named Española, there are mountains of very great size and beauty, vast plains, groves, and very fruitful fields, admirably adapted

---

fluvii : multi quoque et eminentissimi in ea sunt montes. Omnes hæ insulæ sunt pulcherrimæ, et variis distinctæ figuris, perviæ, et maximâ arborum varietate sidera lambentium plenæ, quas nunquam foliis privari credo : quippe vidi eas ita virentes atque decoras, ceu mense Maio in Hispania solent esse ; quarum aliæ florentes, aliæ fructuosæ, aliæ in alio statu, secundum uniuscujusque qualitatem vigebant. Garriebat philomela, et alii passeres varii ac innumeri, mense Novembri, quo ipse per eas deambulabam. Sunt præterea in dicta insula Joanna septem vel octo palmarum genera, quæ proceritate et pulchritudine, quemadmodum ceteræ omnes arbores, herbæ fructusque, nostras facile exsuperant. Sunt et mirabiles pinus, agri, et prata vastissima, variæ aves, varia mella, variaque metalla, ferro excepto. In ea autem, quam Hispanam supra diximus nuncupari, maximi sunt montes ac pulchri, vasta rura, nemora, campi feracissimi, seri pascique et condendis ædificiis aptissimi :

for tillage, pasture, and habitation. The convenience and excellence of the harbours in this island, and the abundance of the rivers, so indispensable to the health of man, surpass anything that would be believed by one who had not seen it. The trees, herbage, and fruits of Española are very different from those of Juana, and moreover it abounds in various kinds of spices, gold, and other metals. The inhabitants of both sexes in this island, and in all the others which I have seen, or of which I have received information, go always naked as they were born, with the exception of some of the women, who use the covering of a leaf, or small bough, or an apron of cotton which they prepare for that purpose. None of them, as I have already said, are possessed of any iron, neither have they weapons, being unacquainted with, and indeed incompetent to use them, not from any deformity of body (for they are well-formed), but because they are timid and full of fear. They carry however in lieu of arms, canes dried in the sun, on the ends of which they fix heads of dried wood sharpened to a point, and even these they dare not use habitually; for it has often occurred when I have sent two or three

---

portuum in hac insula commoditas et præstantia, fluminum copia, salubritate admixta hominum, quod, nisi quis viderit, credulitatem superat. Hujus arbores, pascua et fructus multum ab illis Joannæ differunt. Hæc præterea Hispana diverso aromatis genere, auro metallisque abundat. Hujus quidem et omnium aliarum, quas ego vidi et quarum cognitionem habeo, incolæ utriusque sexûs nudi semper incedunt, quemadmodum eduntur in lucem ; præter aliquas feminas, quæ folio frondeve aliqua aut bombycino velo pudenda operiunt quod ipsæ sibi ad id negotii parant. Carent hi omnes (ut supra dixi) quocumque genere ferri : carent et armis, utpote sibi ignotis, nec ad eas sunt apti, non propter corporis deformitatem (quum sint bene formati), sed quia sunt timidi ac pleni formidine ; gestant tamen pro armis arundines sole perustas, in quarum radicibus hastile quoddam ligneum siccum et in mucronem attenuatum figunt, neque his audent jugiter uti : nam sæpe evenit, quum miserim duos vel tres homines ex meis ad aliquas villas, ut cum eorum

of my men to any of the villages to speak with the natives, that they have come out in a disorderly troop, and have fled in such haste at the approach of our men, that the fathers forsook their children and the children their fathers. This timidity did not arise from any loss or injury that they had received from ůs; for, on the contrary, I gave to all I approached whatever articles I had about me, such as cloth and many other things, taking nothing of theirs in return: but they are naturally timid and fearful. As soon however as they see that they are safe, and have laid aside all fear, they are very simple and honest, and exceedingly liberal with all they have; none of them refusing any thing he may possess when he is asked for it, but on the contrary inviting us to ask them. They exhibit great love towards all others in preference to themselves : they also give objects of great value for trifles, and content themselves with very little or nothing in return. I however forbad that these trifles and articles of no value (such as pieces of dishes, plates, and glass, keys, and leather straps) should be given to them, although if they could obtain them, they imagined themselves to be possessed of the most beautiful trinkets in the world. It even happened that a sailor

---

loquerentur incolis, exisse agmen glomeratum ex Indis, et ubi nostros appropinquare videbant, fugam celeriter arripuisse, despretis à patre liberis, et è contra ; et hoc non quod cuipiam eorum damnum aliquod vel injuria illata fuerit, immo ad quoscumque appuli, et quibuscum verbum facere potui, quidquid habebam sum elargitus pannum aliaque permulta, nulla mihi facta versura ; sed sunt naturâ pavidi ac timidi. Ceterum ubi se cernunt tutos omni metu repulso, sunt admodum simplices ac bonæ fidei, et in omnibus quæ habent liberalissimi : roganti quod possidet inficiatur nemo, quin ipsi nos ad id poscendum invitant. Maximum erga omnes amorem præ se ferunt: dant quæque magna pro parvis, minima licet re nihilove contenti. Ego attamen prohibui, ne tam minima et nullius pretii hisce darentur, ut sunt lancis, paropsidum vitrique fragmenta: item clavi, lingulæ ; quamquam si hoc poterant adipisci, videbatur eis pulcherrima mundi possidere jocalia. Accidit enim quemdam

received for a leather strap as much gold as was worth three
golden nobles, and for things of more trifling value offered
by our men, especially-newly coined blancas, or any gold
coins, the Indians would give whatever the seller required;
as, for instance, an ounce and a half or two ounces of gold, or
thirty or forty pounds of cotton, with which commodity they
were already acquainted. Thus they bartered, like idiots, cotton
and gold for fragments of bows, glasses, bottles, and jars;
which I forbad as being unjust, and myself gave them many
beautiful and acceptable articles which I had brought with me,
taking nothing from them in return; I did this in order that
I might the more easily conciliate them, that they might be
led to become Christians, and be inclined to entertain a regard
for the King and Queen, our Princes and all Spaniards, and
that I might induce them to take an interest in seeking out,
and collecting, and delivering to us such things as they possessed in abundance, but which we greatly needed. They
practise no kind of idolatry, but have a firm belief that all
strength and power, and indeed all good things, are in heaven,
and that I had descended from thence with these ships and
sailors, and under this impression was I received after they

---

navitam tantum auri pondus habuisse pro una ligula, quanti sunt
tres aurei solidi, et sic alios pro aliis minoris pretii, præsertim pro
blanquis novis, et quibusdam nummis aureis, pro quibus habendis
dabant quicquid petebat venditor, puta unciam cum dimidia et duas
auri: vel triginta et quadraginta bombycis pondo, quod ipsi jam
noverant.   Item arcuum, amphoræ, hydriæ, doliique fragmenta
bombyci et auro tamquam bestiæ comparabant; quod quia iniquum
sane erat, vetui, dedique eis multa pulchra et grata, quæ mecum
tuleram, nullo interveniente præmio, ut eos mihi facilius concilia-
rem, fierentque Christicolæ, et ut sint proni in amorem erga Regem,
Reginam Principesque nostros, et universas gentes Hispaniæ, ac
studeant perquirere et coacervare, eaque nobis tradere quibus ipsi
affluunt et nos magnopere indigemus.   Nullam hi norunt idololat-
triam, immo firmissimè credunt omnem vim, omnem potentiam,
omnia denique bona esse in cœlo, meque inde cum his navibus et

had thrown aside their fears. Nor are they slow or stupid, but of very clear understanding; and those men who have crossed to the neighbouring islands give an admirable description of everything they observed; but they never saw any people clothed, nor any ships like ours. On my arrival at that sea, I had taken some Indians by force from the first island that I came to, in order that they might learn our language, and communicate to us what they knew respecting the country; which plan succeeded excellently, and was a great advantage to us, for in a short time, either by gestures and signs, or by words, we were enabled to understand each other. These men are still travelling with me, and although they have been with us now a long time, they continue to entertain the idea that I have descended from heaven; and on our arrival at any new place they published this, crying out immediately with a loud voice to the other Indians, "Come, come and look upon beings of a celestial race": upon which both women and men, children and adults, young men and old, when they got rid of the fear they at first entertained, would come out in throngs, crowding the roads to see us,

---

nautis descendisse; atque hoc animo ibi fui susceptus postquam metum repulerant. Nec sunt segnes aut rudes, quin summi ac perspicacis ingenii; et homines, qui transfretant mare illud, non sine admiratione uniuscujusque rei rationem reddunt; sed nunquam viderunt gentes vestitas, neque naves hujusmodi. Ego statim ac ad mare illud perveni, é prima insula quosdam Indos violenter arripui, qui ediscerent à nobis, et nos pariter docerent ea quorum ipsi in hisce partibus cognitionem habebant, et ex voto successit: nam brevi nos ipsos, et hi nos, tum gestu ac signis, tum verbis intellexerunt, magnoque nobis fuere emolumento. Veniunt modo mecum, tamen qui semper putant me desiluisse è cœlo, quamvis diu nobiscum versati fuerint, hodieque versentur, et hi erant primi, qui id quocumque appellebamus nunciabant, alii deinceps aliis elata voce dicentes, Venite, venite, et videbitis gentes æthereas. Quamobrem tam feminæ quam viri tam impuberes quam adulti, tam juvenes quam senes, deposita formidine paulo ante concepta, nos certatim visebant magna iter

some bringing food, others drink, with astonishing affection
and kindness.   Each of these islands has a great number of
canoes, built of solid wood, narrow and not unlike our double-
banked boats in length and shape, but swifter in their motion:
they steer them only by the oar.   These canoes are of various
sizes, but the greater number are constructed with eighteen
banks of oars, and with these they cross to the other islands,
which are of countless number, to carry on traffic with the
people.   I saw some of these canoes that held as many as
seventy-eight rowers.   In all these islands there is no difference of physiognomy, of manners, or of language, but they
all clearly understand each other, a circumstance very propitious for the realization of what I conceive to be the principal
wish of our most serene King, namely, the conversion of these
people to the holy faith of Christ, to which indeed, as far as I
can judge, they are very favourable and well-disposed.   I said
before, that I went three hundred and twenty-two miles in a
direct line from west to east, along the coast of the island of

stipante caterva, aliis cibum, aliis potum afferentibus, maximo cum
amore ac benevolentia incredibili.   Habet unaquæque insula multas
scaphas solidi ligni, etsi angustas, longitudine tamen ac forma nostris biremibus similes, cursu autem velociores : reguntur remis tantum modo.   Harum quædam sunt magnæ, quædam parvæ, quædam
in medio consistunt: plures tamen biremi qua remigent duo-
deviginti transtris majores, cum quibus in omnes illas insulas quæ
innumeræ sunt trajicitur, cumque his suam mercaturam exercent,
et inter eos commercia fiunt.   Aliquas ego harum biremium seu
scapharum vidi, quæ vehebant septuaginta et octoginta remiges.   In
omnibus his insulis nulla est diversitas inter gentis effigies, nulla in
moribus atque loquela, quin omnes se intelligunt adinvicem, quæ res
perutilis est ad id quod Serenissimum Regem nostrum exoptare
præcipué reor, scilicet eorum ad sanctam Christi fidem conversionem,
cui quidem, quantum intelligere potui, facillimi sunt et proni.   Dixi
quemadmodum sum progressus antea insulam Joannam per rectum
tramitem occassus in orientem milliar. cccxxii.   Secundum quam
viam et intervallum itineris possum dicere hanc Joannam esse ma-

Juana;[8] judging by which voyage, and the length of the passage, I can assert that it is larger than England and Scotland united; for independent of the said three hundred and twenty-two miles, there are in the western part of the island two provinces which I did not visit; one of these is called by the Indians Anam, and its inhabitants are born with tails. These provinces extend to a hundred and fifty-three miles in length, as I have learnt from the Indians whom I have brought with me, and who are well acquainted with the country. But the extent of Española is greater than all Spain from Catalonia to Fontarabia, which is easily proved, because one of its four sides which I myself coasted in a direct line, from west to east, measures five hundred and forty miles. This island is to

---

jorem Anglia et Scotia simul : namque ultra dicta cccxxii milliaria in ea parte quæ ad occidentem prospectat duæ, quas non petii, supersunt provinciæ, quarum alteram Indi Anam vocant, cujus accolæ caudati nascuntur.   Tenduntur in longitudinem ad milliaria cliii, ut ab his quos veho mecum Indis percepi, qui omnes has callent insulas.   Hispanæ vero ambitus major est tota Hispania a Cologna usque ad Fontem Rabidum ; hincque facile arguitur, quod quartum ejus latus, quod ipse per rectam lineam occidentis in orientem trajeci, milliaria continet dxl.   Hæc insula est affectanda, et affectata,

---

8 Here a somewhat similar mistake to that which occurred in page four has been made by Navarrete, in his translation from the Latin ; the accusative "insulam Joannam" comes after the neuter verb "progressus sum" without the intervention of a preposition ; but it is evident from the sense that the missing word was intended to express that Columbus proceeded *along* the island ; whereas Navarrete has translated it thus: " He dicho que anduve en recta direccion de poniente a oriente trescientas veinte y dos millas para llegar a la isla Juanna." *Anglice.* " I have said that I proceeded three hundred and twenty-two miles in a straight line from west to east *to arrive at* the island of Juana," a mode of proceeding which was in the first place geographically impossible, and in the next place would destroy the basis upon which Columbus founds his estimate of the size of the island, when compared with England and Scotland. There is no doubt that " per" is the preposition understood, while Mr. Navarrete has incautiously adopted " versus" instead of it.

be regarded with especial interest, and not to be slighted; for
although as I have said I took possession of all these islands
in the name of our invincible King, and the government of
them is unreservedly committed to his said Majesty, yet there
was one large town in Española of which especially I took
possession, situated in a remarkably favourable spot, and in
every way convenient for the purposes of gain and commerce.
To this town I gave the name of Navidad del Señor, and
ordered a fortress to be built there, which must by this time
be completed, in which I left as many men as I thought
necessary,[9] with all sorts of arms, and enough provisions for
more than a year. I also left them one caravel, and skilful
workmen both in ship-building and other arts, and engaged

---

non spernenda, in qua, etsi aliarum omnium ut dixi pro invictissimo
Rege nostro solemniter possessionem accepi, earumque imperium
dicto Regi penitus committitur, in opportuniori tamen loco, atque
omni lucro et commercio condecenti, cujusdam magnæ villæ, cui
Nativitatis Domini nomen dedimus, possessionem peculiariter accepi:
ibique arcem quamdam erigere extemplo jussi, quæ modo jam debet
esse peracta, in qua homines, qui necessarii sunt visi, cum omni ar-
morum genere, et ultra annum victu opportuno reliqui ; item quamdam caravelam, et pro aliis construendis tam in hac arte quam in
ceteris peritos, ac ejusdem insulæ Regis erga nos benevolentiam et

[9] There appears to be a doubt as to the exact number of men left by
Columbus at Española, different accounts variously giving it as thirty-
seven, thirty-eight, thirty-nine, and forty. There is, however, a list of
their names included in one of the diplomatic documents printed in
Navarrete's work, which makes the number amount to forty, independent
of the governor Diego de Arana, and his two lieutenants Pedro Gutierrez
and Rodrigo de Escobedo. All these men were Spaniards, with the exception of two ; one an Irishman named William Ires, a native of Galway,
and one an Englishman, whose name was given as Tallarte de Lajes, but
whose native designation it is difficult to guess at. The document in
question, was a proclamation to the effect that the heirs of those men
should, on presenting at the office of public business at Seville, sufficient
proof of their being the next of kin, receive payment in conformity with
the royal order to that purpose, issued at Burgos, on the twentieth of
December, 1507.

the favor and friendship of the King of the island in their behalf, to a degree that would not be believed, for these people are so amiable and friendly that even the King took a pride in calling me his brother. But supposing their feelings should become changed, and they should wish to injure those who have remained in the fortress, they could not do so, for they have no arms, they go naked, and are moreover too cowardly; so that those who hold the said fortress, can easily keep the whole island in check, without any pressing danger to themselves, provided they do not transgress the directions and regulations which I have given them. As far as I have learned, every man throughout these islands is united to but one wife, with the exception of the kings and princes, who are allowed to have twenty : the women seem to work more than the men. I could not clearly understand whether the people possess any private property, for I observed that one man had the charge of distributing various things to the rest, but especially meat and provisions and the like. I did not find, as some of us had expected, any cannibals amongst them, but on the contrary men of great deference and kindness. Neither are they black, like the Ethiopians: their hair is smooth and straight:

---

familiaritatem incredibilem. Sunt enim gentes illæ amabiles admodum et benignæ, eo quod rex prædictus me fratrem suum dici gloriabatur. Et si animum revocarent et iis qui in arce manserunt nocere velint, nequeunt, quia armis carent, nudi incedunt, et nimium timidi : ideo dictam arcem tenentes dumtaxat possunt totam eam insulam nullo sibi imminente discrimine, dummodo leges quas dedimus ac regimen non excedant, facile detinere. In omnibus his insulis, ut intellexi, quisque uni tantum conjugi acquiescit, præter Principes aut Reges quibus viginti habere licet. Feminæ magis quam viri laborare videntur, nec bene potui intelligere an habeant bona propria ; vidi enim, quod unus habebat aliis impartiri, præsertim dapes, obsonia et hujusmodi. Nullum apud eos monstrum reperi, ut plerique existimabant, sed homines magnæ reverentiæ atque benignos. Nec sunt nigri velut æthiopes : habent crines planos ac demissos ; non degunt ubi radiorum solaris emicat calor :

for they do not dwell where the rays of the sun strike most
vividly,—and the sun has intense power there, the distance
from the equinoctial line being, it appears, but six-and-twenty
degrees. On the tops of the mountains the cold is very great,
but the effect of this upon the Indians is lessened by their
being accustomed to the climate, and by their frequently in-
dulging in the use of very hot meats and drinks. Thus, as I have
already said, I saw no cannibals, nor did I hear of any, except
in a certain island called Charis,[10] which is the second from
Española on the side towards India, where dwell a people
who are considered by the neighbouring islanders as most
ferocious : and these feed upon human flesh.   The same
people have many kinds of canoes, in which they cross to all
the surrounding islands and rob and plunder wherever they
can ; they are not different from the other islanders, except
that they wear their hair long, like women, and make use of
the bows and javelins of cane, with sharpened spear-points
fixed on the thickest end, which I have before described, and
therefore they are looked upon as ferocious, and regarded by
the other Indians with unbounded fear; but I think no more

permagna namque hic est solis vehementia, propterea quod ab æqui-
noctiali linea distat (ut videtur) gradus sex et viginti. Ex montium
cacuminibus maximum quoque viget frigus, sed id quidem mode-
rant Indi tum loci consuetudine, tum rerum calidissimarum quibus
frequenter et luxuriosè vescuntur præsidio.   Itaque monstra aliqua
non vidi, neque eorum alicubi habui cognitionem, excepta quadam
insula Charis nuncupata, quæ secunda ex Hispana in Indiam trans-
fretantibus existit, quam gens quædam, à finitimis habita ferocior,
incolit : hi carne humana vescuntur.   Habent prædicti biremium
genera plurima, quibus in omnes indicas insulas trajiciunt, depræ-
dant, surripiuntque quæcumque possunt.   Nihil ab aliis differunt,
nisi quod gerunt more femineo longos crines, utuntur arcubus et
spiculis arundineis, fixis, ut diximus, in grossiori parte attenuatis
hastilibus : ideoque habentur feroces ; quare ceteri Indi inexhausto

[10] Query Carib, the Indian name of Porto Rico.

of them than of the rest. These are the men who form unions
with certain women, who dwell alone in the island Matenin,[11]
which lies next to Española on the side towards India; these
latter employ themselves in no labour suitable to their own
sex, for they use bows and javelins as I have already described
their paramours as doing, and for defensive armour have plates
of brass, of which metal they possess great abundance. They
assure me that there is another island larger than Española,
whose inhabitants have no hair, and which abounds in gold
more than any of the rest. I bring with me individuals of
this island and of the others that I have seen, who are proofs
of the facts which I state. Finally, to compress into few words
the entire summary of my voyage and speedy return, and of the
advantages derivable therefrom, I promise, that with a little
assistance afforded me by our most invincible sovereigns, I will
procure them as much gold as they need, as great a quantity
of spices, of cotton, and of mastic (which is only found in Chios),
and as many men for the service of the navy as their Majesties
may require. I promise also rhubarb and other sorts of drugs,

---

metu plectuntur: sed hos ego nihil facio plus quam alios. Hi sunt
qui coeunt cum quibusdam feminis, quæ solæ insulam Mathenim
primam ex Hispana in Indiam trajicientibus inhabitant. Hæ autem feminæ nullum sui sexûs opus exercent: utuntur enim arcubus
et spiculis, sicuti de earum conjugibus dixi, muniunt sese laminis
æneis, quarum maxima apud eas copia exsistit. Aliam mihi insulam affirmant supradicta Hispana majorem; ejus incolæ carent pilis
auroque inter alias potissimum exuberat. Hujus insulæ et aliarum,
quas vidi, homines mecum porto, qui horum quæ dixi testimonium
perhibent. Denique ut nostri discessûs et ceteris reversionis com-
pendium ac emolumentum brevibus astringam, hoc polliceor, me
nostris Regibus invictissimis, parvo eorum fultum auxilio, tantum
auri daturum, quantum eis fuerit opus, tantum vero aromatum,
bombycis, masticis, quæ apud Chium dumtaxat invenitur, tamque
ligni aloes, tantum servorum hydrophilatorum, quantum eorum

[11] One of the Virgin Islands—which, is uncertain.

which I am persuaded the men whom I have left in the aforesaid fortress have found already and will continue to find;
for I myself have tarried no where longer than I was compelled
to do by the winds, except in the city of Navidad, while I provided for the building of the fortress, and took the necessary
precautions for the perfect security of the men I left there. Although all I have related may appear to be wonderful and
unheard of, yet the results of my voyage would have been more
astonishing if I had had at my disposal such ships as I required.
But these great and marvellous results are not to be attributed
to any merit of mine, but to the holy Christian faith, and to the
piety and religion of our Sovereigns; for that which the unaided
intellect of man could not compass, the spirit of God has
granted to human exertions, for God is wont to hear the
prayers of his servants who love his precepts even to the per-
formance of apparent impossibilities. Thus it has happened to
me in the present instance, who have accomplished a task to
which the powers of mortal men had never hitherto attained;
for if there have been those who have anywhere written or
spoken of these islands, they have done so with doubts and
conjectures, and no one has ever asserted that he has seen
them, on which account their writings have been looked upon

---

majestas voluerit exigere: item reubarbarum et aliorum aromatum
genera, quæ ii quos in dicta arce reliqui, jam invenisse atque inven-
turos existimo: quandoquidem ego nullibi magis sum moratus (nisi
quantum me coegerunt venti) præterquam in villa Nativitatis, dum
arcem condere, et tuta omnia esse providi. Quæ etsi maxima et
inaudita sunt multo tamen majora forent, si naves mihi, ut ratio
exigit, subvenissent. Verum multum ac mirabile hoc nec nostris
meritis correspondens, sed sanctæ christianæ fidei, nostrorumque
regum pietati ac religioni, quia, quod humanus consequi non pote-
rat intellectus, id humanis concessit divinus. Solet enim Deus
servos, quique sua præcepta diligunt, etiam in impossibilibus exau-
dire, ut nobis in præsentia contigit, qui consecuti sumus, quæ hac-
tenus mortalium vires minimè attigerant; nam si harum insularum
quidpiam aliqui scripserunt aut locuti sunt, omnes per ambages et

as little else than fables. Therefore let the king and queen, our princes and their most happy kingdoms, and all the other provinces of Christendom, render thanks to our Lord and Saviour Jesus Christ, who has granted us so great a victory and such prosperity. Let processions be made, and sacred feasts be held, and the temples be adorned with festive boughs. Let Christ rejoice on earth, as he rejoices in heaven in the prospect of the salvation of the souls of so many nations hitherto lost. Let us also rejoice, as well on account of the exaltation of our faith, as on account of the increase of our temporal prosperity, of which not only Spain, but all Christendom will be partakers.

Such are the events which I have briefly described. Farewell.

Lisbon, the 14th of March.

CHRISTOPHER COLUMBUS,

Admiral of the Fleet of the Ocean.

---

conjecturas, nemo se eas vidisse asserit: unde prope videbatur fabula. Igitur Rex et Regina, Principes, ac eorum regna felicissima, cunctæque aliæ Christianorum provinciæ, Salvatori Domino nostro Jesu Christo agamus gratias, qui tanta nos victoria munereque donavit. Celebrentur processiones, peragantur solemnia sacra, festâque fronde velentur delubra. Exsultet Christus in terris, quemadmodum in cœlis exsultat, quum tot populorum perditas antehac animas salvatum iri prævidet. Lætemur et nos, tum propter exaltationem nostræ fidei, tum propter rerum temporalium incrementa, quorum non solum Hispania, sed universa Christianitas est futura particeps. Hæc gesta sic breviter enarrata. Vale. Ulisbonæ pridie idus Martii.

CHRISTOFORUS COLOM,

Oceanæ classis præfectus.

SECOND VOYAGE OF COLUMBUS.[1]

A Letter addressed to the Chapter of Seville by Dr. Chanca,[2] native of that city, and physician to the fleet of Columbus, in his second voyage to the West Indies, describing the principal events which occurred during that voyage.

Most noble sir,—Since the occurrences which I relate in private letters to other persons, are not of such general interest as those which are contained in this epistle, I have resolved to give you a distinct narrative of the events of our

SEGUNDA VIAGE DE COLON.

La Carta del Doctor Chanca, que escribió a la Cindad de Sevilla.

Muy magnífico Señor : Porque las cosas que yo particularmente escribo á otros en otras cartas no son igualmente comunicables como las que en esta escritura van, acordé de escribir distintamente las

[1] The description of the second voyage of Columbus, has been given in Latin by Peter Martyr, of Anghiera, in lib. ii, of his "Decades"; but as Doctor Chanca, a native of Seville, who was physician to the fleet in that voyage, and was an eye-witness of the events he related, has written an account of it in a letter to the Chapter of Seville, it has been deemed advisable to take his account in preference to that of Peter Martyr, which is made up only from information gathered from hearsay. Moreover, Dr. Chanca's description, while it in no way contradicts that of Peter Martyr, is more agreeably written, and mentions some few incidents that are omitted in the narrative of the latter.

[2] Doctor Chanca was appointed physician to Columbus's fleet by a dispatch of the 23rd of May, 1493 ; and on the 24th, the chief accountants were instructed to pay him salary and rations as scrivener in the Indies.

voyage, as well as to treat of the other matters which form the subject of my petition to you. The news I have to communicate are as follows : The expedition which their Catholic Majesties sent, by Divine permission, from Spain to the Indies, under the command of Christopher Columbus, admiral of the ocean, left Cadiz on the twenty-fifth of September, of the year ,[3] with wind and weather favorable for the voyage. This wind lasted two days, during which time we managed to make fifty leagues; the weather then changing, we made little or no progress for the next two days; it pleased God, however, after this, to restore us fine weather, so that in two days more we reached the Great Canary. Here we put into harbour, which we were obliged to do, to repair one of the ships which made a great deal of water; we remained all that day, and on the following set sail again, but were several times becalmed, so that we were four or five days before we reached Gomera. We

---

nuevas de acá y las otras que á mi conviene suplicar á vuestra Señoría, é las nuevas son las siguientes: Que la flota que los Reyes Católicos, nuestros Señores, enviaron de España para las Indias é gobernacion del su Almirante del mar Océano Cristóbal Colon por la divina permision, parte de Caliz á veinte y cinco de Setiembre del año de   años con tiempo é viento convenible á nuestro camino, é duró este tiempo dos dias, en los cuales pudimos andar al pie de cincuenta leguas: y luego nos cambió el tiempo otros dos, en los cuales anduvimos muy poco ó no nada; plogó á Dios que pasados los dias nos tornó buen tiempo, en manera que en otros dos llegamos á la Gran Canaria donde tomamos puerto, lo cual nos fue necesario por reparar un navío que hacia mucha agua, y estovimos ende todo aquel dia, é luego otra dia partimos é fizonos algunas calmerías, de manera que estovimos en llegar al Gomero cuatro ó cinco dias, y en la Gomera fue necesario estar

The curate of Los Palacios makes mention of Dr. Chanca, and had this same narration before him, as may be seen in the one hundred and twentieth chapter of his manuscript "History of their Catholic Majesties". (M. F. de Navarrete).

[3] A similar gap in the original : it should say *of the year* 1493.

had to remain at Gomera one day to lay in our stores of meat,
wood, and as much water as we could stow, preparatory to the
long voyage which we expected to make without seeing land:
thus through the delay at these two ports, and being fixed in
a calm one day after leaving Gomera, we were nineteen or
twenty days before we arrived at the Island of Ferro. After
this we had, by the goodness of God, a return of fine weather,
more continuous than any fleet ever enjoyed during so long a
voyage; so that leaving Ferro on the thirteenth of October,
within twenty days we came in sight of land : and we should
have seen it in fourteen or fifteen days, if the ship *Capitana* had
been as good a sailer as the other vessels ; for many times the
others had to shorten sail, because they were leaving us much
behind. During all this time we had great good fortune, for
throughout the voyage we encountered no storm, with the
exception of one on St. Simon's eve, which for four hours put
us in considerable jeopardy.

On the first Sunday after All Saints, namely the third of
November, about dawn, a pilot of the ship *Capitana* cried out:
" The reward, I see the land !"

----

algun dia por facer provisiones de carne, leña é agua la que mas
pudiesen, por la larga jornada que se esperaba hacer sin ver mas
tierra : ansi que en la estada destos puertos y en un dia despues de
partidos de la Gomera, que nos fizo calma, que tardamos en llegar
fasta la isla del Fierro, estovimos diez y nueve ó veinte dias : desde
aqui por la bondad de Dios nos tornó buen tiempo, el mejor que
nunca flota llevó tan largo camino, tal que partidos del Fierro á trece
de Octubre dentro de veinte dias hobimos vista de tierra : y viera-
mosla á catorce ó quince si la nao Capitana fuera tan buena velera
como los otros navíos, porque muchas veces los otros navíos sacaban
velas porque nos dejaban mucho atras. En todo este tiempo hobimos mucha bonanza, que en él ni en todo el camino no hobimos
fortuna, salvo la víspera de S. Simon que nos vino una que por
cuatro horas nos puso en harto estrecho. El primero domingo
despues de Todos Santos, que fue á tres dias de Noviembre, cerca
del alba, dijo un piloto de la nao Capitana : albricias, que tenemos
tierra. Fue el alegría tan grande en la gente que era maravilla oir

The joy of the people was so great, that it was wonderful to hear their cries and exclamations of pleasure; and they had good reason to be delighted ; for they had become so wearied of bad living, and of working the water out of the ships, that all sighed most anxiously for land. The pilots of the fleet, reckoned on that day, that between leaving Ferro and first reaching land, we had made eight hundred leagues ; others said seven hundred and eighty (so that the difference was not great), and three hundred more between Ferro and Cadiz, making in all eleven hundred leagues; I do not therefore feel as one who had not seen enough of the water. On the morning of the aforesaid Sunday, we saw lying before us an island, and soon on the right hand another appeared : the first[4] was high and mountainous, on the side nearest to us ; the other[5] flat, and very thickly wooded : as soon as it became lighter, other islands began to appear on both sides ; so that on that day, there were six islands to be seen lying in different direc-

---

las gritas y placeres que todos hacian, y con mucha razon, que la gente venian ya tan fatigados de mala vida y de pasar agua, que con muchos deseos sospiraban todos por tierra. Contaron aquel dia los pilotos del armada desde la isla de Fierro hasta la primera tierra que vimos unas ochocientas leguas, otros setecientas é ochenta, de manera que la diferencia no era mucha, é mas trescientas que ponen de la isla de Fierro fasta Caliz, que eran por todos mil é ciento ; ansí que no siento quien no fuese satisfecho de ver agua. Vimos el Domingo de mañana sobredicho, por proa de los navíos, una isla y luego á la man derecha parecio otra : la primera era la tierra alta de sierras por aquella parte que vimos, la otra era tierra llana, tambien muy llena de árboles muy espesos, y luego que fue mas de dia comenzó á parecer á una parte é á otra islas ; de manera que aquel dia eran seis islas á diversas partes, y las mas harto grandes. Fuimos enderezados para ver aquella que primero habiamos visto, é

4 The island of Dominica, which is so called from having been discovered on a Sunday. (M. F. de Navarrete.)

5 The island Marigalante, which was so called from the name of the ship in which Columbus sailed. (M. F. de Navarrete.)

tions, and most of them of considerable size. We directed
our course towards that which we had first seen, and reaching
the coast, we proceeded more than a league in search of a
port where we might anchor, but without finding one : all that
part of the island which we could observe, appeared mountainous, very beautiful, and green even up to the water, which
was delightful to see, for at that season, there is scarcely any
thing green in our own country. When we found that there
was no harbour there, the admiral decided that we should
go to the other island, which appeared on the right, and which
was at four or five leagues distance : one vessel however still
remained on the first island all that day seeking for a harbour,
in case it should be necessary to return thither. At length,
having found a good one, where they saw both people and dwellings, they returned that night to the fleet, which had put into
harbour at the other island,[6] and there the admiral, accompanied
by a great number of men, landed with the royal banner in his
hands, and took formal possession on behalf of their Majesties.
This island was filled with an astonishingly thick growth of
wood ; the variety of unknown trees, some bearing fruit and

---

llegamos por la costa andando mas de una legua buscando puerto
para sorgir, el cual todo aquel espacio nunca se pudo hallar.   Era
en todo aquello que parecia desta isla todo montaña muy hermosa y
muy verde, fasta el agua que era alegria en mirarla, porque en aquel
tiempo no hay en nuestra tierra apenas cosa verde.   Despues que
allí no hallamos puerto acordó el Almirante que nos volviesemos á
la otra isla que parescia á la mano derecha, que estaba desta otra
cuatro ó cinco leguas.   Quedó por entonces un navío en esta isla
buscando puerto todo aquel dia para cuando fuese necesario venir á
ella, en la cual halló buen puerto é vido casas é gentes, é luego se
tornó aquella noche para donde estaba la flota que habia tomado
puerto en la otra isla, donde decendió el Almirante é mucha gente
con él con la bandera Real en les manos, adonde tomó posesion por
sus Altezas en forma de derecho. En esta isla habia tanta espesura
de arboledas que era maravilla, é tanta diferencia de árboles no co-

[6] Marigalante.

some flowers, was surprising, and indeed every spot was covered with verdure. We found there a tree whose leaf had the finest smell of cloves that I have ever met with ; it was like a laurel leaf, but not so large : but I think it was a species of laurel. There were wild fruits of various kinds, some of which our men, not very prudently, tasted ; and upon only touching them with their tongues, their countenances became inflamed,[7] and such great heat and pain followed, that they seemed to be mad, and were obliged to resort to refrigerants to cure themselves. We found no signs of any people in this island, and concluded it was uninhabited ; we remained only two hours, for it was very late when we landed, and on the following morning we left for another very large island,[8] situated below this at the distance of seven or eight leagues. We approached it under the side of a great mountain, that seemed almost to reach the skies, in the middle of which rose a peak, higher than all the rest of the mountain, whence many streams diverged into different channels, especially towards the part

nocidos á nadie que era para espantar, dellos con fruto, dellos con flor, ansí que todo era verde. Allí hallamos un arbol, cuya hoja tenia el mas fino olor de clavos que nunca ví, y era como laurel, salvo que no era ansi grande ; yo ansí pienso que era laurel su especia. Allí habia frutas salvaginas de diferentes maneras, de las quales algunos no muy sabios probaban, y del gusto solamente tocándoles con las lenguas se les hinchaban las caras, y les venia tan grande ardor y dolor que parecian que rabiaban, los cuales se remediaban con cosas frias. En esta isla no hallamos gente nin señal della, creimos que era desboblada, en la cual estovimos bien dos horas, porque cuando allí llegamos era sobre tarde, é luego otro dia de mañana partimos para otra isla que parescia en bajo desta que era muy grande, fasta la cual desta que habria siete ú ocho leguas, llegamos á ella hácia la parte de una gran montaña que parecia que queria llegar al cielo, en medio de la cual montaña estaba un pico mas alto que toda la otra montaña, del cual se ver-

[7] One would infer from this that it was the fruit of the manzanillo, which produces similar effects. (M. F. de Navarrete.) [8] Guadaloupe.

at which we arrived. At three leagues distance, we could see
an immense fall of water, which discharged itself from such
a height that it appeared to fall from the sky; it was seen
from so great a distance that it occasioned many wagers to
be laid on board the ships, some maintaining that it was but
a series of white rocks, and others that it was water. When
we came nearer to it, it showed itself distinctly, and it was
the most beautiful thing in the world to see from how great
a height and from what a small space so large a fall of water
was discharged. As soon as we neared the island the admiral
ordered a light caravel to run along the coast to search for a
harbour; the captain put into land in a boat, and seeing some
houses, leapt on shore and went up to them, the inhabitants
fleeing at sight of our men; he then went into the houses
and there found various household articles that had been
left unremoved, from which he took two parrots, very large
and quite different from any we had before seen; he found a
great quantity of cotton, both spun and prepared for spinning,
and articles of food, of all of which he brought away a portion; besides these, he also brought away four or five bones

---

tian á diversas partes muchas aguas, en especial hácia la parte donde
ibamos: de tres leguas paresció un golpe de agua tan gordo como
un buey, que se despeñaba de tan alto como si cayera del cielo .
parescia de tan lejos, que hobo en los navíos muchas apuestas, que
unos decian que eran peñas blancas y otros que era agua.   Desque
llegamos mas á cerca vídose lo cierto, y era la mas hermosa cosa del
mundo de ver de cuan alto se despeñaba é de tan poco logar nacia
tan gran golpe de agua.   Luego que llegamos cerca mandó el Almirante á una carbela ligera que fuese costeando á buscar puerto,
la cual se adelantó y llegando á la tierra vido unas casas, é con la
barca saltó el Capitan en tierra é llegó á las casas, en las cuales
halló su gente, y luego que los vieron fueron huyendo, é entró en
ellas, donde halló las cosas que ellos tienen, que no habian llevado
nada, donde tomó dos papagayos muy grandes y muy diferenciados
de cuantos se habian visto.   Halló mucho algodon hilado é por hilar, é cosas de sus mantenimientos, é de todo trajo un poco, en es-

of human arms and legs. On seeing these we suspected that we were amongst the Caribbee islands, which are inhabited by cannibals; for the admiral, guided by the information respecting their situation which he had received from the Indians of the islands discovered in his former voyage, had directed his course with a view to their discovery, both because they were the nearest to Spain, and because this was the direct track for the island of Española, where he had left some of his people. Thither, by the goodness of God and the wise management of the admiral, we came in as straight a track as if we had sailed by a well known and frequented route. This island is very large, and on the side where we arrived it seemed to us to be twenty-five leagues in length. We sailed more than two leagues along the shore in search of a harbour; on the part towards which we moved appeared very high mountains, and on that which we left extensive plains; on the sea coast there were a few small villages, whose inhabitants fled as soon as they saw the sails : at length after proceeding two leagues we found a port late in the evening. That night the admiral resolved that some of the men should

---

pecial trajo cuatro ó cinco huesos de brazos é piernas de hombres. Luego que aquello vimos sospechamos que aquellas islas eran las de Caribe, que son habitadas de gente que comen carne humana, porque el Almirante por las señas que le habian dado del sitio destas islas, el otro camino, los indios de las islas que antes habian descubierto, habia enderezado el camino por descubrirlas, porque estaban mas cerca de España, y tambien porque por allí se hacia el camino derecho para venir á la isla Española, donde antes habia dejado la gente, á los cuales, por la bondad de Dios y por el buen saber del Almirante, venimos tan derechos como si por camino sabido é seguido vinieramos. Esta isla es muy grande, y por el lado nos pareció que habia de luengo de costa veinte é cinco leguas : fuimos costeando por ella buscando puerto mas de dos leguas ; por la parte donde ibamos eran montañas muy altas, á la parte que dejamos parecian grandes llanos, á la orilla de la mar habia algunos poblados pequeños, é luego que veian las velas huian todos. Andadas dos

land at break of day in order to confer with the natives, and
learn what sort of people they were; although it was suspected, from the appearance of those who had fled at our
approach, that they were naked, like those whom the admiral
had seen in his former voyage. In the morning several de-
tachments under their respective captains sailed forth; one
of them arrived at the dinner hour, and brought away a boy
of about fourteen years of age, as it afterwards appeared, who
said that he was one of the prisoners taken by these people.
The others divided themselves, and one party took a little
boy whom a man was leading by the hand, but who left
him and fled; this boy they sent on board immediately with
some of our men; others remained, and took certain women,
natives of the island, together with other women from among
the captives who came of their own accord. One captain of
this last company, not knowing that any intelligence of the
people had been obtained, advanced farther into the island
and lost himself, with the six men who accompanied him :
they could not find their way back until after four days,
when they lighted upon the sea shore, and following the

---

leguas hallamos puerto y bien tarde. Esa noche acordó el Almirante que á la madrugada saliesen algunos para tomar lengua é saber
que gente era, no embargante la sospecha é los que ya habian visto
ir huyendo, que era gente desnuda como la otra que ya el Almirante habia visto el otro viage. Salieron esa madrugada ciertos
Capitanes; los unos vinieron á hora de comer é trageron un mozo
de fasta catorce años, á lo que despues se sopo, é él dijo que era de
los que esta gente tenian cativos. Los otros se dividieron, los unos
tomaron un mochacho pequeño, al cual llevaba un hombre por la
mano, é por huir lo desamparó. Este enviaron luego con algunos
dellos, otros quedaron, é destos unos tomaron ciertas mugeres naturales de la isla, é otras que se vinieron de grado, que eran de las
cativas. Desta compañia se apartó un Capitan no sabiendo que se
habia habido lengua con seis hombres, el cual se perdió con los que
con él iban, que jamas sopieron tornar, fasta que á cabo de cuatro
dias toparon con la costa de la mar, é siguiendo por ella tornaron á

line of coast returned to the fleet.[8] We had already looked
upon them as killed and eaten by the people that are called
Caribbees, for we could not account for their long absence in
any other way, since they had among them some pilots who by
their knowledge of the stars could navigate either to or from
Spain, so that we imagined that they could not lose themselves
in so small a space. On this first day of our landing several
men and women came on the beach up to the water's edge,
and gazed at the ships in astonishment at so novel a sight;
and when a boat pushed on shore in order to speak with them,
they cried out, " tayno, tayno," which is as much as to say,
" good, good," and waited for the landing of the sailors,
standing by the boat in such a manner that they might
escape when they pleased. The result was, that none of the
men could be persuaded to join us, and only two were taken

---

topar con la flota. Ya los teniamos por perdidos é comidos de
aquellas gentes que se dicen los Caribes, porque no bastaba razon
para creer que eran perdidos de otra manera, porque iban entre
ellos pilotos, marineros que por la estrella saben ir é venir hasta
España, creiamos que en tan pequeño espacio no se podian perder.
Este dia primero que allí decendimos andaban por la playa junto
con el agua muchos hombres é mugeres mirando la flota, é maravillándose de cosa tan nueva, ó llegándose alguna barca á tierra á
hablar con ellos, diciéndolos *tayno tayno*, que quiere decir *bueno*,
esperaban en tanto que no salian del agua, junto con él moran, de
manera que cuando ellos querian se podian salvar : en conclusion,
que de los hombres ninguno se pudo tomar por fuerza ni por grado, salvo dos que se seguraron é despues los trajeron por fuerza

---

9 It was Diego Marquez, the caterer, who with eight other men went
on shore into the interior of the island, without permission from the admiral, who caused him to be sought for by parties of men with trumpets,
but without success. One of those who were sent out with this object,
was Alonzo Ojeda, who took with him forty men, and on their return they
reported that they had found many aromatic plants, a variety of birds, and
some considerable rivers. The wanderers were not able to find their way
to the ships until the eighth of November. (M. F. Navarrete's note, from
Bartholomeo de las Casas' Manuscript History, chap. 84.)

by force, who were secured and led away. More than twenty
of the female captives were taken with their own consent,
and other women natives of the island were surprised and
carried off: several of the boys, who were captives, came to us
fleeing from the natives of the island who had taken them
prisoners. We remained eight days in this port in consequence of the loss of the aforesaid captain, and went many
times on shore, passing amongst the dwellings and villages
which were on the coast; we found a vast number of human
bones and skulls hung up about the houses, like vessels
intended for holding various things. There were very few
men to be seen here, and the women informed us that this was
in consequence of ten canoes having gone to make an attack
upon other islands. These islanders appeared to us to be
more civilized than those that we had hitherto seen; for
although all the Indians have houses of straw, yet the houses
of these people are constructed in a much superior fashion,
are better stocked with provisions, and exhibit more evidences
of industry, both on the part of the men and the women.
They had a considerable quantity of cotton, both spun and

---

allí. Se tomaron mas de veinte mugeres de las cativas, y de su
grado se venian otras naturales de la isla, que fueron salteadas é
tomadas por fuerza. Ciertos mochachos cabtivos se vinieron á
nosotros huyendo de los naturales de la isla que los tenian cabtivos.
En este puerto estovimos ocho dias á causa de la pérdida del sobredicho Capitan, donde muchas veces salimos á tierra andando por sus
moradas é pueblos, que estaban á la costa, donde hallamos infinitos
huesos de hombres, é los cascos de las cabezas colgados por las
casas á manera de vasijas para tener cosas. Aquí no parescieron
muchos hombres ; la causa era, segun nos dijeron las mugeres, que
eran idas diez canoas con gentes á saltear á otras islas. Esta gente
nos pareció mas política que la que habita en estas otras islas que
habemos visto, aunque todos tienen las moradas de paja ; pero estos las tienen de mucho mejor hechura, é mas proveidas de mantenimientos, é parece en ellas mas industria ansi veril como femenil.
Tenian mucho algodon hilado y por hilar, y muchas mantas de al-

prepared for spinning, and many cotton sheets, so well woven as to be no way inferior to those of our country. We enquired of the women, who were prisoners in the island, what people these islanders were : they replied that they were Caribbees. As soon as they learned that we abhorred such people, on account of their evil practice of eating human flesh, they were much delighted; and, after that, if they brought forward any woman or man of the Caribbees, they informed us (but secretly), that they were such, still evincing by their dread of their conquerors, that they belonged to a vanquished nation, though they knew them all to be in our power.

We were enabled to distinguish which of the women were natives, and which were captives, by the Caribbees wearing on each leg two bands of woven cotton, the one fastened round the knee, and the other round the ankle ; by this means they make the calves of their legs large, and the above-mentioned parts very small, which I imagine that they regard as a matter of refinement : by this peculiarity we distinguished them. The habits of these Caribbees are brutal. There are three islands : the one called Turuqueira; the other, which was the

---

godon tan bien tejidas que no deben nada á las de nuestra patria. Preguntamos á las mugeres, que eran cativas en esta isla, que qué gente era esta ; respondieron que eran Caribes. Despues que entendieron que nosotros aborreciamos tal gente por su mal uso de comer carne de hombres, holgaban mucho, y sí de nuevo traian alguna muger ó hombre de los Caribes, secretamente decian que eran Caribes, que allí donde estaban todos en nuestro poder mostraban temor dellos como gente sojuzgada, y de allí conocimos cuáles eran Caribes de las mugeres é cuáles nó, porque las Caribes traian en las piernas en cada una dos argollas tejidas de algodon, la una junto con la rodilla, la otra junto con los tobillos ; de manera que les hacen las pantorrillas grandes, é de los sobredichos logares muy ceñidas, que esto me parece que tienen ellos por cosa gentil, ansi que por esta diferencia conocemos los unos de los otros. La costumbre desta gente de Caribes es bestial : son tres islas, esta se llama Turuqueira, la otra que primero vimos se llama Ceyre, la tercera

first that we saw, is called Ceyre; the third is called Ayay : there is a resemblance amongst all these, as if they were of one race, and they do no injury to each other ; but each and all of them wage war against the other neighbouring islands, and for the purpose of attacking them, make voyages of a hundred and fifty leagues at sea, with their numerous canoes, which are a small kind of craft with one mast. Their arms are arrows, in the place of iron weapons, and as they have no iron, some of them point their arrows with tortoise-shell, and others make their arrow heads of fish spines, which are naturally barbed like coarse saws : these prove dangerous weapons to a naked people like the Indians, and may inflict severe injury, but to men of our nation, are not very formidable. In their attacks upon the neighbouring islands, these people take as many of the women as they can, especially those who are young and beautiful, and keep them as concubines; and so great a number do they carry off, that in fifty houses no men were to be seen; and out of the number of the captives, more than twenty were young girls. These women also say that the Caribbees use them with such cruelty as would scarcely

---

se llama Ayay; estos todos son conformidad como si fuesen de un linage, los cuales no se hacen mal : unos é otros hacen guerra á todas las otras islas comarcanas, los cuales van por mar ciento é cincuenta leguas á saltear con muchas canoas que tienen, que son unas fustas pequeñas de un solo madero. Sus armas son frechas en lugar de hierros ; porque no poseen ningun hierro, ponen unas puntas fechas de huesos de torgugas los unos, otros de otra isla ponen unas espinas de un pez fechas dentadas, que ansi lo son naturalmente, á manera de sierras bien recias, que para gente desarmada, como son todos, es cosa que les puede matar é hacer harto daño ; pero para gente de nuestra nacion no son armas para mucho temer. Esta gente saltea en las otras islas, que traen las mugeres que pueden haber, en especial mozas y hermosas, las cuales tienen para su servicio, é para tener por mancebas, é traen tantas que en cincuenta casas ellos no parecieron, y de las cativas se vinieron mas de veinte mozas. Dicen tambien estas mugeres que estos usan de una cruel-

be believed; and that they eat the children which they bear to them, and only bring up those which they have by their natural wives. Such of their male enemies as they can take alive, they bring to their houses to make a feast of them, and those who are dead they devour at once. They say that man's flesh is so good, that there is nothing like it in the world; and this is pretty evident, for of the bones which we found in their houses, they had gnawed everything that could be gnawed, so that nothing remained of them, but what from its great hardness, could not be eaten: in one of the houses we found the neck of a man, undergoing the process of cooking. When they take any boys prisoners, they dismember them, and make use of them until they grow up to manhood, and then when they wish to make a feast they kill and eat them; for they say that the flesh of boys and women is not good to eat. Three of these boys came fleeing to us thus mutilated.

At the end of four days arrived the captain who had lost himself with his companions, of whose return we had by this time given up all hope; for other parties had been twice sent out to seek him, one of which came back on the same day

---

dad que parece cosa increible; que los hijos que en ellas han se los comen, que solamente crian los que han en sus mugeres naturales. Los hombres que pueden haber, los que son vivos llevánselos á sus casas para hacer carnicería dellos, y los que han muertos luego se los comen. Dicen que la carne del hombre es tan buena que no hay tal coso en el mundo; y bien parece porque los huesos que en estas casas hallamos todo lo que se puede roer todo lo tenian roido, que no habia en ellos sino lo que por su mucha dureza no se podia comer. Allí se halló en una casa cociendo en una olla un pezcuezo de un hombre. Los mochachos que cativan cortanlos el miembro, é sirvense de ellos fasta que son hombres, y despues cuando quieren facer fiesta mátanlos é cómenselos, porque dicen que la carne de los mochachos é de las mogeres no es buena para comer. Destos mochachos se vinieron para nosotros huyendo tres, todos tres cortados sus miembros. E á cabo de cuatro dias vino el Capitan que se habia perdido, de cuya venida estabamos ya bien desesperados,

that he rejoined us, without having gained any information respecting the wanderers : we rejoiced at their arrival, regarding it as a new accession to our numbers. The captain and the men who accompanied him brought back some women and boys, ten in number : neither this party, nor those who went out to seek them, had seen any of the men of the island, which must have arisen either from their having fled, or possibly from there being but very few men in that locality; for, as the women informed us, ten canoes had gone away to make an attack upon the neighbouring islands. The wanderers had returned from the mountains in such an emaciated condition, that it was distressing to see them; when we asked them how it was that they lost themselves, they said that the trees were so thick and close that they could not see the sky; some of them who were mariners had climbed the trees to get a sight of the stars, but could never see them, and if they had not found their way to the sea coast, it would have been impossible to have returned to the fleet. We left this island eight days after our arrival.[9] The next day at noon we saw another

---

porque ya los habian ido á buscar otras cuadrillas por dos veces, é aquel dia vino la una cuadrilla sin saber dellos ciertamente.   Holgamos con su venida como si nuevamente se hobieran hallado : trajo este Capitan con los que fueron con él diez cabezas entre mochachos y mugeres.   Estos ni los otros que los fueron á buscar, nunca hallaron hombres porque se habien huido, ó por ventura que en aquella comarca habia pocos hombres, porque segun se supo de las mugeres eran idas diez canoas con gentes á saltear á otras islas. Vino él é los que fueron con él tan destrozados del monte, que era lástima de los ver : decian, preguntándoles como se habien perdido, dijeron que era la espesura de los árboles tanta que el cielo no podian ver, é que algunos de ellos, que eran marineros, habian subido por los árboles para mirar el estrella, é que nunca la podieron ver, é que si no toparan con el mar fuera imposible tornar á la flota. Partimos desta isla ocho dias despues que allí llegamos.   Luego

[10] They left on Sunday the 10th of November.   (M. F. de Navarrete.)

island,[11] not very large, at about twelve leagues distance from
the one we were leaving; the greater part of the first day of
our departure we were kept close in to the coast of this island
by a calm, but as the Indian women whom we brought with
us said that it was not inhabited, but had been dispeopled by
the Carribees, we made no stay in it. On that evening we
saw another island:[12] and in the night finding there were some
sandbanks near, we dropped anchor, not venturing to proceed
until the morning. On the morrow another island[13] appeared,
of considerable size, but we touched at none of these because
we were anxious to convey consolation to our people who had
been left in Española; but it did not please God to grant us
our desire, as will hereafter appear. Another day at the dinner
hour we arrived at an island[14] which seemed to be worth finding,
for judging by the extent of cultivation in it, it appeared very
populous. We went thither and put into harbour, when the
admiral immediately sent on shore a well manned barge to
hold speech with the Indians, in order to ascertain what race

---

otro dia á medio dia vimos otra isla, no muy grande, que estaria
desta otra doce leguas ; porque el primero dia que partimos lo mas
del dia nos fizo calma, fuimos junto con la costa desta isla, é dijeron
las Indias que llevabamos que no era habitada, que los Caribes la
habian despoblado, é por esto no paramos en ella. Luego esa tarde
vimos otra : á esa noche, cerca desta isla, fallamos unos bajos, por
cuyo temor sorgimos, que no osamos andar fasta que fuese de dia.
Luego á la mañana paresció otra isla harto grande : á ninguna destas no llegamos por consolar los que habian dejado en la Española,
é no plogó á Dios segun que abajo parecerá. Otro dia á hora de
comer llegamos á una isla é pareciónos mucho bien, porque parecia
muy poblada, segun las muchas labranzas que en ella habia. Fuimos allá é tomamos puerto en la costa : luego mandó el Almirante
ir á tierra una barca guarnecida de gente para si pudiese tomar
lengua para saber que gente era, é tambien porque habiamos me-

---

[11] The island Montserrat. (M. F. de Navarrete.)
[12] The admiral called it Santa Maria la Redonda. (M. F. de Navarrete.)
[13] Santa Maria la Antigua.   [14] The island of St. Martin.

they were, and also because we considered it necessary to
gain some information respecting our course; although it
afterwards plainly appeared that the admiral, who had never
made that passage before, had taken a very correct route.
But since doubtful questions ought always by investigation
to be reduced as nearly to a certainty as possible, he wished
that communication should be held with the natives at once,
and some of the men who went in the barge leapt on shore
and went up to a village, whence the inhabitants had already
withdrawn and hidden themselves. They took in this island
five or six women and some boys, most of whom were captives,
like those in the other island; we learned from the women
whom we had brought with us, that the natives of this place also
were Caribbees. As this barge was about to return to the ships
with the capture which they had taken, a canoe came along
the coast containing four men, two women, and a boy; and
when they saw the fleet they were so stupified with amazement, that for a good hour they remained motionless at the
distance of nearly two gunshots from the ships. In this position they were seen by those who were in the barge and also

---

nester informarnos del camino, caso quel Almirante, aunque nunca
habia fecho aquel camino, iba muy bien encaminado segun en cabo
pareció. Pero porque las cosas dubdosas se deben siempre buscar
con la mayor certinidad que haberse pueda, quiso haber allí lengua,
de la cual gente que iba en la barca ciertas personas saltaron en
tierra, é llegaron en tierra á un poblado de donde la gente ya se
habia escondido. Tomaron allí cinco ó seis mugeres y ciertos mochachos, de las cuales las mas eran tambien de las cativas como en
la otra isla, porque tambien estos eran de los Caribes, segun ya sabiamos por la relacion de las mugeres que traiamos. Ya que esta
barca se queria tornar á los navíos con su presa que habia fecho por
parte debajo ; por la costa venia una canoa en que venian cuatro
hombres é dos mugeres é un mochaco, é desque vieron la flota ma-
ravillados se embebecieron tanto que por una grande hora estovieron
que no se movieron de un lugar casi dos tiros de lombarda de los
navíos. En esto fueron vistos de los que estaban en la barca é aun

by all the fleet. Meanwhile those in the barge moved towards the canoe, but so close in shore, that the Indians, in their perplexity and astonishment as to what all this could mean, never saw them, until they were so near that escape was impossible; for our men pressed on them so rapidly that they could not get away, although they made considerable effort to do so.

When the Caribbees saw that all attempt at flight was useless, they most courageously took to their bows, both women and men; I say most courageously, because they were only four men and two women, and our people were twenty-five in number. Two of our men were wounded by the Indians, one with two arrow-shots in his breast, and another with one in his side, and if it had not happened that they carried shields and wooden bucklers, and that they got near them with the barge and upset their canoe, most of them would have been killed with their arrows. After their canoe was upset, they remained in the water swimming and occasionally wading (for there were shallows in that part), still using their bows as much as they could, so that our men had enough to do to take them : and after all there was one of

---

de toda la flota. Luego los de la barca fueron para ellos tan junto con la tierra, que con el embebecimiento que tenian, maravillándose é pensando que cosa seria, nunca los vieron hasta que estovieron muy cerca dellos, que no les pudieron mucho huir aunque harto trabajaron por ello ; pero los nuestros aguijaron con tanta priesa que no se les pudieron ir. Los Caribes desque vieron que el hoir no les aprovechaba, con mucha osadia pusieron mano á los arcos, tambien las mugeres como los hombres ; é digo con mucha osadia porque ellos no eran mas de cuatro hombres y dos mugeres, é los nuestros mas de veinte é cinco, de los cuales firieron dos, al uno dieron dos frechadas en los pechos é al otro una por el costado, é sino fuera porque llevaban adargas é tablachutas, é porque los invistieron presto con la barca é les trastornaron su canoa, asaetearan con sus frechas los mas dellos. E despues de trastornada su canoa quedaron en el agua nadando, é á las veces haciendo pie, que alli habia unos bajos, é tovieron harto que hacer en tomarlos, que to-

them whom they were unable to secure till he had received a
mortal wound with a lance, and whom thus wounded they
took to the ships. The difference between these Caribbees
and the other Indians, with respect to dress, consists in their
wearing their hair very long, while the others have it clipt
irregularly and paint their heads with crosses and a hundred
thousand different devices, each according to his fancy;
which they do with sharpened reeds. All of them, both the
Caribbees and the others, are beardless, so that it is a rare
thing to find a man with a beard: the Caribbees whom we
took had their eyes and eyebrows stained, which I imagine
they do from ostentation and to give them a more formidable
appearance. One of these captives said, that in an island
belonging to them called Cayre (which is the first we saw,
though we did not go to it), there is a great quantity of gold;
and that if we were to take them nails and tools with which
to make their canoes, we might bring away as much gold as
we liked. On the same day we left that island, having been
there no more than six or seven hours; and steering for

---

davía cuanto podian tiraban, é con todo eso el uno no lo pudieron
tomar sino mal herido de una lanzada que murió, el cual trajeron
ansi herido fasta los navíos. La diferencia destos á los otros indios
en el hábito, es que los de Caribe tienen el cabello muy largo, los
otros son tresquilados é fechas cien mil diferencias en las cabezas de
cruces, é de otras pinturas en diversas maneras, cada uno como se
le antoja, lo cual se hacen con cañas agudas. Todos ansi los de
Caribe como los otros es gente sin barbas, que por maravilla halla-
rás hombre que las tenga. Estos Caribes que allí tomaron venian
tiznados los ojos é las cejas, lo cual me parece que hacen por gala,
é con aquello parescian mas espantables; el uno destos dice que en
una isla dellos, llamada Cayre, que es la primera que vimos, á la
cual no llegamos, hay mucho oro; que vayan allá con clavos é con-
tezuelas para hacer sus canoas, é que traerán cuanto oro quisieren.
Luego aquel dia partimos de esta isla, que no estariamos allí mas de
seis ó siete horas, fuemos para otra tierra que pareció á ojo que

another point of land[15] which appeared to lie in our intended course, we reached it by night. On the morning of the following day we coasted along it, and found it to be a large extent of country, but not continuous, for it was divided into more than forty islets.[16] The land was very high and most of it barren, an appearance which we have never observed in any of the islands visited by us before or since: the surface of the ground seemed to suggest the probability of its containing metals. None of us went on shore here, but a small latteen caravel went up to one of the islets and found in it some fishermen's huts; the Indian women whom we brought with us said they were not inhabited. We proceeded along the coast the greater part of that day, and on the evening of the next we discovered another island called Burenquen,[17] which we judged to be thirty leagues in length, for we were coasting along it the whole of one day. This island is very beautiful and apparently fertile: hither the Caribbees come

---

estaba en el camino que habiamos de facer : llegamos noche cerca della. Otro dia de mañana fuimos por la costa della : era muy gran tierra, aunque no era muy continua, que eran mas de cuarenta y tantos islones, tierra muy alta, é la mas della pelada, la cual no era ninguna ni es de las que antes ni despues habemos visto. Parescia tierra dispuesta para haber en ella metales: á esta no llegamos para saltar en tierra, salvo una carabela latina llegó á un islon de estos, en el cual hallaron ciertas casas de pescadores. Las Indias que traiamos dijeron que no eran pobladas. Andovimos por esta costa lo mas deste dia, hasta otro dia en la tarde que llegamos á vista de otra isla llama Burenquen, cuya costo corrimos todo un dia : juzgábase que ternia por aquella banda treinta leguas. Esta isla es muy hermosa y muy fértil á parecer : á esta vienen los de Caribe á con-

[15] The island of *Santa Cruz*, where they anchored on Thursday the fourteenth of November. (M. F. de Navarrete.

[16] The admiral named the largest of these islands *St. Ursula*, and all the others *The eleven thousand Virgins*. (M. F. de Navarrete.)

[17] The island of *Porto Rico*, to which the admiral gave the name of *St. John the Baptist*. (M. F. de Navarrete.)

with the view of subduing the inhabitants, and often carry
away many of the people.   These islanders have no boats nor
any knowledge of navigation ; but, as our captives inform us,
they use bows as well as the Caribbees, and if by chance
when they are attacked they succeed in taking any of
their invaders, they will eat them in like manner as the
Caribbees themselves in the contrary event would devour
them.   We remained two days in this island, and a great
number of our men went on shore, but could never get speech
of the natives, who had all fled, from fear of the Caribbees.   All
the above-mentioned islands were discovered in this voyage,
the admiral having seen nothing of them in his former voyage;
they are all very beautiful and possess a most luxuriant soil,
but this last island appeared to exceed all the others in beauty.
Here terminated the islands, which on the side towards Spain
had not been seen before by the admiral, although we regard
it as a matter of certainty that there is land more than forty
leagues beyond the foremost of these newly discovered islands,
on the side nearest to Spain.   We believe this to be the case,
because two days before we saw land we observed some birds
called rabihorcados (or pelicans, marine birds of prey which

---

quistar, de la cual llevaban mucha gente ; estos no tienen fustas
ningunas nin saben andar por mar ; pero, segun dicen estos Caribes
que tomamos, usan arcos como ellos, é si por caso cuando los vienen
á saltear los pueden prender tambien se los comen como los de
Caribe á ellos.   En un puerto desta isla estovimos dos dias, donde
saltó mucha gente en tierra ; pero jamas podimos haber lengua, que
todos se fuyeron como gente temorizadas de los Caribes.   Todas
estas islas dichas fueron descubiertas deste camino, que fasta aquí
ninguna dellas habia visto el Almirante el otro viage, todos son muy
hermosas é de muy buena tierra ; pero esta paresció mejor á todos :
aquí casi se acabaron las islas que fácia la parte de España habia
dejado de ver el Almirante, aunque tenemos por cosa cierta que
hay tierra mas de cuarenta leguas antes de estas primeras hasta
España, porque dos dias antes que viesemos tierra vimos unas aves
que llaman rabihorcados, que son aves de rapiña marinas é ni si-

do not sit or sleep upon the water), making circumvolutions in the air at the close of evening previous to taking their flight towards land for the night. These birds could not be going to settle at more than twelve or fifteen leagues distance, because it was late in the evening, and this was on our right hand on the side towards Spain; from which we all judged that there was land there still undiscovered; but we did not go in search of it, because it would have taken us round out of our intended route. I hope that in a few voyages it will be discovered. It was at dawn that we left the before-mentioned island of Burenquen,[18] and on that day before nightfall we caught sight of land, which though not recognized by any of those who had come hither in the former voyage, we believed to be Española, from the information given us by the Indian women whom we had with us : and in this island we remain at present.[19] Between Española and Burenquen[20] another island appeared at a distance, but of no great size. When we reached Española the land, at the part where we approached it, was low and very

---

entan ni duermen sobre el agua, sobre tarde rodeando sobir en alto, é despues tiran su via á buscar tierra para dormir, las cuales no podrian ir á caer segun era tarde de doce ó quince leguas arriba, y esto era á la man derecha donde veniamos hasta la parte de España; de donde todos juzgaron allí quedar tierra, lo cual no se buscó porque se nos hacia rodeo para la via que traimos. Espero que á pocos viages se hallará. Desta isla sobredicha partimos una madrugada, é aquel dia, antes que fuese noche, hobimos vista de tierra, la cual tampoco era conocida de ninguno de los que habian venido el otro viage ; pero por las nuevas de las indias que traimos sospechamos que era la Española, en la cual agora estamos. Entre esta isla é la otra de Buriquen parecia de lejos otra, aunque no era grande. Desque llegamos á esta Española, por el comienzo de alla era tierra baja y muy llana, del conocimiento de la cual aun estaban todos

[18] Porto Rico.
[19] On Friday, the twenty-second of November, the admiral first caught sight of the island of Española. (M. F. de Navarrete.)
[20] La Mona and Monito. (M. F. de Navarrete.)

flat, [21] on seeing which, a general doubt arose as to its identity; for, neither the admiral nor his companions, on the previous voyage, had seen it on this side.

The island being large, is divided into provinces ; the part which we first touched at, is called Hayti ; another province adjoining it, they call Xamana ; and the next province is named Bohio, where we now are.   These provinces are again subdivided, for they are of great extent.   Those who have seen the length of its coast, state that it is two hundred leagues long, and I, myself, should judge it not to be less than a hundred and fifty leagues : as to its breadth, nothing is hitherto known ; it is now forty days since a caravel left us with the view of circumnavigating it, and is not yet returned. The country is very remarkable, and contains a vast number of large rivers, and extensive chains of mountains, with broad open valleys, and the mountains are very high : it does not appear that the grass is ever cut throughout the year.   I do not think they have any winter in this part, for near Navidad (at Christmas) were found many birds-nests, some containing the

---

dubdosos si fuese la que es, porque aquella parte nin el Almirante ni los otros que con él vinieron habian visto, é aquesta isla como es grande es nombrada por provincias, e á esta parte que primero llegamos llaman Hayti, y luego á la otra provincia junta con esta llaman Xamaná, é á la otra Bohio, en la cual agora estamos ; ansi hay en ellas muchas provincias porque es gran cosa, porque segun afirman los que la han visto por la costa de largo, dicen que habrá doscientas leguas : á mi me parece que á lo menos habrá ciento é cincuenta ; del ancho della hasta agora no se sabe.   Alla es ido cuarenta dias ha á rodearla una carabela, la cual no es venida hasta hoy.   Es tierra muy singular, donde hay infinitos rios grandes é sierras grandes é valles grandes rasos, grandes montañas : sospecho que nunca se secan las yerbas en todo el año.   Non creo que hay invierno ninguno en esta nin en las otras, porque por Navidad se fallan muchos nidos de aves, dellas con pájaros, é dellas con hue-

---

[21] Cape Engaño, in the island of Española.

young birds, and others containing eggs. No four-footed animal has ever been seen in this or any of the other islands, except some dogs of various colours, as in our own country, but in shape like large house-dogs; and also some little animals, in colour, size, and fur, like a rabbit, with long tails, and feet like those of a rat; these animals climb up the trees, and many who have tasted them, say they are very good to eat :[22] there are not any wild beasts. There are great numbers of small snakes, and some lizards, but not many; for the Indians consider them as great a luxury as we do pheasants : they are of the same size as ours, but different in shape. In a small adjacent island[23] (in which is a port called Monte Christo, where we stayed several days), our men saw an enormous kind of lizard, which they said was as large round as a calf, with a tail as long as a lance, which they often went out to kill; but bulky as it was, it got into the sea, so that they could not catch it. There are, both in this and the other islands, an infinite number of birds like those in our own country, and

---

vos. En ella ni en las otras nunca se ha visto animal de cuatro pies, salvo algunos perros de todas colores como en nuestra patria, la hechura como unos gosques grandes; de animales salvages no hay. Otrosí, hay un hanimal de color de conejo é de su pelo, el grandor de un conejo nuevo, el rabo largo, los pies é manos como de raton, suben por los árboles, muchos los han comido, dicen que es muy bueno de comer: hay culebras muchas no grandes; lagartos aunque no muchos, porque los indios hacen tanta fiesta dellos como hariamos allá con faisanes, son del tamaño de los de allá, salvo que en la hechura son diferentes, aunque en una isleta pequeña, que está junto con un puerto que llaman Monte Christo, donde estovimos muchos dias, vieron muchos dias un lagarto muy grande que decian que seria de gordura de un becerro, é atan complido como una lanza, é muchas veces salieron por lo matar, é con la mucha espesura se les metia en la mar, de manera que no se pudo haber dél derecho. Hay en esta isla y en las otras infinitas aves de las de nuestra patria, é otras muchas que allá nunca se vieron :

[22] In all probability a species of *capromys*.
[23] Cabra, or Goat island, between Puerto de Plata and Cas Rouge Point.

many others such as we had never seen.   No kind of domestic
fowl has been seen here, with the exception of some ducks in
the houses in Zuruquia ; these ducks were larger than those
of Spain, though smaller than geese,—very pretty, with tufts
on their heads, most of them as white as snow, but some black.

We ran along the coast of this island nearly a hundred
leagues, concluding, that within this range we should find
the spot where the admiral had left some of his men, and
which we supposed to be about the middle of the coast.   As
we passed by the province called Xamaná, we sent on shore
one of the Indians, who had been taken in the previous voyage, clothed, and carrying some trifles, which the admiral had
ordered to be given him.   On that day died one of our
sailors, a Biscayan, who had been wounded in the affray with
the Caribbees, when they were captured, as I have already
described, through their want of caution.   As we were proceeding along the coast, an opportunity was afforded for a
boat to go on shore to bury him, the boat being accompanied
by two caravels to protect it.   When they reached the shore,
a great number of Indians came out to the boat, some of
them wearing necklaces and ear-rings of gold, and expressed

---

de las aves domésticas nunca se ha visto acá ninguna, salvo en la
Zuruquia habia en las casas unas ánades, las mas dellas blancas como la nieve é algunas dellas negras, muy lindas, con crestas rasas,
mayores que las de allá, menores que ánsares.   Por la costa desta
isla corrimos al pie de cien leguas porque hasta donde el Almirante
habia dejado la gente, habria en este compás, que será en comedio
ó en medio de la isla.   Andando por la provincia della llamada
Xamaná, en derecho echamos en tierra uno de los indios quel otro
viage habian llevado vestido, é con algunas cosillas quel Almirante
le habia mandado dar.   Aquel dia se nos murió un marinero viz-
caino que habia seido herido de los Caribes, que ya dije que se tomaron, por su mala guarda, é porque ibamos por costa de tierra,
dióse lugar que saliese una barca á enterrarlo, é fueron en reguarda
de la barca dos carabelas cerca con tierra.   Salieron á la barca en
llegando en tierra muchos indios, de los cuales algunos traian oro

a wish to accompany the Spaniards to the ships; but our men refused to take them, because they had not received permission from the admiral. When the Indians found that they would not take them, two of them got into a small canoe, and went up to one of the caravels that had put in to shore; they were received on board with great kindness, and taken to the admiral's ship, where, through the medium of an interpreter, they related that a certain king had sent them to ascertain who we were, and to invite us to land, adding that they had plenty of gold, and also of provisions, to which we should be welcome. The admiral desired that shirts, and caps, and other trifles, should be given to each of them, and said that as he was going to the place where Guacamari dwelt, he would not stop then, but that on a future day he should have the opportunity of seeing him, and with that they departed. We continued our route till we came to an harbour called Monte Cristi, where we remained two days, in order to observe the position of the land; for the admiral had an objection to the spot where his men had been left with the view of forming a station. We went on shore therefore to survey the forma-

---

al cuello, é á las orejas; querian venir con los cristianos á los navíos, é no los quisieron traer, porque no llevaban licencia del Almirante; los cuales desque vieron que no los querian traer se metieron dos dellos en una canoa pequeña, é se vinieron á una carabela de las que se habian acercado á tierra, en la cual los recibieron con su amor, é trajéronlos á la nao del Almirante, é dijeron, mediante un interprete, que un Rey fulano los enviaba á saber que gente eramos, é á rogar que quisiesemos llegar á tierra, porque tenian mucho oro é le darian dello, é de lo que tenian de comer: el Almirante les mandó dar sendas camisas é bonetes é otras cosillas, é les dijo que porque iba á donde estaba Guacamarí non se podria detener, que otro tiempo habria que le pudiese ver, é con esto se fueron. No cesamos de andar nuestro camino fasta llegar á un puerto llamado Monte Cristi, donde estuvimos dos dias para ver la disposicion de la tierra, porque no habia parecido bien al Almirante el logar donde habia dejado la gente para hacer asiento. Decendimos en tierra

tion of the land : there was a large river of excellent water
close by ;[24] but the ground was inundated, and very ill-calcu-
lated for habitation. As we went on making our observations
on the river and the land, some of our men found two dead
bodies by the river's side, one with a rope round his neck,
and the other with one round his foot : this was on the first
day of our landing. On the following day they found two
other corpses farther on, and one of these was observed to
have a great quantity of beard ; this was regarded as a very
suspicious circumstance by many of our people, because, as I
have already said, all the Indians are beardless. This harbour
is twelve leagues[25] from the place where the Spaniards had been
left under the protection of Guacamari, the king of that province, whom I suppose to be one of the chief men of the
island. After two days we set sail for that spot, but as it was
late when we arrived there,[26] and there were some shoals, where
the admiral's ship had been lost, we did not venture to put in

para ver la dispusicion : habia cerca de allí un gran rio de muy
buena agua ; pero es toda tierra anegada é muy indispuesta para
habitar.   Andando veyendo el rio é tierra hallaron algunos de los
nuestros en una parte dos hombres muertos junto con el rio, el uno
con un lazo al pescuezo y el otro con otro al pie, esto fue el primero dia.   Otro dia siguiente hallaron otros dos muertos mas adelante de aquellos, el uno destos estaba en disposicion que se le pudo
conocer tener muchas barbas. Algunos de los nuestros sospecharon
mas mal que bien, é con razon, porque los indios son todos desbar-
bados, como dicho he.   Este puerto está del lugar donde estaba la
gente cristiana doce leguas : pasados dos dias alzamos velas para el
lugar donde el Almirante habia dejado la sobredicha gente, en compañía de un Rey destos indios, que se llamaba Guacamarí, que
pienso ser de los principales desta isla.   Este dia llegamos en derecho de aquel lugar ; pero era ya tarde, é porque allí habia unos
bajos donde el otro dia se habia perdido la nao en que habia ido el

[24] The river of Santiago.   [25] It is only seven leagues.
[26] The admiral anchored at the entrance of the harbour of Navidad, on
Wednesday, the twenty-seventh of November, towards midnight, and on
the following day, in the afternoon, put into the harbour. (Navarrete.)

close to the shore, but remained that night at a little less than a league from the coast, waiting until the morning, when we might enter securely. On that evening, a canoe, containing five or six Indians, came out at a considerable distance from where we were, and approached us with great celerity. The admiral believing that he insured our safety by keeping the sails set, would not wait for them; they, however, perseveringly rowed up to us within gunshot, and then stopped to look at us; but when they saw that we did not wait for them, they put back and went away. After we had anchored that night at the spot in question,[27] the admiral ordered two guns to be fired, to see if the Spaniards, who had remained with Guacamari, would fire in return, for they also had guns with them; but when we received no reply, and could not perceive any fires, nor the slightest symptom of habitations on the spot, the spirits of our people became much depressed, and they began to entertain the suspicion which the circumstances were naturally calculated to excite. While all were in this desponding mood, and when four or five hours of the night had passed

---

Almirante, no osamos tomar el puerto cerca de tierra fasta que otro dia de mañana se desfondase é pudiesen entrar seguramente : quedamos aquella noche no una legua de tierra. Esa tarde, viniendo para allí de lejos, salió una canoa en que parescian cinco ó seis indios, los cuales venian á prisa para nosotros. El Almirante creyendo que nos seguraba hasta alzarnos, no quiso que los esperasemos, é porfiando llegaron hasta un tiro de lombarda de nosotros, é parabanse á mirar, é desde allí desque vieron que no los esperabamos dieron vuelta é tornaron su via. Despues que surgimos en aquel lugar sobredicho tarde, el Almirante mandó tirar dos lombardas á ver si respondian los cristianos que habian quedado con el dicho Guacamarí, porque tambien tenian lombardas, los cuales nunca respondieron ni menos parescian huegos ni señal de casas en aquel lugar, de lo qual se deconsoló mucho la gente é tomaron la sospecha que de tal caso se debia tomar. Estando ansi todos muy tristes, pasadas cuatro ó cinco horas de la noche, vino la misma

[27] The Bay of Caracol, four leagues west of Fort Dauphin.

away, the same canoe which we had seen in the evening, came
up, and the Indians with a loud voice addressed the captain
of the caravel, which they first approached, inquiring for the
admiral; they were conducted to the admiral's vessel, but
would not go on board till he had spoken to them, and they
had asked for a light, in order to assure themselves that it
was he who conversed with them.   One of them was a cousin
of Guacamari, who had been sent by him once before : it appeared, that after they had turned back the previous evening,
they had been charged by Guacamari with two masks of
gold as a present; one for the admiral, the other for a captain who had accompanied him on the former voyage.   They
remained on board for three hours, talking with the admiral
in the presence of all of us, he showing much pleasure in their
conversation, and inquiring respecting the welfare of the
Spaniards whom he had left behind.   Guacamari's cousin replied, that those who remained were all well, but that some
of them had died of disease, and others had been killed in
quarrels that had arisen amongst them : he said also that the
province had been invaded, by two kings named Caonabó and

---

canoa que esa tarde habiamos visto, é venia dando voces, pregun-
tando por el Almirante un Capitan de una carabela donde primero
llegaron : trajéronlos á la nao del Almirante, los cuales nunca quisieron entrar hasta que el Almirante los hablase ; demandaron lum ·
bre para lo conocer, é despues que lo conocieron entraron.   Era
uno dellos primo del Guacamarí, el cual los habia enviado otra vez.
Despues que se habian tornado aquella tarde traian caratulas de oro
que Guacamarí enviaba en presente ; la una para el Almirante é
la otra para un Capitan quel otro viage habia ido con él.   Estovieron en la nao hablando con el Almirante en presencia de todos por
tres horas mostrando mucho placer, preguntándoles por los Cristianos que tales estaban : aquel pariente dijo que estaban todos buenos, aunque entre ellos habia algunos muertos de dolencia é otros
de diferencia que habia contecido entre ellos, é que Guacamarí estaba en otro lugar ferido en una pierna é por eso no habia venido,
pero que otro dia vernia ;   porque otros dos Reyes, llamado el uno

Mayreni, who had burned the habitations of the people ; and that Guacamari was at some distance, lying ill of a wound in his leg, which was the occasion of his not appearing, but that he would come on the next day. The Indians then departed, saying they would return on the following day with the said Guacamari, and left us consoled for that night. On the morning of the next day, we were expecting that Guacamari would come ; and, in the meantime, some of our men landed by command of the admiral, and went to the spot where the Spaniards had formerly been : they found the building which they had inhabited, and which they had in some degree fortified with a palisade, burnt and levelled with the ground ; they found also some rags and stuffs which the Indians had brought to throw upon the house. They observed too that the Indians who were seen near the spot, looked very shy, and dared not approach, but, on the contrary, fled from them. This appeared strange to us, for the admiral had told us that in the former voyage, when he arrived at this place, so many came in canoes to see us, that there was no keeping them off; and as we now saw that they were suspicious of us, it gave us

---

Caonabó y el otro Mayrení, habian venido á pelear con él é que le habian quemado el logar ; é luego esa noche se tornaron diciendo que otra dia vernian con el dicho Guacamarí, é con esto nos dejaron por esa noche consolados. Otro dia en la mañana estovimos esperando que viniese el dicho Guacamarí, é entretanto saltaron en tierra algunos por mandado del Almirante, é fueron al lugar donde solian estar, é halláronle quemado un cortijo algo fuerte con una palizada, donde los Cristianos habitaban, é tenian lo suyo quemado é derribado, é ciertas bernias é ropas que los indios habian traido á echar en la casa. Los dichos indios que por allí parecian andaban muy cahareños, que no se osaban allegar á nosotros, antes huian ; lo cual no nos pareció bien porque el Almirante nos habia dicho que en llegando á quel lugar salian tantas canoas dellos á bordo de los navíos á vernos que no nos podriamos defender dellos, é que en el otro viage ansí lo facian ; é como agora veiamos que estaban sospechosos de nosotros no nos parecia bien, con todo halagándoles

a very unfavourable impression. We threw trifles, such as buttons and beads, towards them, in order to conciliate them, but only four, a relation of Guacamari's and three others, took courage to enter the boat, and were rowed on board. When they were asked concerning the Spaniards, they replied that all of them were dead : we had been told this already by one of the Indians whom we had brought from Spain, and who had conversed with the two Indians that on the former occasion came on board with their canoe, but we had not believed it. Guacamari's kinsman was asked who had killed them : he replied that king Caonabó and king Mayreni had made an attack upon them, and burnt the buildings on the spot, that many were wounded in the affray, and among them Guacamari, who had received a wound in his thigh, and had retired to some distance: he also stated that he wished to go and fetch him; upon which some trifles were given to him, and he took his departure for the place of Guacamari's abode. All that day we remained in expectation of them, and when we saw that they did not come, many suspected that the Indians who had been on board the night before, had been drowned; for

---

aquel dia é arrojándolos algunas cosas, ansi como cascabeles é cuentas, hobo de asegurarse un su pariente del dicho Guacamarí é otros tres, los cuales entraron en la barca é trajéronlos la nao. Despues que le preguntaron por los Cristianos dijeron que todos eran muertos, aunque ya nos lo habia dicho un indio de los que llevabamos de Castilla que lo habian hablado los dos indios que antes habian venido á la nao, que se habian quedado á bordo de la nao con su canao, pero no le habiamos creido. Fue preguntado á este pariente de Guacamarí quien los habia muerto : dijo que el Rey de Canoabó y el Rey Mayrení, é que le quemaron las cosas del lugar, é que estaban dellos muchos heridos, é tambien el dicho Guacamarí estaba pasado un muslo, y él que estaba en otro lugar y que él queria ir luego allá á lo llamar, al cual dieron algunas cosas, é luego se partió para donde estaba Guacamarí. Todo aquel dia los estobimos esperando, é desque vimos que no venian, muchos tenian sospecha que se habian ahogado los indios que antenoche habian venido,

they had had wine given them two or three times, and they had come in a small canoe that might be easily upset. The next morning the admiral went on shore, taking some of us with him; we went to the spot where the settlement had been, and found it utterly destroyed by fire, and the clothes of the Spaniards lying about upon the grass, but on that occasion we saw no dead body. There were many different opinions amongst us; some suspecting that Guacamari himself was concerned in the betrayal and death of the Christians; others thought not, because his own residence was burnt: so that it remained a very doubtful question. The admiral ordered all the ground which had been occupied by the fortifications of the Spaniards to be searched, for he had left orders with them to bury all the gold that they might get. While this was being done, the admiral wished to examine a spot at about a league's distance, which seemed to be suitable for building a town, for there was yet time to do so;—and some of us went thither with him, making our observations of the land as we went along the coast, until we reached a village of seven or eight houses, which the Indians for-

---

porque los habian dado á beber dos ó tres veces de vino, é venian en una canoa pequeña que se les podria trastornar. Otro dia de mañana salió á tierra el Almirante é algunos de nosotros, é fuemos donde solia estar la villa, la cual nos vimos toda quemada é los vestidos de los cristianos se hallaban por aquella yerba. Por aquella hora no vimos ningun muerto. Habia entre nosotros muchas razones diferentes, unos sospechando que el mismo Guacamarí fuese en la traicion ó muerte de los Cristianos, otros les parecia que no, pues estaba quemada su villa, ansí que la cosa era mucho para dudar. El Almirante mandó catar todo el sitio donde los Cristianos estaban fortalecidos porquel los habia mandado que desque toviesen alguna cantidad de oro que lo enterrasen. Entretanto que esto se hacia quiso llegar á ver á cerca de una legua do nos parecia que podria haber asiento para poder edificar una villa porque ya era tiempo, adonde fuimos ciertos con él mirando la tierra por la costa, fasta que llegamos á un poblado donde habia siete ú ocho casas; las

sook when they saw us approach, carrying away what they
could, and leaving the things which they could not remove,
hidden amongst the grass, around the houses. These people
are so degraded that they have not even the sense to select a
fitting place to live in ; those who dwell on the shore, build
for themselves the most miserable hovels that can be imagined,
and all the houses are so covered with grass and dampness,
that I wonder how they can contrive to exist. In these houses
we found many things belonging to the Spaniards, which it
could not be·supposed they would have bartered ; such as a
very handsome Moorish mantle, which had not been unfolded
since it was brought from Spain, stockings and pieces of cloth,
also an anchor belonging to the ship which the admiral had
lost here on the previous voyage ; with other articles, which
the more confirmed our suspicions. On examining some
things which had been very cautiously sewn up in a small
basket, we found a man's head wrapped up with great care ;
this we judged might be the head of a father, or mother, or
of some person whom they much regarded : I have since heard
that many were found in the same state, which makes me

---

quales habian desamparado los indios luego que nos vieron ir, é
llevaron lo que pudieron é lo otro dejaron escondido entre yerbas
junto con las casas, que es gente tan bestial que no tienen discrecion para buscar lugar para habitar, que los que viven á la marina
es maravilla cuan bestialmente edifican, que las casas enderedor
tienen tan cubiertas de yerba ó de humidad, que estoy espantado
como viven.   En aquellas casas hallamos muchas cosas de los Cristianos, las cuales no se creian que ellos hobiesen rescatado, ansí como una almalafa muy gentil, la cual no se habia descogido de como
la llevaron de Castilla, é calzas é pedazos de paños, é una ancla de
la nao quel Almirante habia allí perdido el otro viage, é otras cosas,
de las cuales mas se esforzó nuestra opinion ; y de acá hallamos,
buscando las cosas que tenian guardadas en una esportilla mucho
cosida é mucho á recabdo, una cabeza de hombre mucho guardada.
Allí juzgamos por entonces que seria la cabeza de padre ó madre, ó
de persona que mucho querian. Despues he oido que hayan hallado

believe that our first impression was the true one. After this we returned. We went on the same day to the site of the settlement; and when we arrived, we found many Indians, who had regained their courage, bartering gold with our men: they had bartered to the extent of a mark : we also learned that they had shown where the bodies of eleven of the dead Spaniards were laid, which were already covered with the grass that had grown over them; and they all with one voice asserted that Caonabó and Mayreni had killed them; but notwithstanding all this, we began to hear complaints that one of the Spaniards had taken three women to himself, and another four; from whence we drew the inference that jealousy was the cause of the misfortune that had occurred. On the next morning, as no spot in that vicinity appeared suitable for our making a settlement, the admiral ordered a caravel to go in one direction to look for a convenient locality, while some of us went with him another way. In the course of our explorations, we discovered a harbour, of great security; the neighbourhood of which, so far as regarded the formation of the land, was excellent for habitation ; but as it was far from any mine of gold, the neighbourhood of which was very de-

---

muchas desta manera, por donde creo ser verdad lo que allí juzgamos ; desde allí nos tornamos. Aquel dia venimos por donde estaba la villa, y cuando llegamos hallamos muchos indios que se habian asegurado y estaban rescatando oro : tenian rescatado fasta un marco: hallamos que habian mostrado donde estaban muertos once cristianos, cubiertos ya de la yerba que habia crecido sobre ellos, é todos hablaban por una boca que Caonabó é Mayreni los habian muerto ; pero con todo eso asomaban queja que los Cristianos uno tenia tres mugeres, otro cuatro, donde creemos quel mal que les vino fue de zelos. Otro dia de mañana, porque en todo aquello no habia logar dispuesto para nosotros poder hacer asiento, acordó el Almirante fuese una carabela á una parte para mirar lugar conveniente, é algunos que fuimos con él fuimos á otra parte, á do hallamos un puerto muy seguro é muy gentil disposicion de tierra para habitar, pero porque estaba lejos de donde nos deseabamos que estaba la

sirable, the admiral decided that we should settle in some spot which would give us greater certainty of attaining that object, provided the position of the land should prove equally convenient. On our return, we found the other caravel arrived, in which Melchior and four or five other trustworthy men had been exploring with a similar object. They reported that as they went along the coast, a canoe came out to them in which were two Indians, one of whom was the brother of Guacamari, and was recognized by a pilot who was in the caravel. When he questioned them as to their purpose, they replied that Guacamari sent to beg the Spaniards to come on shore, as he was residing near, with as many as fifty families around him. The chief men of the party then went on shore in the boat, proceeded to the place where Guacamari was, and found him stretched on his bed, complaining of a severe wound. They conferred with him, and inquired respecting the Spaniards; his reply was, in accordance with the account already given by the others, viz.—that they had been killed by Caonabó and Mayreni, who also had wounded him in the thigh; and in confirmation of his assertion, he showed them the limb bound

---

mina de oro, no acordó el Almirante de poblar sino en otra parte que fuese mas cierta si se hallase conveniente disposicion. Cuando venimos deste lugar hallamos venida la otra carabela que habia ido á la otra parte á buscar el dicho lugar, en la cual habia ido Melchior e otros cuatro ó cinco hombres de pro. E yendo costeando por tierra salió á ellos una canoa en que venian dos indios, el uno era hermano de Guacamarí, el cual fue conocido por un piloto que iba en la dicha carabela, é preguntó quien iba allí, al cual, dijeron los hombres prencipales, dijeron que Guacamarí les rogaba que se llegasen á tierra, donde él tenia su asiento con fasta cincuenta casas. Los dichos prencipales saltaron en tierra con la barca é fueron donde él estaba, el cual fallaron en su cama echado faciendo del doliente ferido. Fablaron con él preguntándole por los Cristianos : respondió concertando con la mesma razon de los otros, que era que Caonabó é Mayreni los habian muerto, é que á él habian ferido en un muslo, el cual mostró ligado :

up : on seeing which, they concluded that his statement was correct. At their departure he gave to each of them a jewel of gold, according to his estimation of their respective merits. The Indians beat the gold into very thin plates, in order to make masks of it, and set it in a cement which they make for that purpose : other ornaments they make of it, to wear on the head and to hang in the ears and nostrils, for these also they require it to be thin ; it is not the massiveness of the gold that they admire in their ornaments, but its showy appearance. Guacamari desired them by signs and as well as he was able, to tell the admiral that as he was thus wounded, he prayed him to have the goodness to come to see him. This adventure the aforesaid sailors related to the admiral when he arrived. The next morning he resolved to go thither, for the spot could be reached in three hours, being scarcely three leagues distance from the place where we were ; but as it would be the dinner-hour when we arrived, we dined before we went on shore. After dinner, the admiral gave orders that all the captains should come with their barges to proceed to the shore, for already on that morning, previous to our de-

---

los que entonces lo vieron ansí les pareció que era verdad como él lo dijo : al tiempo del despedirse dió á cada uno dellos una joya de oro, á cada uno como le pareció que lo merescia. Este oro facian en fojas muy delgadas, porque lo quieren para facer carátulas é para poderse asentar en betun que ellos facen, si así no fuese no se asentaria. Otro facen para traer en la cabeza é para colgar en las orejas é narices, ansí que todavía es menester que sea delgado, pues que ellos nada desto hacen por riqueza salvo por buen parecer. Dijo el dicho Guacamarí por señas e como mejor pudo, que porque él estaba ansí herido que dijesen al Almirante que quisiese venir á verlo. Luego quel Almirante llegó los sobredichos le contaron este caso. Otro dia de mañana acordó partir para allá, al cual lugar llegariamos dentro de tres horas, porque apenas habria dende donde estábamos allá tres leguas ; ansí que cuando allí llegamos era hora de comer : comimos ante de salir en tierra. Luego que hobimos comido mandó el Almirante que todos los Capitanes viniesen con

parture, the aforesaid brother of Guacamari had come to speak
with the admiral to urge his visit.   Then the admiral went on
shore accompanied by all the principal officers, so richly
dressed that they would have made a distinguished appearance
even in any of our chief cities : he took with him some articles
as presents, having already received from Guacamari a certain
quantity of gold, and it was reasonable that he should make
a commensurate response to his acts and expressions of good-
will : Guacamari had also provided himself with a present.
When we arrived, we found him stretched upon his bed, which
was made of cotton net-work, and, according to their custom,
suspended. He did not arise, but made from his bed the best
gesture of courtesy of which he was capable.   He showed
much feeling ; with tears in his eyes lamented the death of
the Spaniards, and began speaking on the subject, with explaining to the best of his power, how some died of disease,
others had gone to Caonabó in search of the mine of gold,
and had there been killed, and that the rest had been attacked
and slain in their own town.   According to the appearance
of the dead bodies, it was not two months since this had hap-

---

sus barcas para ir en tierra, porque ya esa mañana antes que parti-
esemos de donde estábamos habia venido el sobredicho su hermano
á hablar con el Almirante, é á darle priesa que fuese al lugar donde
estaba el dicho Guacamarí.   Allí fue el Almirante á tierra é toda
la gente de pro con él, tan ataviados que en una cibdad prencipal
parecieran bien : llevó algunas cosas para le presentar porque ya
habia recibido dél alguna cantidad de oro, é era razon le respondiese
con la obra é voluntad quel habia mostrado.   El dicho Guacamarí
ansí mismo tenia aparejado para hacerle presente.   Cuando llegamos hallámosle echado en su cama, como ellos lo usan, colgado en
el aire, fecha una cama de algodon como de red ; no se levantó,
salvo dende la cama hizo el semblante de cortesia como él mejor
sopo, mostró mucho sentimiento con lágrimas en los ojos por la
muerte de los Cristianos, é comenzó á hablar en ello mostrando,
como mejor podia, como unos murieron de dolencia, é como otros
se habian ido á Caonabó á buscar la mina del oro é que allí los

pened. Then the admiral presented him with eight marks
and a half of gold, six hundred and five pieces of jewellery, of
various colours, and a cap of similar jewel-work, which I think
they ought to value very highly, because in it was a jewel, for
which the admiral, when presenting it, expressed great vene-
ration. It appears to me that these people put more value
upon copper than gold. The surgeon of the fleet and myself
being present, the admiral told Guacamari that we were
skilled in the treatment of human disorders, and wished that
he would shew us his wound; he replied that he was willing;
upon which I said it would be necessary that he should, if
possible, go out of the house, because we could not see well
on account of the place being darkened by the throng of
people; to this he consented, I think more from timidity than
inclination, and left the house leaning on the arm of the
admiral. After he was seated, the surgeon approached him
and began to untie the bandage; then he told the admiral
that the wound was made with a *ciba,* by which he meant
with a stone. When the wound was uncovered, we went up

---

habian muerto, é los otros que se los habian venido á matar allí en
su villa. A lo que parecian los cuerpos de los muertos no habia
dos meses que habia acaecido. Esa hora el presentó al Almirante
ocho marcos y medio de oro, é cinco ó seiscientos labrados de pe-
dreria de diversos colores, é un bonete de la misma pedrería, lo
cual me parece deben tener ellos en mucho. En el bonete estaba un
joyel, lo cual le dió en mucha veneracion. Pareceme que tienen
en mas el cobre quel oro. Estábamos presentes yo y un zurugiano
de armada ; entonces dijo el Almirante al dicho Guacamarí que
nosotros eramos sabios de las enfermedades de los hombres que nos
quisiese mostrar la herida : él respondió que le placia, para lo cual
yo dije que seria necesario, si pudiese, que saliese fuera de casa,
porque con la mucha gente estaba escura é no se podria ver bien ;
lo cual él fizo luego, creo mas de empacho que de gana ; arrimán-
dose á el salió fuera. Despues de asentado, llegó el zurugiano á
él é comenzó de desligarle : entonces dijo al Almirante que era
ferida fecha con ciba, que quiere decir con piedra. Despues que

to examine it : it is certain that there was no more wound on that leg than on the other, although he cunningly pretended that it pained him much. Ignorant as we were of the facts, it was impossible to come to a definite conclusion There were certainly many proofs of an invasion by a hostile people, so that the admiral was at a loss what to do ; he with many others thought, however, that for the present, and until they could ascertain the truth, they ought to conceal their distrust; for after ascertaining it, they would be able to claim whatever indemnity they thought proper. That evening Guacamari accompanied the admiral to the ships, and when they showed him the horses and other objects of interest, their novelty struck him with the greatest amazement: he took supper on board, and returned that evening to his house. The admiral told him that he wished to settle there and to build houses ; to which he assented, but said that the place was not wholesome, because it was very damp: and so it most certainly was.

All this passed through the interpretation of two of the Indians who had gone to Spain in the last voyage,

---

fue desatada llegamos á tentarle. Es cierto que no tenia mas mal en aquella que en la otra, aunque él hacia del raposo que le dolia mucho. Ciertamente no se podia bien determinar porque las razones eran ignotas, que ciertamente muchas cosas habia que mostraban haber venido á él gente contraria. Ansimesmo el Almirante no sabia que se hacer : parescióle, é á otros muchos, que por entonces fasta bien saber la verdad que se debia disimular, porque despues de sabida, cada que quisiesen, se podia dél recibir enmienda. E aquella tarde se vino con el Almirante á las naos, é mostráronle caballos é cuanto ahí habia, de lo cual quedó muy maravillado como de cosa estraña á él ; tomó colacion en la nao, é esa tarde luego se tornó á su casa : el Almirante dijo que queria ir á habitar allí con él é queria facer casas, y él respondió que le placia, pero que el lugar era mal sano porque era muy humido, é tal era él por cierto. Esto todo pasaba estando por intérpretes dos indios de los que el otro viage habian ido á Castilla, los cuales habian que-

who were the sole survivors of seven who had embarked
with us; five died on the voyage, and these but nar-
rowly escaped. The next day we anchored in that port:
Guacamari sent to know when the admiral intended leaving,
and was told that he should do so on the morrow. The same
day Guacamari's brother, and others with him, came on board,
bringing gold to barter: on the day of our departure also they
bartered a great quantity of gold. There were ten women on
board, of those which had been taken in the Caribbee islands,
principally from Boriquen, and it was observed that the
brother of Guacamari spoke with them; we think that he
told them to make an effort to escape that night; for certainly during our first sleep they dropped themselves quietly
into the water, and went on shore, so that by the time they
were missed they had reached such a distance that only four
could be taken by the boats which went in pursuit, and these
were secured when just leaving the water: they had to swim
considerably more than half a league. The next morning the
admiral sent to desire that Guacamari would cause search to
be made for the women who had escaped in the night, and

---

dado vivos de siete que metimos en el puerto, que los cinco se murieron en el camino, los cuales escaparon á uña de caballo. Otro
dia estuvimos surtos en aquel puerto ; é quiso saber cuando se par-
tiria el Almirante : le mandó decir que otro dia. En aquel dia
vinieron á la nao el sobredicho hermano suyo é otros con él, é trajeron algun oro para rescatar. Ansí mesmo el dia que allá salimos
se rescató buena cantidad de oro. En la nao habia diez mugeres
de las que se habian tomado en las islas de Cariby ; eran las mas
dellas de Boriquen. Aquel hermano de Guacamarí habló con ellas :
creemos que les dijo lo que luego esa noche pusieron por obra, y es
que al primer sueño muy mansamente se echaron al agua ó se fueron á tierra, de manera que cuando fueron falladas menos iban tanto
trecho que con las barcas no pudieron tomar mas de las cuatro, las
cuales tomaron al salir del agua ; fueron nadando mas de una gran
media legua. Otro dia de mañana envió el Almirante á decir á
Guacamarí que le enviase aquellas mugeres que la noche antes se

that he would send them back to the ships. When the messengers arrived they found the place forsaken and not a soul
there; this strongly confirmed the suspicions of many, but
others said they might have removed to another village, as
was their custom. That day we remained quiet, because the
weather was contrary for our departure. On the next morning
the admiral resolved that as the wind was adverse, it would
be well to go with the boats to inspect a port on the coast at
two leagues distance further up,[28] to see if the formation of
the land was favourable for a settlement; and we went thither
with all the ship's boats, leaving the ships in the harbour.
As we moved along the coast the people manifested a sense
of insecurity, and when we reached the spot to which we were
bound all the natives had fled. While we were walking about
this place we found an Indian stretched on the hill-side, close
by the houses, with a gaping wound in his shoulder caused by
a dart, so that he had been disabled from fleeing any further.
The natives of this island fight with sharp darts, which they
discharge from cross-bows in the same manner as boys in

---

habian huido, é que luego las mandase buscar. Cuando fueron
hallaron el lugar despoblado, que no estaba persona en el; ahí tornaron muchos fuerte á afirmar su sospecha, otros decian que se
habria mudado á otra poblacion quellos ansí lo suelen hacer. Aquel
dia estovimos allí quedos por que el tiempo era contrario para salir:
otro dia de mañana acordó el Almirante, pues que el tiempo era
contrario, que seria bien ir con las barcas á ver un puerto la costa
arriba, fasta el cual habria dos leguas, para ver si habria dis
pusicion de tierra para hacer habitacion; donde fuemos con
todas las barcas de los navíos dejando los navíos en el puerto.
Fuimos corriendo toda la costa, é tambien estos no se segura-
ban bien de nosotros; llegamos á un lugar de donde todos eran
huidos.   Andando por él fallamos junto con las casas, metido
en el monte, un indio ferido de una vara, de una ferida que
resollaba por las espaldas, que no habia podido huir mas lejos.
Los desta isla pelean con unas varas agudas, las cuales tiran con
unas tiranderas como las que tiran los mochachos las varillas en

[28] Port Dauphin.

Spain shoot their small arrows, and which they send with considerable skill to a great distance; and certainly upon an un-
armed people these weapons are calculated to do serious injury.
The wounded man told us that Caonabó and his people had
wounded him and burnt the houses of Guacamari. Thus we
are still kept in uncertainty respecting the death of our people,
on account of the paucity of information on which to form an
opinion, and the conflicting and equivocal character of the
evidence we have obtained. We did not find the position of
the land in this port favourable for healthy habitation, and
the admiral resolved upon returning along the upper coast by
which we had come from Spain, because we had had tidings
of gold in that direction. But the weather was so adverse
that it cost more labour to sail thirty leagues in a backward
direction than the whole voyage from Spain; so that, what
with the contrary wind and the length of the passage, three
months had elapsed since we first set foot on land. It pleased
God, however, that through the check upon our progress
caused by contrary winds, we succeeded in finding the best
and most suitable spot that we could have selected for a

Castilla, con las cuales tiran muy lejos asaz certero. Es cierto que
para gente desarmada que pueden hacer harto daño. Este nos dijo
que Caonabó é los suyos lo habian ferido, é habian quemado las
casas á Guacamarí. Ansí quel poco entender que los entendemos
é las razones equívocas nos han traido á todos tan afuscados que
fasta agora no se ha podido saber la verdad de la muerte de nuestra
gente, é no hallamos en aquel puerto dispusicion saludable parer
hacer habitacion. Acordó el Almirante nos tornásemos por la
costa arriba por do habiamos venido de Castilla, porque la nueva
del oro era fasta allá. Fuenos el tiempo contrario, que mayor pena
nos fue tornar treinta leguas atrás que venir desde Castilla, que
con el tiempo contrario é la largueza del camino ya eran tres meses
pasados cuando decendimos en tierra. Plugó á nuestro Señor que
por la contrariedad del tiempo que no nos dejó ir mas adelante,
hobimos de tomar tierra en el mejor sitio y dispusicion que pudieramos escoger, donde hay mucho buen puerto é gran pesquería,

settlement, where there was an excellent harbour[29] and abundance of fish, an article of which we stood in great need from
the scarcity of meat. The fish caught here are very singular and more wholesome than those of Spain. The climate
does not allow the fish to be kept from one day to another,
for all animal food speedily becomes unwholesome, on account
of the alternate heat and damp.

The land is very rich for all purposes; near the harbour there
are two rivers; one large,[30] and another of moderate breadth
somewhat near to it: the water is of a very remarkable quality.
On the bank of it is being built a city called Marta,[31] one side of
which is bounded by the water with a ravine of cleft rock, so
that at that part there is no need of fortification; the other half
is girt with a plantation of trees so thick that a rabbit could
scarcely pass through it; and so green that fire will never be
able to burn it. A channel has been commenced for a branch
of the river, which the managers say they will lead through
the middle of the settlement, and will place on it mills of all
kinds requiring to be worked by water. Great quantities of

---

de la cual tenemos mucha necesidad por el carecimiento de las
carnes. Hay en esta tierra muy singular pescado mas sano quel
de España. Verdad sea que la tierra no consiente que se guarde de
un dia para otro porque es caliente é humida, é por ende luego las
cosas introfatibles ligeramente se corrompen. La tierra es muy
gruesa para todas cosas; tiene junto un rio prencipal é otro razonable, asaz cerca de muy singular agua: edificase sobre la ribera dél una cibdad Marta, junto quel lugar se deslinda con el agua,
de manera que la metad de la cibdad queda cercada de agua con
una barranca de peña tajada, tal que por allí no ha menester defensa ninguna; la otra metad está cercada de una arboleda espesa
que apenas podrá un conejo andar por ella; es tan verde que en
ningun tiempo del mundo fuego la podrá quemar: hase comenzado
á traer un brazo del rio, el cual dicen los maestros que trairán por
medio del lugar, é asentarán en él moliendas é sierras de agua, é

[29] Port Isabelique, or Isabella, ten leagues to the east of Monte Cristi.
[30] The river Isabella.   [31] The infant city of Isabella.

vegetables have been planted, which certainly attain a more luxuriant growth here in eight days than they would in Spain in twenty. We were frequently visited by numbers of Indians, among whom were some of their caciques or chiefs, and many women. They all come loaded with *ages*,[32] a sort of turnip, very excellent for food, which we dressed in various ways. This food was so nutritious as to prove a great support to all of us after the privations we endured when at sea, which were more severe then ever were suffered by man; for as we could not tell what weather it would please God to send us on our voyage, we were obliged to limit ourselves most rigorously with regard to food, in order that, at all events, we might at least have the means of supporting life: this *age* the Caribbees call *nabi*, and the Indians *hage*. The Indians barter gold, provisions, and every thing they bring with them, for tags of laces, beads, and pins, and pieces of porringers and dishes. They all, as I have said, go naked as they were born, except the women of this island, who some of them wear a covering of cotton, which they bind round their hips, while others use

cuanto se pudiere hacer con agua. Han sembrado mucha hortaliza, la cual es cierto que crece mas en ocho dias que en España en veinte. Vienen aquí continuamente muchos indios é caciques con ellos, que son como capitanes dellos, é muchas indias : todos víenen cargados de *ages*, que son como nabos, muy excelente manjar, de los cuales facemos acá muchas maneras de manjares en cualquier manera ; es tanto cordial manjar que nos tiene á todos muy consolados, porque de verdad la vida que se trajo por la mar ha seido la mas estrecha que nunca hombres pasaron, é fue ansí necesario porque no sabiamos que tiempo nos haria, ó cuanto permitiría Dios que estoviesemos en el camino ; ansí que fue cordura estrecharnos, porque cualquier tiempo que viniera pudieramos conservar la vida. Rescatan el oro é mantenimientos é todo lo que traen por cabos de agujetas, por cuentas, por alfileres, por pedasos de escudillas é de plateles. A este *age* llaman los de Caribi *nabi*, é los indios *hage*. Toda esta gente, como dicho tengo, andan como nacieron, salvo las

[32] Yams.

VACoAAcBGQ==

GgoAAcBGQ==
AAAAAcBGQ==

grass and leaves of trees. When they wish to appear full-dressed, both men and women paint themselves, some black, others white, and various colours, in so many devices that the effect is very laughable: they shave some parts of their heads, and in others wear long tufts of matted hair, which have an indescribably ridiculous appearance : in short, whatever would be looked upon in our country as characteristic of a madman, is here regarded by the highest of the Indians as a mark of distinction.

In our present position, we are in the neighbourhood of many mines of gold, not one of which, we are told, is more than twenty or twenty-five leagues off : the Indians say that some of them are in Niti, in the possession of Caonabó, who killed the Christians ; the others are in another place called Cibao, which, if it please God, we shall see with our eyes before many days are over; indeed we should go there at once, but that we have so many things to provide that we are not equal to it at present. One third of our people have fallen sick within the last four or five days, which I think has principally arisen from the toil and privations of the journey;

---

mugeres de esta isla traen cubiertas sus verguenzas, dellos con ropa de algodon que les ciñen las caderas, otras con yerbas é fojas de árboles. Sus galas dellos é dellas es pintarse, unos de negro, otros de blanco é colorado, de tantos visajes que en verlos es bien cosa de reir ; las cabezas rapadas en logares, é en logares con vedijas de tantas maneras que no se podria escrebir. En conclusion, que todo lo que allá en nuestra España quieren hacer en la cabeza de un loco; acá el mejor dellos vos lo terná en mucha merced. Aquí estamos en comarca de muchas minas de oro, que segun lo que ellos dicen no hay cada una dellas de veinte ó veinte é cinco leguas: las unas dicen que son en Niti, en poder de Caonabó, aquel que mató los cristianos ; otras hay en otra parte que se llama Cibao, las cuales, si place á nuestro Señor, sabremos é veremos con los ojos antes que pasen muchos dias, porque agora se ficiera sino porque hay tantas cosas de proveer que no bastamos para todo, porque la gente ha adolecido en cuatro ó cinco dias el tercio della, creo la

another cause has been the variableness of the climate; but I hope in our Lord that all will be restored to health. My idea of this people is, that if we could converse with them, they would all become converted, for they do whatever they see us do, making genuflections before the altars at the Ave Maria and the other parts of the devotional service, and making the sign of the cross. They all say that they wish to be Christians, although in truth they are idolaters, for in their houses they have many kinds of figures: when asked what such a figure was, they would reply it is a thing of *Turey*, by which they meant " of Heaven." I made a pretence of throwing them on the fire, which grieved them so that they began to weep: they believe that everything we bring comes from heaven, and therefore call it *Turey*, which, as I have already said, means heaven in their language. The first day that I went on shore to sleep, was the Lord's day: the little time that we have spent on land, has been so much occupied in seeking for a fitting spot for the settlement, and in providing necessaries, that we have had little opportunity of becoming acquainted with the productions of the soil, yet although the

---

mayor causa dello ha seido el trabajo é mala pasada del camino ; allende de la diversidad de la tierra ; pero espero en nuestro Señor que todos se levantarán con salud. Lo que parece desta gente es que si lengua toviesemos que todos se convertirian, porque cuanto nos veen facer tanto facen, en hincar las rodillas á los altares, é al Ave Maria, é á las otras devociones é santiguarse : todos dicen que quieren ser cristianos, puesto que verdaderamente son idólatras, porque en sus casas hay figuras de muchas maneras ; yo les he preguntado que es aquello, dicenme que es cosa de *Turey*, que quiere decir del cielo. Yo acometi á querer echarselos en el fuego é haciaseles de mal que querian llorar : pero ansi piensan que cuanto nosotros traemos que es cosa del cielo, que á todo llaman *Turey*, que quiere decir cielo. El dia que yo salí á dormir en tierra fue el primero dia del Señor : el poco tiempo que habemos gastado en tierra ha seido mas en hacer donde nos metamos, é buscar las cosas necesarias, que en saber las cosas que hay en la tierra, pero aunque ha

time has been so short, many marvellous things have been
seen. We have met with trees bearing wool, of a sufficiently
fine quality (according to the opinion of those who are acquainted with the art) to be woven into good cloth; there are
so many of these trees that we might load the caravels with
wool, although it is troublesome to collect, for the trees are
very thorny,[33] but some means may be easily found of over-
coming this difficulty. There are also cotton trees as large as
peach trees, which produce cotton in the greatest abundance.
We found trees producing wax as good both in colour and smell
as bees-wax and equally useful for burning, indeed there is
no great difference between them. There are vast numbers
of trees which yield surprisingly fine turpentine, and a great
abundance of tragacanth, also very good. We found other
trees which I think bear nutmegs, because the bark tastes and
smells like that spice, but at present there is no fruit on them;
I saw one root of ginger, which an Indian wore hanging
round his neck. There are also aloes; not like those which
we have hitherto seen in Spain, but no doubt they are of the

---

sido poco se han visto cosas bien de maravillar, que se han visto
árboles que llevan lana y harto fina, tal que los que saben del arte
dicen que podrán hacer buenos paños dellas. Destos árboles hay
tantos que se podrán cargar las carabelas de la lana, aunque es tra-
bajosa de coger, porque los árboles son muy espinosos ; pero bien
se puede hallar ingenio para la coger. Hay infinito algodon de árboles perpetuos tan grandes como duraznos. Hay árboles que
llevan cera en color y en sabor é en arder tan buena como la de
abejas, tal que no hay diferencia mucha de la una á la otra. Hay
infinitos árboles de trementina muy singular é muy fina. Hay
mucho alquitira, tambien muy buena. Hay árboles que pienso que
llevan nueces moscadas, salvo que agora estan sin fruto, é digo que
lo pienso porque el sabor y olor de la corteza es como de nueces
moscadas. Vi una raiz de gengibre que la traía un indio colgada
al cuello. Hay tambien linaloe, aunque no es de la manera del que

[33] A spices of the *N. O. Bombaceæ;* perhaps the *Eriodendron an-
fractuosum.*

same kind as those used by us doctors. A sort of cinnamon also has been found; but, to speak the truth, it is not so fine as that with which we are already acquainted in Spain. I do not know whether this arises from ignorance of the proper season to gather it, or whether the soil does not produce better. We have also seen some yellow mirabolans; at this season they are all lying under the trees, and have a bitter flavour, arising, I think, from the rottenness occasioned by the moisture of the ground; but the taste of such parts as have remained sound, is that of the genuine mirabolan. There is also very good mastic. None of the natives of these islands, as far as we have yet seen, possess any iron; they have, however, many tools, such as hatchets and axes, made of stone, which are so handsome and well finished, that it is wonderful how they contrive to make them without the use of iron. Their food consists of bread, made of the roots of a vegetable which is between a tree and a vegetable, and the *age*, which I have already described as being like the turnip, and very good food; they use, to season it, a spice

---

fasta agora se ha visto en nuestras partes ; pero no es de dudar que sea una de las especias de linaloes que los dotores ponemos. Tambien se ha hallado una manera de canela, verdad es que no es tan fina como la que allá se ha visto, no sabemos si por ventura lo hace el defeto de saberla coger en sus tiempos como se ha de coger, ó si por ventura la tierra no la lleva mejor. Tambien se ha hallado mirabolanos cetrinos, salvo que agora no estan sino debajo del ár- bol, como la tierra es muy humida estan podridos, tienen el sabor mucho amargo, yo creo sea del podrimiento ; pero todo lo otro, salvo el sabor que está corrompido, es de mirabolanos verdaderos. Hay tambien almástica muy buena. Todas estas gentes destas islas, que fasta agora se han visto, no poseen fierro ninguno. Tienen muchas ferramientas, ansi como hachas é azuelas hechas de piedra tan gentiles é tan labradas que es maravilla como sin fierro se pue- den hacer. El mantenimiento suyo es pan hecho de raices de una yerba que es entre árbol é yerba, é el age, de que ya tengo dicho que es como nabos, que es muy buen mantenimiento : tienen por

called *agi*, which they also eat with fish, and such birds as they can catch of the many kinds which abound in the island. They have, besides, a kind of grain like hazel-nuts, very good to eat. They eat all the snakes, and lizards, and spiders, and worms, that they find upon the ground; so that, to my fancy, their bestiality is greater than that of any beast upon the face of the earth. The admiral had at one time determined to leave the search for the mines until he had first despatched the ships which were to return to Spain[34] on account of the great sickness which had prevailed among the men, but afterwards he resolved upon sending two bands under the command of two captains, the one to Cibao,[35] and the other to Niti, where, as I have already said, Caonabó lived. These parties went, one of them returning on the twentieth, and the other on the twenty-first of January. The party that went to Cibao saw gold in so many places as to seem almost incredible, for in truth they found it in more

---

especia, por lo adobar, una especia que se llama *agi*, con la cual comen tambien el pescado, como aves cuando las pueden haber, que hay infinitas de muchas maneras. Tienen otrosí unos granos como avellanas, muy buenos de comer. Comen cuantas culebras é lagartos é arañas é cuantos gusanos se hallan por el suelo ; ansi que me parece es mayor su bestialidad que de ninguna bestia del mundo. Despues de una vez haber determinado el Almirante de dejar el descobrir las minas fasta primero enviar los navíos que se habian de partir á Castilla, por la mucha enfermedad que habia seido en la gente, acordó de enviar dos cuadrillas con dos Capitanes, el uno á Cibao y el otro á Niti, donde está Caonabó, de que ya he dicho, los cuales fueron é vinieron el uno á veinte dias de Enero, é el otro á veinte é uno : el que fue á Cibao halló oro en tantas partes que

[34] In fact he sent twelve vessels under the command of Antonio de Torres, who set sail from the port of Navidad, on the second of February, 1494, charged with an account of all that had occurred. (Navarrete.)

[35] This was Alonzo de Ojeda, who went out with fifteen men, in the month of January 1494, to seek the mines of Cibao, and returned a few days after with good news, having been well received everywhere by the natives. (Navarrete.)

than fifty streamlets and rivers, as well as upon their banks; so that, the captain said they had only to seek throughout that province, and they would find as much as they wished. He brought specimens from the different parts, namely, from the sand of the rivers and small springs. It is thought, that by digging, it will be found in greater pieces, for the Indians neither know how to dig nor have the means of digging more than a hand's depth. The other captain, who went to Niti, returned also with news of a great quantity of gold in three or four places; of which he likewise brought specimens.

Thus, surely, their Highnesses the King and Queen may henceforth regard themselves as the most prosperous and wealthy Sovereigns in the world; never yet, since the creation, has such a thing been seen or read of; for on the return of the ships from their next voyage, they will be able to carry back such a quantity of gold as will fill with amazement all who hear of it. Here I think I shall do well to break off my narrative. I think those who do not know me will consider me prolix, and somewhat an exaggerator, but

---

no lo osa hombre decir, que de verdad en mas de cincuenta arroyos é rios hallaban oro, é fuera de los rios por tierra ; de manera que en toda aquella provincia dice que do quiera que lo quieran buscar lo hallarán. Trajo muestra de muchas partes como en la arena de los rios é en las hontizuelas, que estan sobre tierra, creese que cabando, como sabemos hacer, se hallará en mayores pedazos, porque los indios no saben cabar ni tienen con que puedan cabar de un palmo arriba. El otro que fue á Niti trajo tambien nueva de mucho oro en tres ó cuatro partes; ansi mesmo trajo la muestra dello. Ansi que de cierto los Reyes nuestros Señores desde agora se pueden tener por los mas prósperos é mas ricos Príncipes del mundo, porque tal cosa hasta agora no se ha visto ni leido de ninguno en el mundo, porque verdaderamente á otro camino que los navíos vuelvan pueden llevar tanta cantidad de oro que se puedan maravillar cualesquiera que lo supieren. Aquí me parece será bien cesar el cuento : creo los que no me conocen que oyeren éstas cosas, me ternán por prolijo é por hombre que ha alargado algo ;

God is my witness, that I have not exceeded, by one tittle, the bounds of truth.

The preceding is the translation of that part of Doctor Chanca's letter, which refers to intelligence respecting the Indies.[36] The remainder of the letter does not bear upon the subject, but treats of private matters, in which Doctor Chanca requests the interference and support of the Chapter of Seville (of which city he was a native), in behalf of his family and property, which he had left in the said city. This letter reached Seville in the month of[37]   in the year fourteen hundred and ninety-three.

---

pero Dios es testigo que yo no he traspasado una jota los términos de la verdad.

Hasta aquí es el treslado de lo que conviene á nuevas de aquellas partes é Indias. Lo demas que venia en la carta no hace al caso, porque son cosas particulares que el dicho Dotor Chanca, como natural de Sevilla, suplicaba y encomendaba á los del Cabildo de Sevilla que tocaba á su hacienda y á los suyos, que en la dicha cibdad habia dejado, y llegó esta á Sevilla en el mes de
año de mil é cuatrocientos énoventa y tres años.

[36] It is to be regretted, Navarrete here justly remarks, that Dr. Chanca should not have described the subsequent occurrences in Hispaniola, which are very important, and which have been related by cotemporary historians.

[37] A similar gap in the original. The date of the year is a mistake. This letter must have been brought by the ships commanded by Torres, and consequently must have been written at the end of January 1494, after the first expedition of Ojeda. (Navarrete.)

MEMORIAL.

Memorial of the results of the Second Voyage of the Admiral, Christopher Columbus, to the Indies, drawn up by him for their Highnesses King Ferdinand and Queen Isabella; and addressed to Antonio de Torres, from the City of Isabella, the 30th of January 1494. The reply of their Highnesses is affixed at the end of each chapter.[1]

THE report which you, Antonio de Torres, captain of the ship Marigalante, and Governor of the city of Isabella, have to make, on my behalf, to the King and Queen our sovereigns, is as follows :

Imprimis : after having delivered the credentials which you bear from me to their Highnesses, you will do homage in my name, and commend me to them as to my natural sovereigns,

---

MEMORIAL.

Que para los Reyes Católicos dió el Almirante D. Cristobal Colon, en la ciudad Isabela, á 30 de Enero de 1494 á Antonio de Torres, sobre el suceso de su segundo viage á las Indias; y al final de cada capítulo la respuesta de sus Altezas.

Lo que vos Antonio de Torres, capitan de la nao Marigalante, é Alcaide de la ciudad Isabela, habeis de decir é suplicar de mi parte al Rey é la Reina nuestros Señores es lo siguiente :

Primeramente, dadas las cartas de creencia que llevais de mí para sus Altezas, besareis por mí sus reales pies é manos, é me encomendareis en sus Altezas como á Rey é Reina mis señores naturales, en cuyo servicio yo deseo fenecer mis dias, como esto mas

---

[1] In the original, the replies are affixed in the margin of each chapter. (Navarrete.)

in whose service I desire to continue till death; and you will furthermore be able to lay before them all that you have yourself seen and known respecting me.

Their Highnesses accept aud acknowledge the service.

Item. Although, by the letters which I have written to their Highnesses, as well as to Father Buil and to the Treasurer, a clear and comprehensive idea may be formed of all that has transpired since our arrival; you will, notwithstanding, inform their Highnesses, on my behalf, that God has been pleased to manifest such favour towards their service, that not only has nothing hitherto occurred to diminish the importance of what I have formerly written or said to their Highnesses; but on the contrary I hope, by God's grace, shortly to prove it more clearly by facts; because we have found upon the sea shore, without penetrating into the interior of the country, some spots showing so many indications of various spices, as naturally to suggest the hope of the best results for the future. The same holds good with respect to the gold mines; for two parties only, who were sent out in different directions to discover them, and who, because they had few people with

---

largamente vos podreis decir á sus altezas, segun lo que en mi vistes é supistes.

Sus Altezas se lo tienen en servicio.

Item: Como quiera que por las cartas que á sus altezas escribo y aun el Padre Fray Buil y el Tesorero, podrán comprender todo lo que acá despues de nuestra llegada se fizo, y esto harto por menudo y extensamente; con todo direis á sus altezas de mi parte, que á Dios ha placido darme tal gracia para en su servicio, que hasta aquí no hallo yo menos ni se ha hallado en cosa alguna de lo que yo escribí y dije, y afirmé á sus Altezas en los dias pasados, antes por gracia de Dios espero que aun muy mas claramente y muy presto por la obra parecerá, porque las cosas de especeria en solas las orillas de la mar, sin haber entrado dentro en la tierra, se halla tal rastro é principios della, que es razon que se esperen muy mejores fines, y esto mismo en las mínas del oro, porque con solos dos que fueron á descubrir cada uno por su parte, sin detenerse

them, remained out but a short time, found, nevertheless, a great number of rivers whose sands contained this precious metal in such quantity, that each man took up a sample of it in his hand; so that our two messengers returned so joyous, and boasted so much of the abundance of gold, that I fear I should weary the attention of their Highnesses, were I to repeat all that they said. But as Gorbalan, who was one of the persons who went on the discovery, is returning to Spain, he will be able to relate all that he has seen and observed; although there remains here another individual,—named Hojeda, formerly servant of the Duke of Medinaceli, and a very discreet and pains-taking youth,—who without doubt discovered, beyond all comparison, more than the other, judging by the account which he gave of the rivers he had seen; for he reported, that each of them contained things that appeared incredible. It results from all this, that their highnesses ought to return thanks to God, for the favour which He thus accords to all their highnesses' enterprises.

Their Highnesses return thanks to God for all that is here recorded, and regard as a very signal service all that the Admiral has already done, and is yet doing; for they are

---

allá porque era poca gente, se han descubierto tantos rios tan poblados de oro, que cualquier de los que lo vieron é cogieron, solamente con las manos por muestra, vinieron tan alegres, y dicen tantas cosas de la abundancia dello, que yo tengo empacho de las decir y escribir á sus altezas ; pero porque allá v Gorbalan, que fue uno de los descubridores, el dirá lo que vió aunque acá queda otro que llaman Hojeda, criado del Duque de Medinaceli, muy discreto mozo y de muy gran recabdo, que sin duda y aun sin comparacion, descubrió mucho mas, segun el memorial de los rios que él trajo, diciendo que en cada uno de ellos hay cosa de no creella ; por lo cual sus altezas pueden dar gracias á Dios, pues tan favorablemente se ha en todas sus cosas.

Sus Altezas dan muchas gracias a Dios por esto, y tienen en muy senalado servicio al Almirante todo lo que en esto ha fecho y hace,

sensible that, under God, it is he who has procured for them
their present and future possessions in these countries ; and as
they are about to write to him on this subject more at length,
they refer to their letter.

Item.   You will repeat to their Highnesses what I have
already written to them, that I should have ardently desired
to have been able to send them, by this occasion, a larger
quantity of gold than what they have any hope of our being
able to collect, but that the greater part of the people we
employed fell suddenly ill.   Moreover, the departure of this
present expedition could not be delayed any longer, for two
reasons: namely, on account of the heavy expense which their
stay here occasioned ; and because the weather was favourable for their departure, and for the return of those who
should bring back the articles of which we stand in the most
pressing need.   If the former were to be put off the time of
their starting, and the latter were to delay their departure,
they would not be able to reach here by the month of
May.   Besides, if I wished now to undertake a journey to
the rivers with those who are well,—whether with those who

---

porque conocen que despues de Dios á él son en cargo de todo lo que
en esto han habido y hobieren ; y porque cerca desto le escriben mas
largo, á su carta se remiten.

Item: Direis á sus Altezas, como quier que ya se les escribe, que yo
deseaba mucho en esta armada poderles enviar mayor cuantidad de
oro del que acá seespera poder coger, si la gente que acá está nuestra, la mayor parte subitamente no cayera doliente ; pero porque
ya esta armada non se podia detener acá mas, siquiera por la costa
grande que hace, siquiera porque el tiempo es este propio para ir y
poder volver los que han de traer acá las cosas que aquí hacen mucha mengua, porque si tardasen de irse de aquí non podrian vol-
verse para Mayo los que han de volver, y allende desto si con los
sanos que acá se hallan, así en mar como en tierra en la poblacion,
yo quisiera emprender de ir á las minas ó rios agora, habia muchas
dificultades é aun peligros, porque de aquí á veinte y tres ó veinte
y cuatro leguas, en donde hay puertos é rios para pasar y para tan

are at sea, or those who are on land in the huts,—I should
experience great difficulties, and even dangers; because, in
traversing three or four-and-twenty leagues, where there are
bays and rivers to pass, we should be obliged to carry, as
provision for so long a journey, and for the time necessary
for collecting the gold, many articles of food, &c., which
could not be carried on our backs, and there are no beasts
of burden to be found, to afford the necessary assistance.
Moreover, the roads and passes are not in such a condition
as I should wish for travelling over; and, first of all, I have
turned my attention to this point. It would be also extremely inconvenient to leave the sick men here in the open
air, or in huts, with such food and defences as they have on
shore; although these Indians appear every day to be more
simple and harmless to those who land for the purpose of
making investigations. In short, although they come every
day to visit us, it would nevertheless be imprudent to risk
the loss of our men and our provisions, which might very
easily happen, if an Indian were only, with a lighted coal, to
set fire to the huts, for they ramble about both night and
.day; for this reason, we keep sentinels constantly on the
watch while the dwellings are exposed and undefended.

---

largo camino, y para estar allá al tiempo que seria menester para
coger el oro, habia menester llevar muchos mantenimientos, los
cuales non podrian llevar á cuestas, ni hay bestias acá que á esto
pudiesen suplir, ni los caminos é pasos non estan tan aparejados,
como quier que se han comenzado á adobar para que se podiesen
pasar; y tambien era grande inconveniente dejar acá los dolientes
en lugar abierto y chozas, y las provisiones y mantenimientos que
estan en tierra, que como quier que estos indios se hayan mostrado
á los descubridores, y se muestran cada dia muy simples y sin malicia; con todo, porque cada dia vienen acá entre nosotros non
pareció que fuera buen consejo meter á riesgo y á ventura de per-
derse esta gente y los mantenimientos, lo que un indio con un tizon
podria hacer poniendo huego á las chozas, porque de noche y de dia
siempre van y vienen: á causa dellos tenemos guardas en el campo
mientras la poblacion está abierta y sin defension.

He has done well.

Further, as we have remarked that the greatest part of those who have gone out to make discoveries, have fallen sick on their return, and that some have even been obliged to abandon the undertaking in the middle of their journey, and return, it was equally to be feared that the same would occur to those who were at the time enjoying good health, if they were also to go.   There were two evils to fear:—one, the chance of falling ill in undertaking the same work, in a place where there were no houses nor any kind of protection, and of being exposed to the attacks of the cacique called Caonabo, who, by all accounts, is a badly-disposed man, and extremely daring; who, if he were to find us in a dispirited condition and sick, might venture upon what he would not dare to do if we were well.   The other evil consisted in the difficulty of carrying the gold; for, either we should have to carry it in small quantities, and go and return every day, and thus daily expose ourselves to the chance of sickness; or we should have to send it under the escort of a party of our people, and equally run the risk of losing them.

He has done well.

These are the reasons, you will tell their Highnesses, why

Que lo hizo bien.

Otrosí : Como habemos visto en los que fueron por tierra á descobrir que los mas cayeron dolientes despues de vueltos, y aun algunos se hobieron de volver del camino, era tambien razon de temer que otro tal conteciese á los que agora irian destos sanos que se hallan, y seguirse hian dos peligros de allí, el uno de adolecer allá en la misma obra dó no hay casa ni reparo alguno de aquel Cacique que llaman Caonabó, que es hombre, segun relacion de todos, muy malo y muy mas atrevido, el cual viéndonos allá así desbaratados y dolientes, podria emprender lo que non osaria si fuesemos sanos : y con esto mismo se allega otra dificultad de traer acá lo que llegasemos de oro, porque ó habiamos de traer poco y ir y venir cada dia, y meterse en el riesgo de las dolencias, ó se habia de enviar con alguna parte de la gente con el mismo peligro de perderlo.

Lo hizo bien.

the departure of the expedition has not been delayed, and why only a sample of the gold is sent to them; but I trust in the mercy of God, who in all things and in every place has guided us hitherto, that all our men will be soon restored to health, as, indeed, they are already beginning to be; for there are but a few places which agree with them, but when they are in these places, they speedily recover their health. One thing is certain, that if they could have fresh meat, they would very quickly, by the help of God, be up and doing; and those who are most sickly, would speedily recover. I hope that they may be restored. The small number of those who continue well, are employed every day in barricading our dwelling, so as to put it in a state of defence, and in taking necessary measures for the safety of our ammunition; which will be finished now in a few days, for all our fortifications will consist simply of stone walls.[2] These precautions will be sufficient, as the Indians are not a people to be much afraid of; and, unless they should find us asleep, they would not dare to undertake any hostile movement against us, even if they should entertain the idea of so doing. The misfortune which happened to those who remained here, must be

---

Así que, direis á sus Altezas, que estas son las cabsas porque de presente non se ha detenido el armada, ni se les envia oro mas de las muestras; pero confiando en la misericordia de Dios, que en todo y por todo nos ha guiado hasta aquí, esta gente convalescerá presto, como ya lo hace, porque solamente les prueba la tierra de algunas ceciones, y luego se levantan; y es cierto que si toviesen algunas carnes frescas para convalescer muy presto serian todos en pie con ayuda de Dios, é aun los mas estarian ya convalescidos en este tiempo, espero que ellos convalescerán : con estos pocos sanos que acá quedan, cada dia se entiende en cerrar la poblacion y meterla en alguna defensa, y los mantenimientos en seguro, que será fecho en breves dias, porque non ha de ser sino albarradas que non son gente los indios, que si dormiendo non nos fallasen para emprender cosa ninguna, aunque la toviesen pensada, que así hicieron á los otros

[2] *Albarrada*—an Arabic word implying a stone wall without mortar.

attributed to their want of vigilance; for however few they were in number,—however favourable the opportunities that the Indians had for doing what they did,—they would never have ventured to do them any injury, if they had only seen that they took proper precautions against an attack. As soon as that object is gained, I will undertake to go in search of these rivers; either by going by land from hence, and employing the best means we can devise, or else by sea, rounding the island, until we come to the place which is described as being only six or seven leagues from where these rivers that I speak of are situated; so that we may collect the gold in safety, and put it in security against all attacks in some stronghold or tower, which may be quickly built for that purpose : and thus, when the two caravels shall return thither, the gold may be taken away and finally sent home in safety at the first favourable season for making the voyage.

This is well, and exactly as he should have done.

Item.   You will inform their Highnesses (as indeed has been already done), that the cause of the sickness so general among us, is the change of air and water, for we find that all

---

que acá quedaron por su mal recabdo, los cuales por pocos que fuesen, y por mayores ocasiones que dieran á los indios de haber é de hacer lo que hicieron, nunca ellos osaran emprender de dañarles si los vieran á buen recabdo : y esto fecho luego se entenderá en ir á los dichos rios, ó desde aquí tomando el camino, y buscando los mejores expedientes que se puedan, ó por la mar rodeando la isla fasta aquella parte de donde se dice que no debe haber mas de seis ó siete leguas hasta los dichos rios ; por forma que con seguridad se pueda cojer el oro y ponerlo en recabdo de alguna fortaleza ó torre que allí se haga luego, para tenerlo cogido al tiempo que las dos carabelas volverán acá, é para que luego con el primer tiempo que sea para navegar este camino se envie á buen recabdo.

Que está bien, y así lo debe hacer.

Item : Direis á sus altezas, como dicho es, que las causas de las dolencias tan general de todos es de mudamiento de aguas y aires,

of us are affected, though few dangerously; consequently, the preservation of the health of the people will depend, under God, on their being provided with the same food that they are accustomed to in Spain : without this precaution, neither those who are here now, nor those that shall come, will be in a position to be of service to their Highnesses, unless they enjoy good health. We ought to have fresh supplies of provisions until the time that we may be able to gather a sufficient crop from what we shall have sown or planted here : I speak of wheat, barley, and grapes, towards the cultivation of which not much has been done this year, from our being unable earlier to choose a convenient settlement. When we had chosen it, the small number of labourers that were with us fell sick ; and, even when they recovered, we had so few cattle, and these cattle were so lean and weak, that the utmost they could do was very little; however, they have sown a few plots of ground, rather for the sake of trying the soil, which seems excellent, than with any other object, and the result of our attempt makes us look forward to a remedy for our necessities. We are very certain, as the fact has shown, that wheat and grapes will grow very well in this

---

porque vemos que á todos arreo se extiende y peligran pocos ; por consiguiente la conservacion de la sanidad, despues de Dios, está que esta gente sea proveida de los mantenimientos que en España acostumbrada, porque dellos, ni de otros que viniesen de nuevo sus Altezas se podrián servir si no estan sanos ; y esta provision ha de durar hasta que acá se haya fecho cimiento de lo que acá se sembrare é plantare, digo de trigos y cebadas, é viñas, de lo cual para este año se ha fecho poco, porque no se pudo de antes tomar asiento, y luego que se tomó adolescieron aquellos poquitos labradores que acá estaban, los cuales aunque estovieran sanos tenian tan pocas bestias y tan magras y flacas, que poco es lo que pudieran hacer : con todo, alguna cosa han sembrado, mas para probar la tierra, que parece muy maravillosa, para que de alli se puede esperar remedio alguno en nuestras necesidades. Somos bien ciertos, como la obra lo muestra, que en esta tierra así el trigo como el vino nacerá muy

country. We must, however, wait for the fruit; and if it grows as quickly and well as the corn, in proportion to the number of vines that have been planted, we shall certainly not sigh for these productions as the produce of Andalusia and Sicily. There are also sugar-canes, of which the small quantity that we have planted has succeeded very well. The beauty of the country in these islands,—the mountains, the valleys, the streams, the fields watered by broad rivers,—in short, everything is so wonderful, that there is no country on which the sun sheds his beams that can present such an appearance, together with so productive a soil.

Since the land is so fertile, it is desirable to sow as much as possible; and Don Juan de Fonseca has been desired to send over immediately everything requisite for that purpose.

Item. You will say, that as a large portion of the wine that we brought with us has run away, and that, as all the men say, in consequence of the bad cooperage of the butts made at Seville, the article that fails us most at this moment, and yet which we most want, is wine; and although we have biscuit and corn for some time longer, it is nevertheless

---

bien; pero hase de esperar el fruto, el cual si tal será como muestra la presteza del nacer del trigo, y de algunos poquitos de sarmientos que se pusieron, es cierto que non fará mengua el Andalucía ni Secilia aquí, ni en las cañas de azucar, segun unas poquitas que se pusieron han prendido; porque es cierto que la hermosura de la tierra de estas islas, así de montes é sierras y aguas, como de vegas donde hay rios cabdales, es tal la vista que ninguna otra tierra que sol escaliente puede ser mejor al parecer ni tan fermosa.

Pues la tierra es tal, que debe procurar que se siembre lo mas que ser pudiere de todas cosas, y á D. Juan de Fonseca se escribe que envie de contino todo lo que fuere menester para esto.

Item : Direis que á cabsa de haberse derramado mucho vino en este camino del que la flota traia, y esto, segun dicen los mas, á culpa de la mala obra que los toneleros ficieron en Sevilla, la mayor mengua que agora tenemos aquí, ó esperamos por esto tener, es de vinos, y como quier que tengamos para mas tiempo así vizcocho

necessary that a reasonable quantity of these be sent to us, for the voyage is a long one, and it is impossible to make a calculation for every day; the same holds good with respect to pork and salt meat, which should be better than what we have had on our voyage hitherto; sheep, lambs, both male and female, young calves and heifers, also are necessary. Consequently it would be expedient that every caravel that may be dispatched hither, should bring a stock of these necessaries; and at the same time some asses, both male and female, and some mares that can be put to work; for here there are no beasts that can be employed to assist man in his labour. As I fear that their Highnesses may not be at Seville, and that their officers or ministers will not, without their express instructions, make any movement towards the carrying out of the necessary arrangements for the return voyage; and that, in the interval between the report and the reply, the favourable moment for the departure of the vessels which are to return hither (and which should be in all the month of May) may elapse, you will tell their Highnesses that I have given strict orders that the gold that you carry

---

como trigo, con todo es necesario que tambien se envie alguna cuantidad razonable, porque el camino es largo y cada dia no se puede proveer, é asimismo algunas canales, digo tocinos, y otra cecina que sea mejor que la que habemos traido este camino. De carneros vivos y aun antes corderos y cordericas, mas fembras que machos, y algunos becerras pequeños son menester, que cada vez vengan en cualquier carabela que acá se enviare, y algunas asnas y asnos, y yeguas para trabajo y simiente, que acá ninguna de estas animalias hay de que hombre se pueda ayudar ni valer. Y porque recelo que sus Altezas no se fallarán en Sevilla, ni los Oficiales ó Ministros suyos sin expreso mandamiento non proveerían en lo porque agora con este primero camino es necesario que venga, porque en la consulta y en la respuesta se pasaria la sazon del partir los navíos que acá por todo Mayo es necesario que sean; direis á sus Altezas, como yo vos dí cargo y mandé, que del oro que allá llevais empeñándolo, ó poniéndolo en poder de algun mercader en

with you be placed in the hands of some merchant in Seville,
in order that he may therefrom disburse the sums that shall
be necessary for loading the two caravels with wine, corn,
and the other articles detailed in this memorial; and this
merchant shall convey or send the said gold to their Highnesses, that they may see it, receive it, and from it cause to
be defrayed the expenses that may arise from the fitting-up
and loading of the said two caravels. It is necessary, for the
encouragement of the men who remain here, and for the
support of their spirits, that an effort should be made to let
the expedition arrive in the course of the month of May, so
that they may have the fresh provisions, and other necessaries, before summer, especially for the sick people. We
particularly stand in need of raisins, sugar, almonds, honey,
and rice, of which we ought to have had a great quantity,
but brought very little with us, and what we had is now consumed. It is the same with the greater part of the medicines
that we brought from Spain; which is not to be wondered
at, when it is considered how many of our number have been
sick. For all these articles, which are intended as much for

Sevilla, el cual distraya y ponga los maravedis que serán menester
para cargar dos carabelas de víno y de trigo, y de las otras cosas
que llevais por memorial, el cual mercader lleve ó envie el dicho
oro para sus Altezas, que le vean, resciban y hagan pagar lo que
hobiere distraido é puesto para el despacho y cargazon de las dichas
dos carabelas, las cuales por consolar y esforzar esta gente que acá
queda, cumple que fagan mas de poder de ser ac vueltas por todo
el mes de Mayo, porque la gente antes de entrar en el verano vea
é tengan algun refrescamiento destas cosas, en especial para las dolencias ; de las cuales cosas acá ya tenemos gran mengua, cómo son
pasas, azucar, almendras, miel é arroz, que debiera venir en gran
cuantidad y vino muy poca, é aquello que vino es ya consumido é
gastado, y aun la mayor parte de las medecinas que de allá tro-
jieron, por la muchedumbre de los muchos dolientes ; de las cuales
cosas, como dicho es, vos llevais memoriales así para sanos, como
para dolientes, fermados de mi mano, los cuales cumplidamente si

the sick as for those who are in good health, you carry, as I have already said, memorials signed by my hand; you will execute my orders to the full, if there be sufficient money wherewith to do so, or you will at least procure what is more immediately necessary, and which ought, consequently, to come as speedily as possible by the two vessels. With respect to such articles as cannot be sent off by them, you will, in submission to their Highnesses' pleasure, look to it that they be sent by other vessels without loss of time.

Their Highnesses will give instructions to Don Juan de Fonseca to make immediate inquiry respecting the imposition in the construction of the casks, in order that a sufficient levy be made on the makers to cover the losses occasioned by the waste of the wine, as well as all the other expenses. He will have to see that sugar-canes of good quality be sent, and will immediately look to the despatch of the other articles herein required.

Item. You will tell their Highnesses, that as we are not acquainted with the language of these people, so as to make them acquainted with our holy faith, as their Highnesses and we ourselves desire, and as we will do so soon as we are able, we send by these two vessels some of these cannibal men and women, as well as some children, both male and female.

---

el dinero bastare, ó á lo menos lo que mas necesario sea para agora despachar, es para que lo puedan luego traer los dichos dos navíos, y lo que quedare procurareis con sus Altezas que con otros navíos venga lo mas presto que ser pudiere.

Sus Altezas enviaron á mandar á D. Juan de Fonseca que luego haya informacion de los que hicieron ese engano en los toneles, y de sus bienes haga que se cobre todo el dano que vino en el vino, con las costas; y en lo de las canas vea como las que se enviaren sean buenas, y en las otras cosas que aquí dice que las provea luego.

Item : Direis á sus Altezas que á cabsa que acá no hay lengua por medio de la cual á esta gente se pueda dar á entender nuestra santa Fé, como sus Altezas desean, y aun los que acá estamos, co- mo quiere que se trabajará cuanto pudieren, se envian de presente con estos navíos así de los canibales, hombres y mugeres y niños y

Their Highnesses can order them to be placed under the care of the most competent persons to teach them the language, giving instructions, at the same time, that they may be employed in useful occupations; and that by degrees more care be bestowed upon them than would be given to other slaves, in order that afterwards one may learn from the other. By not seeing or speaking to each other for a long time, they will learn much sooner in Spain than they will here, and become much better interpreters. We will, however, do what we can; it is true, that as there is but little communication between one of these islands and another, there is some difference in their mode of expressing themselves, which mainly depends on the distance between them. But as amongst all these islands, those inhabited by the cannibals are the largest and the most populous, I have thought it expedient to send to Spain men and women from the islands which they inhabit, in the hope that they may one day be led to abandon their barbarous custom of eating their fellow-creatures. By learning the Spanish language in Spain, they will much earlier receive baptism and ensure the salvation of their souls; moreover, it will be a great happiness to the

---

niñas, los cuales sus Altezas pueden mandar poner en poder de personas con quien puedan mejor aprender la lengua, ejercitándolos en cosas de servicio, y poco á poco mandando poner en ellos algun mas cuidado que en otros esclavos para que deprendan unos de otros, que no se hablen ni se vean sino muy tarde, que mas presto deprenderán allá que no acá, y serán mejores intérpretes, como quier que acá non se dejará de hacer lo que se pueda; es verdad que como esta gente platican poco los de la una isla con los de la otra, en las lenguas hay alguna diferencia entre ellos, segun como estan mas cerca ó mas lejos; y porque entre las otras islas las de los canibales son mucho grandes, y mucho bien pobladas, parecerá acá que tomar dellos y dellas y enviarlos allá á Castilla non seria sino bien, porque quitarse hian una vez de aquella inhumana costumbre que tienen de comer hombres, y allá en Castilla entendiendo la lengua muy mas presto rescibirian el Bautismo, y farian el provecho de sus animas: aun entre estos pueblos que non son de esas cos-

Indians who do not practise the above-mentioned cruel custom, when they see that we have seized and led captive those who injure them, whom they dread so much, that their name alone fills them with horror. You will assure their Highnesses, that our arrival in this country, and the sight of so fine a fleet, have produced the most desirable effect and ensured our future safety; for all the inhabitants of this great island, and of those around it, when they see the good treatment that we shall shew to those who do well, and the punishment that we shall inflict on those who do wrong, will hasten to submit, and their Highnesses will shortly be able to reckon them among the number of their subjects. And as even now they not only readily comply with every wish that we express, but also spontaneously endeavour to do what they think will prove agreeable to us; I think that their Highnesses may rest certain, that on many accounts, both for the present and the future, the arrival of this fleet has secured for them a wide renown amongst all Christian Princes; but they themselves will be able to form a much better judgment on this subject than it is in my power to put into language.

———————

tumbres, se ganaria gran crédito por nosotros viendo que aquellos prendiesemos y cativasemos, de quien ellos suelen rescibir daños, y tienen tamaño miedo que del hombre solo se espantan ; certificando á sus Altezas que la venida é vista de esta flota acá en esta tierra así junta y hermosa, ha dado muy grande autoridad á esto y muy grande seguridad para las cosas venideras, por que toda esta gente de esta grande isla y de las otras, viendo el buen tratamiento que á los bueno se fará, y el castigo que á los malos se dará, verná á obediencia prestamente para poderlos mandar como vasallos de sus Altezas. Y como quier que ellos agora donde quier que hombre se halle non solo hacen de grado lo que hombre quiere que fagan mas ellos de su voluntad se ponen á todo lo que entienden que nos puede placer, y tambien pueden ser ciertos sus Altezas que non menos allá, entre los cristianos Principes haber dado gran reputacion la venida desta armada por muchos respetos, así presentes como venideros, los cuales sus Altezas podrán mejor pensar y entender que non sabria decir.

Let him be informed of what has transpired respecting the
cannibals that came over to Spain. He has done well and his sug-
gestions are good; but let him endeavour by all possible means to
convert them to our holy Catholic religion, and do the same with
respect to the inhabitants of all the islands to which he may go.

Item. You will tell their Highnesses, that for the good of
the souls of the said cannibals, and even of the inhabitants
of this island, the thought has suggested itself to us, that
the greater the number that are sent over to Spain the better,
and thus good service may result to their Highnesses in the
following manner : considering what great need we have of
cattle and of beasts of burthen, both for food and to assist
the settlers in their work, their Highnesses will be able to
authorize a suitable number of caravels to come here every
year to bring over the said cattle, etc., in order that the fields
may become covered with people and cultivation; these
cattle, etc., might be sold at moderate prices for account of
the bearers, and the latter might be paid with slaves, taken
from among the Caribbees, who are a wild people, fit for any
work, well proportioned and very intelligent, and who, when

Decirle heis lo que acá habido en lo de los canibales que acá
vinieron.

Que está muy bien, y asi lo debe hacer ; pero que procure allá, como
si ser pudiere, se reduzgan á nuestra santa Fé católica, y asimismo
lo procure con los de las islas donde está.

Item : Direis á sus Altezas, que el provecho de las almas de los
dichos canibales, y aun destos de acá, ha traido el pensamiento que
cuantos mas allá se llevasen seria mejor, y en ello podrian sus Altezas ser servidos desta manera : que visto cuanto son acá menester
los ganados y bestias de trabajo para el sostenimiento de la gente
que acá ha de estar, y bien de todas estas islas, sus Altezas podrán
dar licencia e permiso á un número de carabelas suficiente que
vengan acá cada año, y trayan de los dichos ganados y otros mantenimientos y cosas para poblar el campo y aprovechar la tierra, y esto
en precios razonables á sus costas de los que las trugieren, las cuales
cosas se les podrian pagar en esclavos de estos canibales, gente tan

they have got rid of the cruel habits to which they have
become accustomed, will be better than any other kind of
slaves. When they lose sight of their country, they will forget their cruel customs; and it will be easy to obtain plenty
of these savages by means of row-boats that we propose to
build. It is taken for granted, that each of the caravels sent
by their Highnesses, will have on board a confidential man,
who will take care that the vessels do not stop anywhere else
than here, where they are to unload and reload their vessels.
Their Highnesses might fix duties on the slaves that may be
taken over, upon their arrival in Spain. You will ask for a
reply upon this point, and bring it to me, in order that I may
be able to take the necessary measures, should the proposition merit the approbation of their Highnesses.

*The consideration of this subject has been suspended for a
time, until some other measure may be suggested with reference
to the island: the Admiral will do well to write what further
he thinks upon the subject.*

Item. You will also tell their Highnesses, that freighting
the ships by the ton, as the Flemish merchants do, will be

---

fiera y dispuesta, y bien proporcionada y de muy buen entendimi-
ento, los cuales quitados de aquella inhumanidad creemos que serán
mejores que otros ningunos esclavos, la cual luego perderán que
sean fuera de su tierra, y de estos podrán haber muchos con las
fustas de remos que acá se entienden de hacer, fecho empero pre-
supuesto que cada una de las carabelas que viniesen de sus Altezas
pusiesen una persona fiable, la cual defendiese las dichas carabelas
que non descendiesen á ninguna otra parte ni isla salvo aquí donde
ha de estar la carga y descarga de toda la mercaduría; y aun destos
esclavos que se llevaren, sus Altezas podrian haber sus derechos allá;
y desto traeres ó enviareis respuesta, porque acá se hagan los aparejos que son menester con mas confianza, si á sus Altezas pareciere
bien.

*En esto se ha suspendido por agora hasta que venga otro camino
de allá, y escriba el Almirante lo que en esto le paresciere.*

Item: Tambien direis á sus Altezas que mas provechoso es, y

more advantageous and less expensive than any other mode, and for this reason I have given instructions to freight the caravels in this manner that you have to send off. It will be well to adopt this plan with all the others that their Highnesses may send if it meets their approbation ; but I do not mean to say that this measure should be applied to the vessels that shall come over licensed for the traffic of slaves.

Their Highnesses have given directions to Don Juan de Fonseca, to have the caravels freighted in the manner described, if it can be done.

Item. You will tell their Highnesses, that in order to save any extra expense, I have purchased the caravels mentioned in the memorial of which you are the bearer, in order to keep them here with the two vessels, the " Gallega" and the " Capitana", of which, by advice of the pilot its commander, I purchased the three-eighths for the price declared in the said memorial, signed by my hand. These vessels will not only afford strength and security to those who will have to remain on shore and whose duty it will be to make arrangements with the Indians for collecting the gold ; but they will be also very useful to ward off any attack that may be made

---

menos costa, fletar los navíos como los fletan los mercaderes para Flandes por toneladas que non de otra manera ; por ende que yo vos dí cargo de fletar á este respecto las dos carabelas que habeis luego de enviar : y así se podrá hacer de todas las otras que sus Altezas enviaren, si de aquella forma se ternán por servidos ; pero non entiendo decir esto de las que han devenir con su licencia por la mercaduría de los esclavos.

Sus Altezas mandan á D. Juan de Fonseca que en el fletar de las carabelas tenga esta forma si ser pudiere.

Item : Direis á sus Altezas que á causa de escusar alguna mas costa, yo merqué estas carabelas que llevais por memorial para retenerlas acá con estas dos naos, conviene á saber, la Gallega y esa otra Capitana, de la cual merqué por semejante del Maestre della los tres ochavos por el precio que en el dicho memorial destas copias llevais firmado de mi mano, los cuales navíos non solo darán

upon them by strangers; moreover, the caravels will be required for the task of making the discovery of terra firma, and of the islands which lie scattered about in this vicinity. You will therefore beg their Highnesses to pay, at the term of credit arranged with the sellers, the sums which these vessels shall cost, for without doubt their Highnesses will be very soon reimbursed for what they may expend; at least, such is my belief and hope in the mercy of God.

The Admiral has done well. You will tell him that the sum mentioned has been paid to the seller of the vessels, and that Don Juan de Fonseca has been ordered to pay the cost of the caravels purchased by the Admiral.

Item. You will speak to their Highnesses, and beseech them on my behalf, in the most humble manner possible, to be pleased to give mature reflection to the observations I make (and which I have most at heart) with reference to the peacefulness, harmony, and good feeling of those who come hither; and you will beg them to make choice of persons in whom they can place full confidence for all matters connected with their service. You will beseech them to hold in view

---

autoridad y gran seguridad á la gente que ha de estar dentro y conversar con los indios para cojer el oro, mas aun para otra cualquier cosa de peligro que de gente estraña pudiese acontescer, allende que las carabelas son necesarias para el descubrir de la tierra firme y otras islas que entre aquí é allá estan; y suplicareis á sus Altezas que los maravedis que estos navíos cuestan manden pager en los tiempos que se les ha prometido, porque sin dubda ellos ganará bien su costa, segun yo creo y espero en la misericordia de Dios.

El Almirante lo hizo bien, y decirle heis como acá se pago al que venidó la nao, y mandaron á D. Juan de Fonseca que pague lo de las carabelas que el Almirante compró.

Item : Direis á sus Altezas y suplicareis de mi parte cuanto mas humilmente pueda, que les plega mucho mirar en ló que por las cartas y otras escripturas verán mas largamente tocante á la paz é sosiego e concordia de los que acá estan, y que para las cosas del servicio de sus Altezas escojan tales personas que non se tenga recelo dellas y

the purpose for which these men are sent, rather than their own interest; and since you yourself have seen and are acquainted with these matters, you will speak to their Highnesses upon this subject, and will tell them the truth on every point exactly as you have understood it; you will also take care that the orders which their Highnesses shall give on this point be put into effect, if possible, by the first vessels, in order that no further injury occur here in the matters that affect their service.

Their Highnesses are well informed of all that takes place, and will see to it that everything is done as it should be.

Item.   You will describe to their Highnesses the position of this city, the beauty of the province in which it is situated, as you have seen it, and as you can honestly speak of it; and you can inform them, that in virtue of the powers which I have received from them, I have made you governor of the said city; and you will tell them also that I humbly beseech them, out of consideration for your services, to receive your nomination favourably, which I sincerely hope they may do.

Their Highnesses are pleased to sanction your appointment as governor.

---

que miren mas á lo por que se envian que non á sus propios intereses; y en esto, pues que todas las cosas vistes é supistes, hablareis é direis á sus Altezas la verdad de todas las cosas como las comprendistes, y que la provision de sus Altezas que sobre ello mandaren facer venga con los primeros navíos si posible fuere, á fin que acá non se hagan escándalos en cosa que tanto va en el servicio de sus Altezas.

Sus Altezas estan bien informados desto, y en todo se proveerá como conviene.

Item: Direis á sus Altezas el asiento de esta ciudad, é la fermosura de la provincia alderedor como lo vistes y compreendistes, y como yo vos hice Alcayde della por los poderes que de sus Altezas tengo para ello, á las cuales humilmente suplico que en alguna parte de satisfaccion de vuestros servicios tengan por bien la dicha provision, como de sus Altezas yo espero.

A sus Altezas plaze que vos seais Alcayde.

Item. As Moses Pedro Margarite, an officer of the household to their Highnesses, has done good service, and will, I hope, continue to do so for the future in all matters which may be entrusted to him, I have felt great pleasure in his continuing his stay in this country; and I have been much pleased to find that Gaspar and Beltran also remain : and as they are all three well known to their Highnesses as faithful servants, I shall place them in posts or employments of trust. You will beg their Highnesses especially to have regard to the situation of the said Moses Pedro Margarite, who is married and the father of a family, and beseech them to give him some vacant command in the order of St. James, of which he is a knight, in order that his wife and children may thus have a competence to live upon. You will also make mention of Juan Aguado, a servant of their Highnesses ; you will inform them of the zeal and activity with which he has served them in all matters that have been entrusted to him ; and also that I beseech their Highnesses on his behalf, as well as on behalf of those above mentioned, not to forget my recommendation, but to give it full consideration.

Their Highnesses grant an annual pension of thirty thousand maravedis to Moses Pedro Margarite, and pensions of

---

Item : Porque Mosen Pedro Margarité, criado de sus Altezas, há bien servido, y espero que así lo hara adelante en las cosas que le fueren encomendadas, he habido placer de su quedada aqui, y tambien de Gaspar y de Beltran por ser conocidos criados de sus Altezas para los poner en cosas de confianza : suplicareis á sus Altezas que especial al dicho Mosen Pedro, que es casado y tiene hijos le provean de alguna encomienda en la Orden de Santiago, de la cual él tiene el hábito, porque su muger é hijos tengan en que vivir. Asimismo hareis relacion de Juan Aguado, criado de sus Altezas, cuan bien é diligentemente ha servido en todo lo que le ha seido mandado ; que suplico á sus Altezas á él é á los sobredichos los hayan por encomendados é por presentes.

Sus Altezas mandan asentar á Mosen Pedro 30000 *maravedis cada ano, y á Gaspar y Beltran á cada uno* 15000 *maravedis cada año*

fifteen thousand maravedis to Gaspard and Beltran, which will be reckoned from this day, the 15th of August 1494. They give orders that the said pensions be paid by the Admiral out of the sums to be paid in the Indies, and by Don Juan de Fonseca out of the sums to be paid in Spain. With respect to the matter of Juan Aguado, their Highnesses will not be forgetful.

Item. You will inform their Highnesses of the continual labour that Doctor Chanca has undergone, from the prodigious number of sick and the scarcity of provisions: and that, in spite of all this, he exhibits the greatest zeal and benevolence in everything that relates to his profession. As their Highnesses have entrusted me with the charge of fixing the salary that is to be paid to him while out here (although it is certain that he neither receives, nor can receive anything from any one, and does not receive anything from his position, equal to what he did, and could still do in Spain, where he lived peaceably and at ease, in a very different style from what he does here; and, although he declares that he earned more in Spain, exclusive of the pay which he received from their Highnesses), I have, nevertheless, not ventured to place to the credit of his account more than fifty thousand mara-

---

desde hoy 15 de Agosto de 94 en adelante, y así les hagar pagar el Almirante en lo que allá se hobiere de pagar, y D. Juan de Fonseca en lo que acá se hobiere de pagar: y en lo de Juan Aguado sus Altezas habrán memoria de él.

Item: Direis á sus Altezas el trabajo que el Doctor Chanca tiene con el afruenta de tantos dolientes, y aun la estrechura de los mantenimientos, é aun con todo ello se dispone con gran diligencia y caridad en todo lo que cumple á su oficio, y porque sus Altezas remitieron á mí el salario que acá se le habia de dar, porque estando acá es cierto quel non toma ni puede haber nada de ninguno, ni ganar de su oficio como en Castilla ganaba, ó podria ganar estando á su reposo é viviendo de otra manera que acá no vive; y así que como quiera que él jura que es mas lo que allá ganaba allende el salario que sus Altezas le dan, y non me quise estender mas de

vedis per annum, as the sum which he is to receive for his yearly labour during the time of his stay in this country. I beg their Highnesses to give their sanction to this salary, exclusive of his maintenance while here; and I do so, because he asserts that all the medical men who attend their Highnesses in the royal yachts, or in any of their expeditions, are accustomed to receive by right the day's pay out of the annual salary of each individual. Let this be as it may, I am informed for certain, that on whatever service they are engaged, it is the custom to give them a certain fixed sum, settled at the will and by order of their Highnesses, in compensation for the said day's pay. You will, therefore, beg their Highnesses to decide this matter, as well with respect to the annual pay as to the above-mentioned usage, so that the said doctor may be reasonably satisfied.

Their Highnesses acknowledge the justice of Doctor Chanca's observations, and it is their wish that the Admiral shall pay him the sum which he has allowed him, exclusive of his fixed annual salary. With respect to the day's pay allowed to medical men, it is not the custom to authorize them to receive it, except when they are in personal attendance upon the King.

---

cincuenta mil maravedis por el trabajo que acá pasa cada un año mientras acá estoviere ; los cuales suplico á sus Altezas le manden librar con el sueldo de acá y eso mismo, porque él dice y afirma que todos los fisicos de vuestras Altezas, que andan en reales ó semejantes cosas que estas, suelen haber de derecho un dia de sueldo en todo el año de toda la gente : con todo he seido informado, y dicenme, que como quier que esto sea, la costumbre es de darles cierta suma tasada á voluntad y mandamiento de sus Altezas en compensa de aquel dia de sueldo. Suplicareis á sus Altezas que en ello manden proveer, así en lo del salario como de esta costumbre, por forma que el dicho Doctor tenga razon de ser contento.

A sus Altezas place desto del Doctor Chanca, y que se le pague esto desde quel Almirante gelo asentó, y que gelos pague con lo del sueldo.

En esto del dia del sueldo de los fisicos, non lo acostumbran haber sino donde el Rey nuestro Senor esté en persona.

Item.   You will tell their Highnesses what great devotion Coronel has shown to the service in many respects, and what great proofs he has given of it in every important matter that has been trusted to him, and how much we feel his loss now that he is sick.   You will represent to them how just it is that he should receive the recompense of such good and loyal services, not only in the favours which may hereafter be shown to him, but also in his present pay, in order that he, and all those that are with us, may see what profit will accrue to them from their zeal in the service; for the importance and difficulty of exploring the mines should call for great consideration towards those to whom such extensive interests are entrusted ; and, as the talents of the said Coronel have made me determine upon appointing him principal constable of this portion of the Indies,—and, as I have given him *carte blanche* for fixing the salaries of those who come under his charge,—I beg their Highnesses to condescend to sanction these grants as fully as they may think proper, upon consideration of his services, and to confirm his nomination to the service which I have allotted to him, by giving him an official appointment thereto.

Their Highnesses grant him, besides his salary, an annnal

Item : Direis á sus Altezas de Coronel cuanto es hombre para servir, á sus Altezas en muchas cosas, y cuanto ha servido hasta aquí en todo lo mas necesario, y la mengua que dél sentimos agora que está doliente, y que sirviendo de tal manera es razon quel sienta el fruto de su servicio, non solo en las mercedes para despues mas en lo de su salario en lo presente, en manera quél é los que acá estan sientan que les aprovecha el servicio, y porque segun el ejercicio que acá se ha de tener en cojer este oro, no son de tener en poco las personas en quien tanta diligencia hay : porque por su habilidad se proveyó acá por mí del oficio de Alguacil´mayor destas Indias, y en la provision va el salario en blanco, que suplico á sus Altezas gelo manden henchir como mas sea su servicio, mirando sus servicios, confirmándole la provision que acá se le dió, e proveyéndole de él de juro.

*pension of fifteen thousand maravedis; the same to be paid him
at the same time as the said salary.*

Item. You will, at the same time, tell their Highnesses
that the bachelor, Gil Garcia, came out here in quality of
principal alcalde, without having any salary fixed or allowed
to him : that he is a good man, well-informed, correct in his
conduct, and one that is very necessary to us; and that I beg
their Highnesses to be pleased to give him such appointments
as shall enable him to support himself honourably; and that
such may be granted to him extra the funds due to the
appointments given to him beyond the sea.

*Their Highnesses grant him an annual pension of twenty
thousand maravedis during his stay in the Indies, and that over
and above his fixed appointments ; and it is their order that
this pension be paid to him at the same time as his salary.*

Item. You will tell their Highnesses, as I have already
told them in writing, that I think it will be impossible to go
this year to make discoveries until arrangements have been
made to work the two rivers in which the gold has been found
in the most profitable manner for their Highnesses' interest ;
and this may be done more effectively hereafter, because it is

---

*Sus Altezas mandan que le asienten quince mil maravedis cada año
mas de su sueldo, é que se le paguen cuando le pagaren su sueldo.*

Asimismo direis á sus Altezas como aquí vino el Bachiller Gil
García por Alcalde mayor é non se le ha consignado ni nombrado
salario, y es persona de bien y de buenas letras, é diligente, é es acá
bien necesario ; que suplico á sus Altezas le manden nombrar é
consignar su salario, por manera que él se pueda sostener, é le sea
librado con el dinero del sueldo de acá.

*Sus Altezas le mandan asentar cada año veinte mil maravedis en
tanto que allá estoviere y mas su sueldo, y que gelo paguen cuando
pagaren el sueldo.*

Item : Direis á sus Altezas como quier que ya se lo escribo por
las cartas, que para este año non entiendo que sea posible ir á descobrir hasta que esto destos rios que se hallaron de oro sea puesto en
el asiento debido á servicio de sus Altezas, que despues mucho mejor

not a thing that every one can do to my satisfaction, or with
advantage to their Highnesses' service, unless I be present;
for whatever is to be done always turns out best under the
eye of the party interested.

*Let him continue to carry on his operations, as well as he is
able, and let him try to discover the places where the gold is
hidden.*

Item.   You will tell their Highnesses, that the horse-soldiers that came from Grenada to the review which took place
at Seville, offered good horses, but that at the time of their
being sent on board, they took advantage of my absence (for
I was somewhat indisposed), and changed them for others,
the best of which does not seem worth two thousand maravedis, for they sold the first and bought these; and this deception on the part of the horse soldiers, is very like what I
have known to occur to many gentlemen in Seville of my
acquaintance.   It seems that Juan de Sorias, after having
settled an advantageous price for himself, put other horses in
the place of those that I expected to find, and when I came
to see them, there were horses there that had never been

---

se podrá facer, porque no es cosa que nadie la podiese facer sin mi
presencia á mi grado, ni á servicio de sus Altezas, por muy bien
que lo ficiese, como es en dubda segun lo que hombre vee por su
presencia.

*Trabaje como lo mas preciso que ser pueda se sepa lo adito de ese
oro.*

Item: Direis á sus Altezas como los escuderos de caballo que
vinieron de Granada, en el alarde que ficieron en Sevilla mostraron
buenos caballos, é despues al embarcar, yo no lo vi porque estaba un
poco doliente, y metiéronlos tales quel mejor dellos non parece que
vale dos mil maravedis, porque vendieron los otros y compraron
estos, y esto fue de la suerte que se hizo lo de mucha gente que allá
en los alardes de Sevilla yo vi muy buena; parece que Juan de
Soria, despues de dado el dinero del sueldo, por algun interese suyo
puso otros en lugar de aquellos que yo acá pensaba fallar, y fallo
gente que yo nunca habia visto: en esto ha habido gran maldad, de

offered to me for sale. In all this the greatest dishonesty has been shown, so that I do not know whether I ought to complain of him alone, since these horse-soldiers have been paid their expenses up to the present day, besides their salary and the hire of their horses, and when they are ill, they will not allow their horses to be used, because they are not present. Their Highnesses did not wish the horses to be purchased, but desired that the men should be taken into their service, but only to be employed in work which required them to ride on horse-back, which is not the case at present. All these considerations lead me to think, that it would be more convenient to buy their horses, which are worth but little, and thus avoid being exposed daily to new disputes; finally, their Highnesses will decide on what plan is best for their own interests.

Their Highnesses order Don Juan de Fonseca to make enquiries respecting the matter of the horses, and if it be true that such a deception has been practised, to send up the culprits to be punished as they deserve; also to gain information respecting the other people that the admiral speaks of, and to send the result of the information to their Highnesses. With respect

---

tal manera que yo no sé si me queje del solo : por esto, visto que á estos escuderos se ha fecho la costa hasta aqui, allende de sus sueldos y tambien á sus caballos, y se hace de presente y son personas que cuando ellos estan dolientes, ó non se les antoja, non quieren que sus caballos sirvan sin ellos mismos ; sus Altezas no quieren que se les compren estos caballos sino que sirvan á sus Altezas, y esto mismo no les paresce que deban servir ni cosa ninguna sino á caballo ; lo cual agora de presente non face mucho al caso, é por esto parece que seria mejor comprarles los caballos, pues que tan poco valen, y non estar cada dia con ellos en estas pendencias ; por ende que sus Altezas determinen esto como fuere su servicio.

Sus Altezas mandan á D. Juan de Fonseca, que se informe de esto de estos caballos, y si se hallare que es verdad que hicieron ese engano, lo envien á sus Altezas porque lo mandarán castigar; tambien se informe deso que dice de la otra gente, y envie la pesquisa á sus Altezas: y

to the horse soldiers, it is their Highnesses' wish and command, that they continue where they are, and remain in service, because they belong to the guards and to the class of their Highnesses' servants. Their Highnesses also command the said horse soldiers to give up their horses into the charge of the Admiral on all occasions when they shall be required, and if the use of the horses should occasion any loss, their Highnesses direct that compensation shall be made for the amount of the injury, through the medium of the Admiral.

Item. You will mention to their Highnesses, that more than two hundred persons have come here without fixed salaries, and that some of them are very useful to the service; and in order to preserve system and uniformity, the others have been ordered to imitate them. For the three first years, it is desirable that we should have here a thousand men, in order to keep a safeguard upon the island and upon the rivers that supply the gold : and even when we are able to mount a hundred men on horse-back, so far from being an evil, it will be a very necessary thing for us; but their Highnesses might pass by the question of the horse-men until gold shall be sent. In short, their Highnesses should give instructions

---

en lo destos escuderos sus Altezas mandan que esten allá y sirvan, pues son de las guardas y criados de sus Altezas ; y á los escuderos mandan sus Altezas qne den los caballos cada vez que fueren menester y el Almirante lo mandare, y si algun dano recibieren los caballos yendo otros en ellos, por medio del Almirante mandan sus Altezas que gelo paguen.

Item : Direis á sus Altezas como aqui han venido mas de doscientas personas sin sueldo, y hay algunos dellos que sirven bien, y aun los otros por semejante se mandan que lo hagan así y porque para estos primeros tres años será gran bien que aqui esten mil hombres para asentar y poner en muy gran seguridad esta Isla y rios de oro, y aunque hobiese ciento de caballo non se perderia nada, antes parece necesario, aunque en estos de caballo fasta que oro se envie sus Altezas podrán sobrecer : con todo á estas doscientas personas, que vienen sin sueldo, sus Altezas deben enviar á decir si

as to whether the two hundred people who have come over without pay, should receive pay like the others, if they do their work well; for we certainly have great need of them to commence our labours, as I have already shown.

It is their Highnesses' wish and command, that the two hundred persons without pay shall replace such of those who are paid as have failed, or as shall hereafter fail, in their duty, provided they are fit for the service and please the Admiral; and their Highnesses order the Accomptant to enter their names in the place of those who shall fail in their duty, as the Admiral shall determine.

Item. As there are means of diminishing the expenses that these people occasion, and of saving a considerable portion of the expenditure, by imitating the plans which other princes have been able to employ with great effect, it would be desirable that we should do likewise.

I think it would be well that all ships that come here should be ordered to bring, besides the ordinary stores and medicines, shoes, and leather for making shoes, shirts, both of common and superior quality, doublets, laces, some peasants' clothing, breeches, and cloth for making clothes, all at moderate prices;

---

se les pagará sueldo como á los otros sirviendo bien, porque cierto son necesarios como dicho tengo para este comienzo.

De estas doscientas personas que aquí dice que fueron sin sueldo, mandan sus Altezas que entren en lugar de los que han faltado y faltaren de los que iban á sueldo, seyendo habiles y á contentamiento del Almirante, y sus Altezas mandan al Contador que los asiente en lugar de los que faltaren como el Almirante lo dijere.

Item : Porque en algo la costa de esta gente se puede aliviar con industria y formas que otros Principes suelen tener en otras, lo gastado mejor que acá se podria escusar, paresce que seria bien mandar traer en los navíos que vinieren allende de las otras cosas que son para los mantenimientos comunes, y de la botica, zapatos y cueras para los mandar facer ; camisas comunes y de otras, jubones, lienzo, sayos, calzas. paños para vestir en razonables precios ; y otras cosas, como son conservas, que son fuera de racion, y para conservacion de la

they might also bring other articles, such as sweetmeats, which do not enter into the daily ration, nor are absolutely necessary to health. The Spaniards that are here would always be happy to receive such articles as these in lieu of part of their pay; and if they were purchased by men who were selected for their known loyalty, and who take an interest in the service of their Highnesses, great economy would result from this arrangement. If their Highnesses find that this plan is expedient for the service, it is desirable that it should be adopted immediately.

It would have been desirable that the Admiral had entered more fully into the details of this subject; meanwhile, Don Juan de Fonseca shall be ordered to instruct Don Ximenes de Bribiesca to make the necessary arrangements for the execution of the proposed plans.

Item. You will tell their Highnesses that, in a review that was holden yesterday, it was remarked that a great number of the people were without arms, which I think must be attributed partly to the exchange made at Seville, or in the harbour, when those who presented themselves armed were left for a while, and for a trifle exchanged their arms for others of an inferior quality. I think it would be desirable that two

---

salud, las cuales cosas todas la gente de ac rescibiria de grado en descuento de su sueldo, y si allá esto se mercase por Ministros leales y que mirasen el servicio de sus Altezas, se ahorraria algo: por ende sabreis la voluntad de sus Altezas cerca desto, y si les pareciere ser su servicio luego se debe poner en obra.

Por este camino se solia ser fasta que mas escriba el Almirante, y ya enviarán á mandar á D. Juan de Fonseca con Jimeno de Bribiesca que provea en esto.

Item : Tambien direis á sus Altezas, que por cuanto ayer en el alarde que se tomó se falló la gente muy desarmada, lo cual pienso que en parte contesció por aquel trocar que allá se fizo en Sevilla ó en el puerto cuando se dejaron los que se mostraron armados, y tomaron otros que daban algo á quien los trocaba, paresce que seria bien que se mandasen traer doscientas corazas, y cien espingardas

hundred cuirasses, a hundred arquebuses, a hundred arbalists, and many other articles of defensive armour, should be sent over to us; for we have great need of them to arm those who are at present without them.

Don Juan de Fonseca has already been written to, to provide them.

Item. Many married persons have come over here, and are engaged in regular duties, such as masons and other tradesmen, who have left their wives in Spain, and wish that the pay that falls due to them may be paid to their wives, or whomsoever they may appoint, in order that they may purchase for them such articles as they may need. I therefore beseech their Highnesses to take such measures as they may deem expedient on this subject; for it is of importance to their interests that these people be well provided for.

Their Highnesses have already ordered Don Juan de Fonseca to attend to this matter.

Item. Besides the other articles which I have begged from their Highnesses in the memorial which you bear, signed by my hand, and which articles consist of provisions and other stores, both for those who are well and for those who are sick,

---

y cien ballestas, y mucho almacen, que es la cosa que mas menester habemos, y de todas estas armas se podrán dar á los desarmados.

Ya se escribe á D. Juan de Fonseca que provea en esto.

Item : Por cuanto algunos oficiales que acá vinieron como son albañies y de otros oficios, que son casados y tienen sus mugeres allá, y querrian que allá lo que se les debe de su sueldo se diese á sus mugeres ó á las personas á quien ellos enviaren sus recabdos, para que les compren las cosas que acá han menester ; que á sus Altezas suplico les mande librar, porque su servicio es que estos esten proveidos acá.

Ya enviaron á mandar sus Altezas á D. Juan, de Fonseca que provea en esto.

Item : Porque allende las otras cosas que allá se envian á pedir por los memoriales que llevais de mi mano firmados, así para mantenimiento de los sanos como para los dolientes, seria muy bien que

it would be very serviceable that fifty pipes of molasses should be sent hither from the island of Madeira; for it is the most nutritious food in the world, and the most wholesome. A pipe of it does not ordinarily cost more than two ducats, exclusive of the casks; and if their Highnesses would order one of the caravels to call at the said island on the return voyage, the purchase might be made, and they might, at the same time, buy ten casks of sugar, of which we stand greatly in need. It is the most favourable season of the year to obtain it at a cheap rate, that is to say, between this and the month of April. The necessary orders might be given, if their Highnesses think proper, and yet the place of destination be carefully concealed.

Don Juan de Fonseca will see to it.

Item. You will tell their Highnesses that, although the rivers contain in their beds the quantity of gold described by those who have seen it, there is no doubt that this metal is produced in the bosom of the earth; and that the water happening to come in contact with the mines, washes it away mingled with the sand. And as among the great number of rivers that have been already discovered

---

se hobiesen de la isla de la Madera cincuenta pipas de miel de azúcar, porque es el mejor mantenimiento del mundo y mas sano, y non suele costar cada pipa sino á dos ducados sin el casco, y si sus Altezas mandan que á la vuelta pase por allí alguna carabela las podrá mercar, y tambien diez cajas de azúcar que es mucho menester, que esta es la mejor sazon del año, digo entre aquí é el mes de Abril para fallarlo, é haber dello buena razon y podriase dar orden mandándolo sus Altezas, é que non supiesen allá para donde lo quieren.

D. Juan de Fonseca que provea en esto.

Item : Direis á sus Altezas, por cuanto aunque los rios tengan en la cuantidad que se dice por los que lo han visto, pero que lo cierto dello es quel oro non se engendra en los rios mas en la tierra, quel agua topando con las minas lo trae envuelto en las arenas, y porque en estos tantos rios se han descubierto, como quiera que hay

there are some of considerable magnitude, there are also some
so small that they might rather be called brooks than rivers,
only two fingers' breadth deep, and very short in their course ;
there will, therefore, be some men wanted to wash the gold
from the sand, and others to seek for it in the bosom of the
earth. This latter operation will be the principal and the
most productive ; it will be expedient, therefore, that their
Highnesses send men both for the washing and for the mining,
from among those who are employed in Spain in the mines
at Almaden,[4] so that, by one means or another, the work
may be managed. We shall not, however, wait for the arrival
of these workmen, but hope, with the aid of God and with the
washers that we have here with us, when they shall be restored
to health, to send a good quantity of gold by the first caravels
that shall leave for Spain.

*This shall be completely provided for by other means; mean-
while, Don Juan de Fonseca has their Highnesses' orders to send
the best miners that he can find. Their Highnesses write also
to Almaden, with instructions to select the greatest number that
can be spared, and to send them up.*

---

algunos grandecitos hay otros tan pequeños que son mas fuentes que
no rios, que non llevan de dos dedos de agua, y se falla luego el cabo doede nasce ; para lo cual non solo serán provechosos los lavadores para cogerlo en el arena, mas los otros para cavarlo en la
tierra, que será lo mas especial é de mayor cuantidad ; é por esto
será bien que sus Altezas envien lavadores, é de los que andan en
las minas allá en Almaden, porque en la una manera y en la otra
se faga el ejercicio, como quier que acá non esperaremos á ellos,
que con los lavadores que aquí tenemos, esperamos con la ayuda
de Dios, si una vez la gente está sana, allegar un buen golpe de oro
para las primeras carabelas que fueren.

*A otro camino se proveerá en esto cumplidamente; en tanto man-
dan sus Altezas á D. Juan de Fonseca que envie luego los mas mi-
nadores que pudiere haber, y escriben al Almaden, que de alli tomen
los que mas pudieren y los envien.*

[4] In La Mancha, New Castile, famous for mines of quicksilver.

Item. You will beseech their Highnesses very humbly in my name, to condescend to pay regard to my strong recommendation of Villacorta, who, as their Highnesses are in some degree aware, has been extremely useful, and has shown the greatest possible zeal in this affair. From all that I have observed in him, I consider him a man of strict integrity,— zealous and devoted to their Highnesses' service. I shall feel very grateful if they would deign to grant him some confidential employment adapted to his qualifications, and in which he might evince his industry and warm desire to serve their Highnesses : and you will take care that Villacorta shall have practical evidence that none of this work which he has done for me, or under my orders, has remained without recompense.

This shall be done as he wishes.

Item. That the said Moses Pedro, Gaspar, Beltran, and others remaining here, came to command caravels which have already gone back, and are in receipt of no salary whatever : as these are people who should be employed in matters of principal importance, and requiring the greatest confidence, their pay has not been fixed, because it ought to be different

---

Item : Suplicareis á sus Altezas de mi parte muy humildemente, que quieran tener por muy encomendado á Villacorta, el cual, como sus Altezas saben, ha mucho servido en esta negociacion, y con muy buena voluntad, y segun le conozco persona diligente y aficionada á su servicio ; rescebiré merced que se le dé algun cargo de confianza, para lo cual él ser suficiente, y pueda mostrar su deseo de servir y diligencia, y esto procurareis por forma que el Villacorta conozca por la obra que lo que ha trabajado por mí en lo que yo le hobe menester le aprovecha en esto.

Así se hará.

Item : Que los dichos Mosen Pedro y Gaspar y Beltran, y otros que han quedado acá, trajieron capitanías de carabelas, que son agora vueltas, y non gozan del sueldo ; pero porque son tales personas, que se han de poner en cosas principales y de confianza, non se les ha determinado el sueldo que sea diferenciado de los otros:

from that of the rest. You will beg their Highnesses, on my behalf, to settle what ought to be given them either yearly or monthly, with respect to their Highnesses' service.

Given in the City of Isabella, the thirtieth of January, in the year fourteen hundred and ninety-four.

This point has been already replied to above; but as in the said clause it is said that they should receive their pay, it is their Highnesses' command that their salary shall be paid to them from the time that the command was issued.

---

suplicareis de mi parte á sus Altezas determinen lo que se les ha de dar en cada un año, ó por meses, como mas fueren servidos. Fecho en la ciudad Isabela á treinta dias de Enero de mil cuatrocientos y noventa y cuatro años.

Ya está respondido arriba, pero porque en el dicho capitulo que en esto habia dice que gozan del salario, desde agora mandan sus Altezas que se les cuenten á todos sus salarios desde que dejaron las capitanias.

THIRD VOYAGE OF COLUMBUS.

The History of a Voyage which Don Christopher Columbus made the third time that he came to the Indies, when he discovered terra firma, and which he sent to their Majesties from the Island of Hispaniola.

MOST serene and most exalted and powerful Princes, the King and Queen, our Sovereigns. The Blessed Trinity moved your Highnesses to the encouragement of this enterprise to the Indies; and of its infinite goodness has made me your messenger therein; as ambassador for which undertaking I approached your royal presence, moved by the consideration that I was appealing to the most exalted monarchs in Christendom, who exercised so great an influence over the Christian faith, and its advancement in the world : those who heard of it looked upon it as impossible, for they fixed

TERCER VIAGE DE COLON.

La historia del viage quel Almirante D. Cristobal Colon hizo la tercera vez que vino á las Indias cuando descubrió la tierra firme, como lo envió á los Reyes desde la Isla Espanola.

SERENÍSIMOS é muy altos é muy poderosos Príncipes Rey é Reina nuestros Señores : La Santa Trinidad movió á vuestras Altezas á esta empresa de las Indias, y por su infinita bondad hizo á mí mensagero dello, al cual vine con el embajada á su Real conspetu, movido como á los mas altos Príncipes de cristianos y que tanto se ejercisaban en la fé y acrecentamiento della ; las personas que entendieron en ello lo tuvieron por imposible, y el caudal hacian sobre bienes de fortuna, y allí echaron el clavo. Puse en esto seis ó siete

all their hopes on the favours of fortune, and pinned their faith solely upon chance. I gave to the subject six or seven years of great anxiety, explaining, to the best of my ability, how great service might be done to our Lord, by this undertaking, in promulgating His sacred name and our holy faith among so many nations;—an enterprise so exalted in itself, and so calculated to enhance the glory and immortalize the renown of the greatest sovereigns. It was also requisite to refer to the temporal prosperity which was foretold in the writings of so many trustworthy and wise historians, who related that great riches were to be found in these parts. And at the same time I thought it desirable to bring to bear upon the subject, the sayings and opinions of those who have written upon the geography of the world. And finally, your Highnesses came to the determination that the undertaking should be entered upon. In this your Highnesses exhibited the noble spirit which has been always manifested by you on every great subject; for all others who had thought of the matter or heard it spoken of, unanimously treated it with contempt, with the exception of two friars,[1] who always

---

años de grave pena, amostrando lo mejor que yo sabia cuanto servicio se podia hacer á nuestro Señor en esto en divulgar su santo nombre y Fé á tantos pueblos; lo cual todo era cosa de tanta excelencia y buena fama y gran memoria para grandes Príncipes fue tambien necesario de hablar del temporal adonde se les amostró el escrebir de tantos sabios dignos de fé, los cuales escribieron historias. Los cuales contaban que en estas partes habia muchas riquezas, y asimismo fue necesario traer á esto el decir é opinion de aquellos que escribieron é situaron el mundo : en fin vuestras Altezas determinaron questo se pusiese en obra. Aquí mostraron el grande corazon que siempre ficieron en toda cosa grande, porque todos los que habian entendido en ello y oido esta platica todos á una mano lo tenian á burla, salvo dos frailes que siempre fueron

[1] These were Fray Juan Perez de Marchena, a Franciscan, keeper of the Convent de la Rabida, and Fray Diejo de Deza, a Dominican, afterwards Archbishop of Seville.

remained constant in their belief of its practicability.   I, myself, in spite of fatiguing opposition, felt sure that the enterprise would nevertheless prosper, and continue equally con-
fident of it to this day, because it is a truth, that though
everything will pass away, the Word of God will not; and I
believe, that every prospect which I hold out will be accomplished; for it was clearly predicted concerning these lands,
by the mouth of the prophet Isaiah, in many places in Scripture, that from Spain the holy name of God was to be spread
abroad.   Thus I departed in the name of the Holy Trinity,
and returned very soon, bringing with me an account of the
practical fulfilment of everything I had said.   Your Highnesses
again sent me out, and in a short space of time, by God's mercy,
not by[2]   I discovered three hundred and thirty-three
leagues of terra firma on the eastern side, and seven hundred
islands,[3] besides those which I discovered on the first voyage;

constantes.   Yo, bien que llevase fatiga, estaba bien seguro que
esto no vernia á menos, y estoy de contino, porque es verdad que
todo pasará, y no la palabra de Dios, y se complirá todo lo que
dijo; el cual tan claro habló de estas tierras por la boca de Isaías
en tantos lugares de su Escriptura, afirmando que de España les
seria divulgado su santo nombre.   E partí en nombre de la Santa
Trinidad, y volví muy presto con la experiencia de todo cuanto yo
habia dicho en la mano : tornáronme á enviar vuestras Altezas, y
en poco espacio digo, no de   le descubri por virtud divinal
trescientas y treinta y tres leguas de la tierra firme, fin de Oriente,
y setcentas islas de nombre, allende de lo descubierto en el primero

[2] A similar gap in the original.
[3] He did not discover terra firma in the second voyage as he here says,
but imagined the island of Cuba to be terra firma, because he was unable
to explore it fully ; nor did he ascertain that it was an island, until, by
order of the king, the Comendador Mayor Nicolas Ovando gave Sebastian
de Ocampo a commission to circumnavigate the island, and he explored
the whole coast in the year 1508.   (See Herrera, Dec. i, lib. 7, cap. i.)
Amongst the number of these islands, Columbus doubtless included many
of those to the south of Cuba, lying in the part which he called the *Queen's
Gardens*.

I also succeeded in circumnavigating the island of Española, which is larger in circumference than all Spain, the inhabitants of which are countless, and all of whom may be laid under tribute. It was then that complaints arose, disparaging the enterprise that I had undertaken, because, forsooth, I had not immediately sent the ships home laden with gold,—no allowance being made for the shortness of the time, and all the other impediments of which I have already spoken. On this account (either as a punishment for my sins, or, as I trust, for my salvation), I was held in detestation, and had obstacles placed in the way of every thing I said or for which I petitioned. I therefore resolved to apply to your Highnesses, to inform you of all the wonderful events that I had experienced, and to explain the reason of every proposition that I made, making reference to the nations that I had seen, among whom, and by whose instrumentality, many souls may be saved. I related how the natives of Española had been laid under tribute to your Highnesses, and regarded you as their sovereigns. And I laid before your Highnesses abundant samples of gold and copper,—proving the existence of extensive mines of those metals. I also laid before your Highnesses many sorts of spices, too

---

víage, y le allané la Isla Española que boja mas que España, en que la gente della es sin cuento, y que todos le pagasen tributo. Nació allí mal decir y menosprecio de la empresa comenzada en ello, porque no habia yo enviado luego los navíos cargados de oro, sin considerar la brevedad del tiempo, y lo otro que yo dije de tantos inconvenientes ; y en esto por mis pecados ó por mi salvacion creo que será, fue puesto en aborrecimiento y dado impedimento á cuanto yo decia y demandaba ; por lo cual acordé de venir á vuestras Altezas, y maravillarme de todo, y mostrarles la razon que en todo habia, y les dige de los pueblos que yo habia vesto, en qué ó de qué se podrian salvar muchas animas, y les truje las obligaciones de la gente de la Isla Española, de como se obligaban á pagar tributo é les tenian por sos Reyes y Señores, y les truje abastante muestra de oro, y que hay mineros y granos muy grandes, y asi-

numerous to detail; and I spoke of the great quantity of bra-
zil-wood, and numberless other articles found in those lands.
All this was of no avail with some persons; who began, with
determined hatred, to speak ill of the enterprise, not taking
into account the service done to our Lord in the salvation of
so many souls, nor the enhancement of your Highnesses'
greatness to a higher pitch than any earthly prince has yet
enjoyed; nor considering, that from the exercise of your
Highnesses' goodness, and the expense incurred, both spiritual
and temporal advantage was to be expected, and that Spain
must in the process of time derive from thence, beyond all
doubt, an unspeakable increase of wealth. This might be
manifestly seen by the evidences already given in writing in
the descriptions of the voyages already made, which also
prove that the fulfilment of every other hope may be reasonably expected. Nor were they affected by the consideration
of what great princes throughout the world have done to increase their fame : as, for example, Solomon, who sent from
Jerusalem, to the uttermost parts of the east, to see Mount
Sopora, in which expedition his ships were detained three
years; and which mountain your Highnesses now possess in

---

mismo de cobre ; y les truje de muchas maneras de especerias, de
que seria largo de escrebir, y les dije de la gran cantidad de brasil,
y otras infinitas cosas.   Todo no aprovechó para con algunas personas que tenian gana y dado comienzo á mal decir del negocio, ni
entrar con fabla del servicio de nuestro Señor con se salvar tantas
animas, ni á decir questo era grandeza de vuestras Altezas, de la
mejor calidad que hasta hoy haya usado Príncipe, por quel ejercicio
é gasto era para el espiritual y temporal, y que no podiá ser que
andando el tiempo no hobiese la España de aquí grandes provechos,
pues que se veian las señales que escribieron de lo de estas partidas
tan manifiestas : que tambien se llegaria á ver todo el otro complimi-
ento, ni á decir cosas que usaron grandes Principes en el mundo
para crecer su fama, así como de Salomon que envió desde Hierusalem en fin de Oriente á ver el monte Sopora, en que se detovieron
los navíos tres años, el cual tienen vuestras Altezas agora en la Isla

the island of Española. Nor, as in the case of Alexander,
who sent to observe the mode of government in the island
of Taprobana,[4] in India; and Cæsar Nero, to explore the
sources of the Nile,[5] and to learn the causes of its increase in
the spring,[6] when water is needed; and many other mighty
deeds that princes have done, and which it is allotted to
princes to achieve.   Nor was it of any avail that no prince
of Spain, as far as I have read, has ever hitherto gained possession of land out of Spain; and that the world of which I
speak is different from that in which the Romans, and Alexander, and the Greeks, made mighty efforts with great armies
to gain the possession of.   Nor have they been affected by
the recent noble example of the kings of Portugal, who have
had the courage to explore as far as Guinea, and to make the
discovery of it, expending so much gold and so many lives in
the undertaking, that a calculation of the population of the
kingdom would show, that one half of them have died in
Guinea : and though it is now a long time since they com-

Española ; ni de Alejandre, que envió á ver el regimiento de la Isla
de Trapobana en India, y Noro Cooar á ver las fuentes del Nilo, y
la razon porque crecian en el verano, cuando las aguas son pocas, y
otras muchas grandezas que hicieron Príncipes, y que á Príncipes
son estas cosas dadas de hacer ; ni valia decir que yo nunca habia
leido que Príncipes de Castilla jamas hobiesen ganado tierra fuera
della, y que esta de acá es otro mundo en que se trabajaron Romanos y Alejandre y Griegos, para la haber con grandes ejercicios, ni
decir del presente de los Reyes de Portugal, que tovieron corazon
para sostener á Guinea, y del descobrir della, y que gastaron oro y
gente á tanta, que quien contase toda la del Reino se hallaria que
otra tanta como la mitad son muertos en Guinea, y todavia la con-
tinuaron hasta que les salió dello lo que parece, lo cual todo comen-

   [4] Ceylon.
   [5] These examples quoted by the admiral from ancient history, are com-
mented upon very learnedly, and at considerable length, by his historian,
Las Casas, in the hundred and twenty-eighth and hundred and twenty-ninth
chapters of his unpublished history.   (Navarrete.)
   [6] Columbus should have said summer.

menced these great exertions, the return for their labour and
expense has hitherto been but trifling; this people has
also dared to make conquests in Africa, and to carry on their
exploits to Ceuta, Tangier, Algiers, and Alcazar, repeatedly
giving battle to the Moors; and all this at great expense;
simply because it was an exploit worthy of a prince, undertaken for the service of God, and to advance the enlarge-
ment of His kingdom.   The more I said on the subject, the
more two-fold was reproach cast upon it, even to the expression of abhorrence, no consideration being given to the
honour and fame that accrued to your Highnesses throughout
all Christendom, from your Highnesses having undertaken
this enterprise; so that there was neither great nor small
who did not desire to hear tidings of it.   Your Highnesses
replied to me encouragingly, and desired that I should pay
no regard to those who spoke ill of the undertaking, inas-
much as they had received no authority or countenance
whatever from your Highnesses.

I started from San Lucar, in the name of the most Holy
Trinity, on Wednesday the 30th of May,[7] much fatigued with

---

zaron de largo tiempo, y ha muy poco que les da renta; los cuales
tambien osaron conquistar en Africa, y sostener la empresa á Cepta,
Tanjar y Arcilla, é Alcazar, y de contino dar guerra á los moros, y
todo esto con grande gasto, solo por hacer cosa de Príncipe servir á
Dios y acrecentar su Señorío.

Cuanto yo mas decia tanto mas se doblaba á poner esto á vituperio,
amostrando en ello aborrecimiento, sin considerar cuánto bien parecio en todo el mundo, y cuánto bien se dijo en todos los cristianos
de vuestras Altezas por haber tomado esta empresa, que no hobo
grande ni pequeño que no quisiese dello carta.   Respondiéronme
vuestras Altezas riéndose y diciendo que yo no curase de nada porque no daban autoridad ni creencia á quien les mal decia de esta
empresa.

Partí en nombre de la santísima Trinidad, Miercoles 30 de Mayo
de la villa de S. Lúcar, bien fatigado de mi viage, que adonde es-

[7] Of the year 1498.

my voyage, for I had hoped, when I left the Indies, to find
repose in Spain; whereas, on the contrary, I experienced
nothing but opposition and vexation. I sailed to the island
of Madeira by a circuitous route, in order to avoid any encounter with an armed fleet from France,[8] which was on the
look out for me off Cape St. Vincent. Thence I went to
the Canaries,[9] from which islands I sailed with but one ship
and two caravels, having dispatched the other ships to Española by the direct road to the Indies ;[10] while I myself moved
southward, with the view of reaching the equinoctial line,
and of then proceeding westward, so as to leave the island of
Española to the north.   But having reached the Cape Verde
islands[11] (an incorrect name, for they are so barren that nothing

---

peraba descanso, cuando yo partí de estas Indias, se me dobló la
pena, y navegué á la Isla de la Madera por camino no acostum-
brado, por evitar escándalo que pudiera tener con un armada de
Francia, que me aguardaba al Cabo de S. Vicente, y de allí á las
Islas de Canaria, de adonde me partí con una nao y dos carabelas,
y envié los otros navíos á derecho camino á las Indias á la Isla Española, y yo navegué al Austro con propósito de llegar á la línea
equinocial, y de allí seguir al Poniente hasta que la Isla Española
me quedase al Septentrion, y llegado á las Islas de Cabo Verde,
falso nombre, porque son atan secas que no ví cosa verde en ellas,

8 Herrera says (Dec. i, lib. 3, cap. 9) that it was a Portuguese squad-
ron ; but Las Casas (cap. 30) distinctly states it to have been French.
(Navarrete.)

9 Herrera and Don Ferdinand Columbus say that he reached the island
of Puerto Santo on the seventh of June, from which island he sailed directly for Madeira, and thence to Gomera, which he reached on the nineteenth, and put to sea again on the twenty-first.

10 The commanders of the three ships which the admiral despatched to
Española, were Pedro de Arana, native of Cordova, brother to the mother
of Ferdinand Columbus ; Alonzo Sanchez de Carabajal, magistrate of
Baeza ; and Juan Antonio Columbus, a relative of the admiral; all of
whom were known to and are spoken of by F. Bartolomé de Las Casas, in
the hundred and thirtieth chapter of his history. (Navarrete.)

11 This was on the twenty-seventh of June. He anchored in the island
of Sal, and on the thirtieth proceeded to the island of Santiago, from
whence he put to sea again on the fourth of July. (Navarrete.)

green was to be seen there, and the people so sickly that I did not venture to remain among them), I sailed away four hundred and eighty miles, which is equivalent to a hundred and twenty leagues, towards the south-west, where, when it grew dark, I found the north star to be in the fifth degree. The wind then failed me, and I entered a climate where the intensity of the heat was such, that I thought both ships and men would have been burnt up, and everything suddenly got into such a state of confusion, that no man dared go below deck to attend to the securing of the water-cask and the provisions. This heat lasted eight days; on the first day the weather was fine, but on the seven other days it rained and was cloudy, yet we found no alleviation of our distress; so that I certainly believe, that if the sun had shone as on the first day, we should not have been able to escape in any way.

I recollect, that in sailing towards the Indies, as soon as I passed a hundred leagues to the westward of the Azores, I found the temperature change: and this is so all along from north to south. I determined, therefore, if it should please the Lord to give me a favourable wind and good weather, so that I might leave the part where I then was, that I would

---

y toda la gente enferma, que no osé detenerme en ellas, y navegué al Sudueste cuatrocientas y ochenta millas, que son ciento y veinte leguas, adonde en anocheciendo tenia la estrella del norte en cinco grados ; alli me desamparó el viento y entré en tanto ardor y tan grande que creí que se me quemasen los navíos y gente, que todo de un golpe vino á tan desordenado, que no habia persona que osase descender debajo de cubierta á remediar la vasija y mantenimientos ; duró este ardor ocho dias ; al primer dia fue claro, y los siete dias siguientes llovió é hizo ñumblado, y con todo no fallamos remedio, que cierto si así fuera de sol como el primero, yo creo que no pudiera escapar en ninguna manera.

Acórdome que navegando á las Indias siempre que yo paso al Poniente de las Islas de los Azores cien leguas, alli fallo mudar la temperanza, y esto es todo de Septentrion en Austro, y determiné que si á nuestro Señor le pluguiese de me dar viento y buen tiempo

give up pursuing the southward course, yet not turn backwards, but sail towards the west, moving in that direction in the hope of finding the same temperature that I had experienced when I sailed in the parallel of the Canaries,—and then, if it proved so, I should still be able to proceed more to the south. At the end of these eight days it pleased our Lord to give me a favourable east wind, and I steered to the west, but did not venture to move lower down towards the south, because I discovered a very great change in the sky and the stars, although I found no alteration in the temperature. I resolved, therefore, to keep on the direct westward course, in a line from Sierra Leone, and not to change it until the chance offered of more speedily reaching land on another tack, which I was very desirous to do, for the purpose of repairing the vessels, and of renewing, if possible, our stock of provisions, and taking in what water we wanted. At the end of seventeen days, during which our Lord gave me a propitious wind, we saw land at noon of Tuesday the 31st of July.[12] This I had expected on the Monday before,

---

que pudiese salir de adonde estaba, de dejar de ir mas al Austro, ni volver tampoco atrás, salvo de navegar al Poniente, á tanto que ya llegase á estar con esta raya con esperanza que yo fallaria allí así temperamiento, como habia fallado cuando yo navegaba en el paralelo de Canaria. E que si así fuese que entonces yo podria ir mas al Austro, y plugó á nuestro Señor que al cabo de estos ocho dias de me dar buen viento Levante, y yo seguí al Poniente, mas no osé declinar abajo al Austro porque fallé grandísimo mudamiento en el cielo y en las estrellas, mas non fallé mudamiento en la temperancia; así acordé de proseguir delante siempre justo al Poniente, en aquel derecho de la Sierra Lioa, con propósito de non mudar derrota fasta adonde yo habia pensado que fallaria tierra, y allí adobar los navíos, y remediar si pudiese los mantenimientos y tomar agua que no tenia; y al cabo de diez y siete dias, los cuales nuestro Señor me dió de próspero viento, Martes 31 de Julio á medio dia

[12] It was first seen by a mariner of Huelva, a servant of the admiral, named Alonzo Perez. (Navarrete.)

and held that route up to this point; but as the sun's strength increased, and our supply of water was failing, I resolved to make for the Carribee Islands, and set sail in that direction; when, by the mercy of God, which He has always extended to me, one of the sailors went up to the main-top and saw to the westward a range of three mountains. Upon this we repeated the " Salve Regina", and other prayers, and all of us gave many thanks to our Lord. I then gave up our northward course, and put in for the land : at the hour of complines we reached a cape, which I called Cape Galea,[13] having already given to the island the name of Trinidad, and here we found a harbour, which would have been excellent but that there was no good anchorage. We saw houses and people on the spot, and the country around was very beautiful, and as fresh and green as the gardens of Valencia in the month of March. I was disappointed at not being able to put into the harbour, and ran along the coast to the westward. After sailing five leagues I found very good bottom, and anchored. The next day I set sail in the same direction,

---

nos amostró tierra, é yo la esperaba el Lunes antes, y tuve aquel camino fasta entonces, que en saliendo el sol, por defecto del agua que no tenia, determiné de andar á las Islas de los Caribales, y tomé esa vuelta ; y como su alta Magestad haya siempre usado de misericordia conmigo, por acertamiento subió un marinero á la gavia, y vido al Poniente tres montañas juntas : dijimos la Salve Regina y otras prosas, y dimos todos muchas gracias á nuestro Señor, y despues dejé el camino de Septentrion, y volví hácia la tierra, adonde yo llegué á hora de completas á un Cabo á que dije de la Galea despues de haber nombrado á la Isla de la Trinidad, y allí hobiera muy buen puerto si fuera fondo, y habia casas y gente, y muy lindas tierras, atan fermosas y verdes como las huertas de Valencia en Marzo. Pesóme cuando no puede entrar en el puerto, y corri la costa de esta tierra del luengo fasta el poniente, y andadas cinco leguas fallé muy buen fondo y surgí, y en el otro dia dí la vela á este

[13] It is now called Cape Galeota, and is the most south-eastern point of the island of Trinidad.

in search of a harbour where I might repair the vessels and
take in water, as well as improve the stock of provisions which
I had brought out with me.   When we had taken in a pipe
of water, we proceeded onwards till we reached the cape,
and there finding good anchorage and protection from the
east wind, I ordered the anchors to be dropped, the water-
cask to be repaired, a supply of water and wood to be taken
in, and the people to rest themselves from the fatigues which
they had endured for so long a time.   I gave to this point
the name of Sandy Point (Punta del Arenal).   All the ground
in the neighbourhood was filled with foot-marks of animals,
like the impression of the foot of a goat; but although it
would have appeared from this circumstance that they were
very numerous, only one was seen, and that was dead.   On
the following day a large canoe came from the eastward,
containing twenty-four men, all in the prime of life, and
well provided with arms, such as bows, arrows, and wooden
shields; they were all, as I have said, young, well-propor-
tioned, and not dark black, but whiter than any other Indians
that I had seen,—of very graceful gesture and handsome
forms, wearing their hair long and straight, and cut in the

---

camino buscando puerto para adobar los navíos y tomar agua, y remediar el trigo y los bastimentos que llevaba solamente.   Allí tomé una pipa de agua, y con ella anduve ansi hasta llegar al cabo, y
allí fallé abrigo de Levante y buen fondo, y así mandé surgir y
adobar la vasija y tomar agua y leña, y descendir la gente á des-
cansar de tanto tiempo que andaban penando.
    A esta punta llamé del Arenal, y allí se falló toda la tierra fol-
lada de unas animalías que tenian la pata como de cabra, y bien que
segun parece ser allí haya muchas, no se vido sino una muerta.
El dia siguiente vino de hácia oriente una grande canoa con veinte
y cuatro hombres, todos mancebos é muy ataviados de armas, arcos
y flechas y tablachinas, y ellos, como dije, todos mancebos, de buena
disposicion y no negros, salvo mas blancos que otros que haya visto
en las Indias, y de muy lindo gesto, y fermosos cuerpos, y los cabellos largos y llanos, cortados á la guisa de Castilla, y traian la

Spanish style. Their heads were bound round with cotton scarfs elaborately worked in colours, which resembled the Moorish head-dresses. Some of these scarfs were worn round the body and used as a covering in lieu of trousers. The natives spoke to us from the canoe while it was yet at a considerable distance, but none of us could understand them; I made signs to them, however, to come nearer to us, and more than two hours were spent in this manner,—but if by any chance they moved a little nearer, they soon pushed off again. I caused basins and other shining objects to be shewn to them to tempt them to come near; and after a long time, they came somewhat nearer than they had hitherto done,— upon which, as I was very anxious to speak with them, and had nothing else to shew them to induce them to approach, I ordered a drum to be played upon the quarter-deck, and some of our young men to dance, believing the Indians would come to see the amusement. No sooner, however, did they perceive the beating of the drum and the dancing, than they all left their oars, and strung their bows, and each man laying hold of his shield, they commenced discharging their arrows at us; upon this, the music and dancing soon ceased,

---

cabeza atada con un pañuelo de algodon tejido á labores y colores, el cual creia yo que era almaizar. Otro de estos pañuelos traían ceñido é se cobijaban con él en lugar de pañetes. Cuando llegó esta canoa habló de muy lejos, é yo ni otro ninguno no los entendiamos, salvo que yo les mandaba hacer señas que se allegasen, y en esto se pasó mas de dos horas, y si se llegaban un poco luego se desviaban. Yo les hacia mostrer bacines y otras cosas que lucian por enamorarlos porque viniesen, y á cabo de buen rato se allegaron mas que hasta entonces no habian, y yo deseaba mucho haber lengua, y no tenia ya cosa que me pareciese que era de mostrarles para que viniesen; salvo que hice sobir un tamborin en el castillo de popa que tañesen, é unos mancebos que danzasen, creyendo que se allegarian á ver la fiesta; y luego que vieron tañer y danzar todos dejaron los remos y echaron mano á los arcos y los encordaron, y embrazo cada uno su tablachina, y comenzaron á tirarnos flechas:

and I ordered a charge to be made from some of our cross-
bows; they then left us, and went rapidly to the other caravel, and placed themselves under its poop. The pilot of
that vessel received them courteously, and gave to the man
who appeared to be their chief, a coat and hat; and it was
then arranged between them, that he should go to speak with
him on shore. Upon this the Indians immediately went
thither and waited for him; but as he would not go without
my permission, he came to my ship in the boat, whereupon
the Indians got into their canoe again and went away, and I
never saw any more of them or of any of the other inhabitants of the island. When I reached the point of Arenal,
I found that the island of Trinidad formed with the land of
Gracia[14] a strait of two leagues' width from east to west, and
as we had to pass through it to go to the north, we found
some strong currents which crossed the strait, and which
made a great roaring, so that I concluded there must be a
reef of sand or rocks, which would preclude our entrance;
and behind this current was another and another, all making

---

cesó luego el tañer y danzar, y mandé luego sacar unas ballestas, y
ellos dejáronme y fueren á mas andar á otra carabela, y de golpe
se fueron debajo la popa della, y el piloto entró con ellos, y dió un
sayo é un bonete á un hombre principal que le pareció dellos, y
quedó concertado que le iria hablar allí en la playa, adonde ellos
luego fueron con la canoa esperándole, y él como no quiso ir sin mi
licencia, como ellos le vieron venir á la nao con la barca, tornaron
á entrar en la canoa é se fueron, é nunca mas los vide ni á otros de
esta isla.

Cuando yo llegué á esta punta del Arenal, allí se hace una boca
grande de dos leguas de Poniente á Levante, la Isla de la Trinidad
con la tierra de Gracia, y que para haber de entrar dentro para
pasar al Septentrion habia unos hileros de corrientes que atrave-
saban aquella boca y traían un rugir muy grande, y creí yo que
sería un arrecife de bajos é peñas, por el cual no se podria entrar
dentro en ella, y detras de este hilero habia otro y otro que todos

[14] Coast of Cumaná.

a roaring noise like the sound of breakers against the rocks. I anchored there, under the said point of Arenal, outside of the strait, and found the water rush from east to west with as much impetuosity as that of the Guadalquivir at its conflux with the sea; and this continued constantly day and night, so that it appeared to be impossible to move backwards for the current or forwards for the shoals. In the dead of night, while I was on deck, I heard an awful roaring that came from the south towards the ship; I stopped to observe what it might be, and I saw the sea rolling from west to east like a mountain as high as the ship, and approaching by little and little; on the top of this rolling sea came a mighty wave roaring with a frightful noise, and with all this terrific uproar were other conflicting currents, producing, as I have already said, a sound as of breakers upon the rocks.[15] To this day I have a vivid recollection of the dread I then felt, lest the ship might founder under the force of that tremendous sea; but it passed by, and reached the mouth of the before-mentioned passage, where the uproar lasted for a considerable

---

traian un rugir grande como ola de la mar que va á romper y dar en peñas. Surgí allí á la dicha punta del Arenal, fuera de la dicha boca, y fallé que venia el agua del Oriente fasta el Poniente con tanta furia como hace Guadalquivir en tiempo de avenida, y esto de contino noche y dia, que creí que no podria volver atrás por la corriente, ni ir adelante por los bajos; y en la noche ya muy tarde, estando al bordo de la nao, oí un rugir muy terrible que venia de la parte del Austro hácia la nao, y me paré á mirar, y ví levantando la mar de Poniente á Levante, en manera de una loma tan alta como la nao, y todavia venia hácia mi poco á poco, y encima della venia un filero de corriente que venia rugiendo con muy grande estrépito con aquella furia de aquel rugir que de los otros hileros que yo dije que me parecian ondas de mar que daban en peñas, que hoy en dia tengo el miedo en el cuerpo que no me trabucasen la nao cuando llegasen debajo della, y passó y llegó fasta la boca adonde allí se

---

15 Produced by the confluence of the Orinoco with the sea. See Rapin, Hist. Phil. vol. iv, p. 272.

time. On the following day I sent out boats to take sound-
ings, and found that in the strait, at the deepest part of the
embouchure, there were six or seven fathoms of water, and
that there were constant contrary currents, one running in-
wards, and the other outwards. It pleased the Lord, however, to give us a favourable wind, and I passed through the
middle of the strait, after which I recovered my tranquillity.
The men happened at this time to draw up some water from
the sea, which, strange to say, proved to be fresh. I then
sailed northwards till I came to a very high mountain, at
about twenty-six leagues from the Punta del Arenal; here
two lofty headlands appeared, one towards the east, and
forming part of the island of Trinidad,[16] and the other, on
the west, being part of the land which I have already called
Gracia;[17] we found here a channel still narrower than that of
Arenal,[18] with similar currents, and a tremendous roaring of
water; the water here also was fresh. Hitherto I had held
no communication with any of the people of this country,
although I very earnestly desired it; I therefore sailed along
the coast westwards, and the further I advanced, the fresher

---

detuvo grande espacio. Y el otro dia siguiente envie las barcas á
sondar y fallé en el mas bajo de la boca, que habia seis ó siete brazas de fondo, y de contino andaban aquellos hileros unos por entrar
y otros por salir, y plugo á nuestro Señor de me dar buen viento, y
atravesé por esa boca adentro, y luego hallé tranquilidad, y por
acertamiento se sacó del agua de la mar y la hallé dulce. Navegué
al Septentrion fasta una sierra muy alta, adonde serian veinte y seis
leguas de esta punta del Arenal, y allí habia dos cabos de tierra muy
alta, el uno de la parte del Oriente, y era de la misma Isla de la
Trinidad, y el otro del Occidente de la tierra que dije de Gracia, y
allí hacia una boca muy angosta mas que aquella de la punta del
Arenal, y allí habia los mismos hileros y aquel rugir fuerte del agua
como era en la punta del Arenal, y asimismo allí la mar era agua
dulce; y fasta entonces yo no habia habido lengua con ninguna
gente de estas tierras, y lo descaba en gran manera, y por esto na-

[16] Point Peña Blanca.   [17] Point Peña.   [18] Boca Grande.

and more wholesome I found the water; and when I had proceeded a considerable distance, I reached a spot where the land appeared to be cultivated. There I anchored, and sent the boats ashore, and the men who went in them found the natives had recently left the place; they also observed that the mountain was covered with monkeys. They came back, and as the coast at that part presented nothing but a chain of mountains, I concluded that further west we should find the land flatter, and consequently in all probability inhabited. Actuated by this thought I weighed anchor, and ran along the coast until we came to the end of the cordillera; I then anchored at the mouth of a river, and we were soon visited by a great number of the inhabitants, who informed us, that the country was called Paria, and that further westward it was more fully peopled. I took four of these natives, and proceeded on my westward voyage; and when I had gone eight leagues further, I found on the other side of a point which I called the Needle,[19] one of the most lovely countries in the world, and very thickly peopled: it

---

vegué al luengo de la costa de esta tierra hácia el Poniente, y cuanto mas andaba hallaba el agua de la mar mas dulce y mas sabrosa, y andando una gran parte llegué á un lugar donde me parecian las tierras labradas y surgí y envié las barcas á tierra, y fallaron que de fresco se habia ido de allí gente, y fallaron todo el monte cubierto de gatos paules : volviéronse, y como esta fuese sierra me pareció que mas allá al Poniente las tierras eran mas llanas, y que allí seria poblado, y por esto seria poblado, y mandé levantar las anclas y corrí esta costa fasta el cabo de esta sierra, y allí á un rio surgi, y luego vino mucha gente, y me dijeron como llamaron á esta tierra Paria, y que de allí mas al Poniente era mas poblada ; tomé dellos cuatro, y despues navegué al Poniente, y andadas ocho leguas mas al Poniente allende una punta á que yo llamé del Aguja : hallé unas tierras las mas hermosas del mundo, y muy pobladas: llegué allí una mañana á hora de tercia, y por ver esta verdura y esta hermosura acordé surgir y ver esta gente, de los cuales luego vinieron en

[19] It is now called Point Alcatraz, or Point Pelican.

was three o'clock in the morning when I reached it, and seeing its verdure and beauty, I resolved to anchor there and communicate with the inhabitants. Some of the natives soon came out to the ship, in canoes, to beg me, in the name of their king, to go on shore; and when they saw that I paid no attention to them, they came to the ship in their canoes in countless numbers, many of them wearing pieces of gold on their breasts, and some with bracelets of pearls on their arms; on seeing which I was much delighted, and made many inquiries with the view of learning where they found them. They informed me, that they were to be procured in their own neighbourhood, and also at a spot to the northward of that place. I would have remained here, but the provisions of corn, and wine, and meats, which I had brought out with so much care, for the people whom I had left behind, were nearly wasted, so that all my anxiety was to get them into a place of safety, and not to stop for any thing. I wished, however, to get some of the pearls that I had seen, and with that view sent the boats on shore. The natives are very numerous, and for the most part handsome in person, and of the same colour as the Indians we had already seen; they

---

canoas á la nao á rogarme, de partes de su Rey, que descendiese en tierra ; é cuando vieron que no curé dellos vinieron á la nao infinitísimos en canoas, y muchos traían piezas de oro al pescuezo, y algunos atados á los brazos algunas perlas : holgué mucho cuando las ví é procuré mucho de saber donde las hallaban, y me dijeron que allí, y de la parte del Norte de aquella tierra.

Quisiera detenerme, mas estos bastimentos, que yo traía, trigo y vino é carne para esta gente que acá esta se me acababan de perder, los cuales hobe allá con tanta fatiga, y por esto yo no buscaba sino á mas andar á venir á poner en ellos cobro, y no me detener para cosa alguna : procuré de haber de aquellas perlas, y envié las barcas á tierra : esta gente es muy mucha, y toda de muy buen parecer, de la misma color que los otros de antes, y muy tratables : la gente nuestra que fue á tierra los hallaron tan convenibles, y los recibieron muy honradamente : dicen que luego que llegaron las barcas

are, moreover, very tractable, and received our men who went on shore most courteously, seeming very well disposed towards us. These men relate, that when the boats reached shore, two of the chiefs, whom they took to be father and son, came forward in advance of the mass of the people, and conducted them to a very large house with façades, and not round and tent-shaped as the other houses were; in this house were many seats, on which they made our men sit down, they themselves sitting on other seats. They then caused bread to be brought, with many kinds of fruits, and various sorts of wine, both white and red, not made of grapes, but apparently produced from different fruits. The most reasonable inference is, that they use maize, which is a plant that bears a spine like an ear of wheat, some of which I took with me from Spain, where it grows abundantly; this they seemed to regard as most excellent, and set a great value upon it. The men remained together at one end of the house, and the women at the other. Great vexation was felt by both parties that they could not understand each other, for they were mutually anxious to make inquiries respecting each other's country. After our men had been entertained at the

---

á tierra que vinieron dos personas principales cón todo el pueblo, creen que el uno el padre y el otro era su hijo, y los llevaron á una casa muy grande hecha á dos aguas, y no redonda, como tienda de campo, como son estas otras, y allí tenian muchas sillas á donde los ficieron asentar, y otras donde ellos se asentaron ; y hicieron traer pan, y de muchas maneras frutas é vino de muchas maneras blanco é tinto, mas no de uvas : debe él de ser de diversas maneras uno de una fruta y otro de otra ; y asimismo debe de ser dello de maiz, que es una simiente que hace una espiga como una mazorca de que llevé yo allá, y hay ya mucho en Castilla, y parece que aquel que lo tenia mejor lo traía por mayor excelencia, y lo daba en gran precio : los hombres todos estaban juntos á un cabo de la casa, y las mugeres en otro. Recibieron ambas las partes gran pena porque no se entendian, ellos para preguntar á los otros de nuestra patria, y los nuestros por saber de la suya. E despues que hobieron resce-

house of the elder Indian, the younger took them to his house, and gave them an equally cordial reception; after which they returned to their boats and came on board. I weighed anchor forthwith, for I was hastened by my anxiety to save the provisions which were becoming spoiled, and which I had procured and preserved with so much care and trouble, as well as to attend to my own health, which had been affected by long watching; and although on my former voyage, when I discovered terra firma, I passed thirty-three days without natural rest, and was all that time deprived of sight, yet never were my eyes so much affected or so painful as at this period. These people, as I have already said, are very graceful in form,—tall, and elegant in their movements, wearing their hair very long and smooth, they also bind their heads with handsome worked handkerchiefs, which from a distance look like silk or gauze; others use the same material in a longer form, wound round them so as to cover them like trousers, and this is done by both the men and the women. These people are of a whiter skin than any that I have seen in the Indies. It is the fashion among all classes to wear something at the breast, and on the arms, and many wear

---

bido colacion allí en casa del mas viejo, los llevó el mozo á la suya, e fizo otro tanto, é despues se pusieron en las barcas é se vinieron á la nao, é yo luego levanté las anclas porque andaba mucho de priesa por remediar los mantenimientos que se me perdian que yo habia habido con tanta fatiga, y tambien por remediarme é mí que habia adolescido por el desvelar de los ojos, que bien quel viage que yo fuí á descubrir la tierra firme estuviese treinta y tres dias sin concebir sueño, y estoviese tanto tiempo sin vista, non se me dañaron los ojos, ni se me rompieron de sangre y con tantos dolores como agora.

Esta gente, como ya dije, son todos de muy linda estatura, altos de cuerpos, é de muy lindos gestos, los cabellos muy largos é llanos, y traen las cabezas atadas con unos pañuelos labrados, como ya dije, hermosos, que parecen de lejos de seda y almaizares: otro traen ceñido mas largo que se cobijan con él en lugar de pañetes, ansi

pieces of gold hanging low on the bosom. Their canoes are larger, lighter, and of better build than those of the islands which I have hitherto seen, and in the middle of each they have a cabin or room, which I found was occupied by the chiefs and their wives. I called this place " Jardines", that is, "the Gardens", for the place and the people corresponded with that appellation. I made many inquiries as to where they found the gold, in reply to which, all of them directed me to an elevated tract of land at no great distance, on the confines of their own country, lying to the westward; but they all advised me not to go there, for fear of being eaten, and at the time, I imagined that by their description they wished to imply, that they were cannibals who dwelt there, but I have since thought it possible, that they meant merely to express, that the country was filled with beasts of prey. I also inquired of them where they obtained the pearls? and in reply to this question likewise, they directed me to the westward, and also to the north, behind the country they occupied. I did not put this information to the test, on account of the provisions, and the weakness of my eyes, and because the

---

hombres como mugeres. La color de esta gente es mas blanca que otra que haya visto en las Indias ; todos traían al pescuezo y á los brazos algo á la guisa de estas tierras, y muchos traían piezas de oro bajo colgado al pescuezo. Las canoas de ellos son muy grandes y de mejor hechura que no son estas otras, y mas livianas, y en el medio de cada una tienen un apartamiento como cámara en que ví que andaban los principales con sus mugeres. Llamé allí á este lugar Jardines, porque así conforman por el nombre. Procuré mucho de saber donde cogian aquel oro, y todos me aseñalaban una tierra frontera dellos al Poniente, que era muy alta, mas no lejos ; mas todos me decian que no fuese allá porque allí comian los hombres, y entendí entonces que decian que eran hombres caribales, é que serian como los otros, y despues he pensado que podria ser que lo decian porque allí habria animalias. Tambien les preg anté adonde cogian las perlas, y me señalaron tambien que al Poniente, y al Norte detrás de esta tierra donde estaban. Dejélo de probar por

large ship that I had with me was not calculated for such an undertaking. The short time that I spent with them was all passed in putting questions; and at evening, as I have already said, we returned to the ships, upon which I weighed anchor and sailed to the westward. I proceeded onwards on the following day, until I found that we were only in three fathoms water; at this time I was still under the idea that it was but an island, and that I should be able to make my exit by the north. Upon which I sent a light caravel in advance of us, to see whether there was any exit, or whether the passage was closed; the caravel proceeded a great distance, until it reached a very large gulf, in which there appeared to be four smaller gulfs, from one of which debouched a large river; they invariably found ground at five fathoms, and a great quantity of very fresh water, indeed, I never tasted any equal to it. I felt great anxiety when I found that I could make no exit, either by the north, south, or west, but that I was enclosed on all three sides by land; I therefore weighed anchor, and sailed in a backward direction, with the hope of finding a passage to the north by the strait, which I have al-

---

esto de los mantenimientos, y del mal de mis ojos, y por una nao grande que traigo que no es para semejante hecho.

Y como el tiempo fue breve se pasó todo en preguntas, y se volvieron á los navíos, que seria hora de vísperas, como ya dije, y luego levanté las anclas y navegué al Poniente ; y asimesmo el dia siguiente fasta que me fallé que no habia si non tres brazas de fondo, con creencia que todavía esta seria isla, y que yo podria salir al Norte ; y así visto envié una carabela sotil adelante á ver si habia salida ó si estaba cerrado, y ansi anduvo mucho camino fasta un golfo muy grande en el cual parecia que habia otros cuatro medianos, y del uno salia un rio grandísimo : fallaron siempre cinco brazas de fondo y el agua muy dulce, en tanta cantidad que yo jamas bebíla pareja della. Fuí yo muy descontento della cuando ví que no podia salir al Norte ni podia andar ya al Austro ni al Poniente porque yo estaba cercado por todas partes de la tierra, y así levanté las anclas, y torne atrás para salir al Norte por la boca que yo arriba dije, y

ready described ; but I could not return along the inhabited part where I had already been, on account of the currents, which drove me entirely out of my course.   But constantly, at every headland, I found the water sweet and clear, and we were carried eastwards very powerfully towards the two straits already mentioned; I then conjectured, that the currents and the overwhelming mountains of water which rushed into these straits with such an awful roaring, arose from the contest between the fresh water and the sea.   The fresh water struggled with the salt to oppose its entrance, and the salt contended against the fresh in its efforts to gain a passage outwards.   And I formed the conjecture, that at one time there was a continuous neck of land from the island of Trinidad and with the land of Garcia, where the two straits now are, as your Highnesses will see, by the drawing which accompanies this letter.   I passed out by this northern strait, and found the fresh water come even there ; and when, by the aid of the wind, I was enabled to proceed, I remarked, while on one of the watery billows which I have described, that in the channel, the water on the inner side of the current was fresh, and on the outside salt.

---

no pude volver por la poblacion adonde yo habia estado, por causa de las corrientes que me habian desviado della, y siempre en todo cabo hallaba el agua dulce y clara, y que me llevaba al Oriente muy recio fácia las dos bocas que arriba dije, y entonces conjeture que los hilos de la corriente, y aquellas lomas que salian y entraban en estas bocas con aquel rugir tan fuerte que era pelea del agua dulce con la salada.   La dulce empujaba á la otra porque no entrase, y la salada porque la otra no saliese ; y conjeturé que allí donde son estas dos bocas que algun tiempo seria tierra continua á la Isla de la Trinidad con la tierra de Gracia, como podrán ver vuestras Altezas por la pintura de lo que con esta les envio.   Salí yo por esta boca del Norte y hallé quel agua dulce siempre vencia, y cuando pasé, que fue con fuerza de viento, estando en una de aquellas lomas, hallé en aquellos hilos de la parte de dentro el agua dulce, y de fuera salada.

When I sailed from Spain to the Indies, I found, that as soon as I had passed a hundred leagues westward of the Azores, there was a very great change in the sky and the stars, in the temperature of the air, and in the water of the sea; and I have been very diligent in observing these things. I remarked, that from north to south, in traversing these hundred leagues from the said islands, the needle of the compass, which hitherto had turned towards the north-east, turned a full quarter of the wind to the north-west, and this took place from the time when we reached that line. At the same time an appearance was presented, as if the sea shore had been transplanted thither, for we found the sea covered all over with a sort of weed, resembling pine branches, and with fruits like that of the mastic tree, so thick, that on my first voyage I thought it was a reef, and that the ships could not avoid running aground; but until I reached this line, I did not meet with a single bough. I also observed, that at this point the sea was very smooth, and that though the wind was rough, the ships never rolled. I likewise found, that within the same line, towards the west, the temperature was always mild, and that it did not vary summer or winter.

Cuando yo navegué de España á las Indias fallo luego en pasando cien leguas á Poniente de los Azores grandísimo mudamiento en el cielo é en las estrellas, y en la temperancia del aire, y en las aguas de la mar, y en esto he tenido mucha diligencia en la experiencia.

Fallo que de Septentrion en Austro, pasando las dichas cien leguas de las dichas islas, que luego en las agujas de marear, que fasta entonces nordesteaban, noruestean una cuarta de viento todo entero, y esto es en allegando allí á aquella línea, como quien traspone una cuesta, asimesmo fallo la mar toda llena de yerba de una calidad que parece ramitos de pino y muy cargada de fruta como de lantisco, y es tan espesa que al primer viage pensé que era bajo, y que daria en seco con los navíos, y hasta llegar con esta raya no se falla un solo ramito: fallo tambien en llegando allí la muy suave y llana, y bien que vente recio nunca se levanta. Asimismo hallo dentro de la dicha raya hácia Poniente la temperancia del cielo muy suave, y

While I was there, I observed that the north star described
a circle five degrees in diameter; that when its satellites[20] are
on the right side, then the star was at its lowest point, and
from this point it continues rising until it reaches the left
side, where it is also at five degrees, and then again it sinks
until it at length returns to the right side. In this voyage I
proceeded immediately from Spain to the island of Madeira,
thence to the Canaries, and then to the Cape Verde isles, and
from the Cape Verde isles I sailed southwards, even below the
equinoctial line, as I have already described. When I reached
the parallel of Sierra Leone, in Guinea, I found the heat so
intense, and the rays of the sun so fierce, that I thought that
we should have been burnt; and although it rained and the
sky was heavy with clouds, I still suffered the same oppres-
sion, until our Lord was pleased to grant me a favourable
wind, giving me an opportunity of sailing to the west, so that
I reached a latitude where I experienced, as I have already
said, a change in the temperature. Immediately upon my
reaching this line, the temperature of the sky became very
mild, and the more I advanced, the more this mildness in-

---

no discrepa de la cantidad quier sea invierno, quier sea en verano.
Cuando allí estoy hallo que la estrella del Norte escribe un círculo
el cualo tiene en el diámetro cinco grados, y estando las guardas en
el brazo derecho estonces está la estrella en el mas bajo, y se vá al-
zando fasta que llega albrazo izquierdo, y estonces está cinco grados, y de allí se vá abajando fasta llegar á volver otra vez al brazo
derecho.

Yo allegué agora de España á la Isla de la Madera, y de allí á
Canaria, y dende á las Islas de Cabo Verde, de adonde cometí el
viage para navegar al Austro fasta debajo la linea equinocial, como
ya dije : allegado á estar en derecho con el paralelo que pasa por la
Sierra Leoa en Guinea, fallo tan grande ardor, y los rayos del sol
tan calientes que pensaba de quemar, y bien que lloviese y el cielo
fuese muy turbado siempre yo estaba en esta fatiga, fasta que nuestro Señor proveyó de buen viento y á mi puso en voluntad que yo

[20] He doubtless alludes to the constellation of Ursa Minor.

creased; but I did not find the positions of the stars correspond with these effects.   I remarked at this place, that when
night came on, the polar star was five degrees high, and then
the satellites were over head; afterwards, at midnight, I
found the north star elevated ten degrees, and when morning
was advancing, the satellites were fifteen feet below.   I found
the smoothness of the sea continue, but not so the weeds; as
to the polar star, I watched it with great wonder, and devoted
many nights to a careful examination of it with the quadrant,
and I always found that the lead and line fell to the same
point.   I look upon this as something new, and I think my
opinion will be supported by that of others, that it is a short
distance for so great a change to take place in the temperature.   I have always read, that the world comprising the land
and the water was spherical, as is testified by the investigations of Ptolemy, and others, who have proved it by the
eclipses of the moon, and other observations made from east
to west, as well as by the elevation of the pole from north to
south.   But I have now seen so much irregularity, as I have

---

navegase al Occidente con este esfuerzo, que en llegando á la raya
de que yo dije que allí fallaria mudamiento en la temperancia.
Despues que yo emparejé á estar en derecho de esta raya luego
falle la temperancia del cielo muy suave, y cuanto mas andaba adelante mas multiplicaba ; mas no hallé conforme á esto las estrellas.

Fallé allí que en anocheciendo tenia yo la estrella del Norte alta
cinco grados, y estonces las guardas estaban encima de la cabeza, y
despues á la media noche fallaba la estrella alta diez grados, y en
amaneciendo que las guardas estaban en los pies quince.

La suavelidad de la mar fallé conforme, mas no en la yerba : en
esto de la estrella del Norte tomé grande admiracion, y por esto
muchas noches con mucha diligencia tornaba yo á repricar la vista
della con el cuadrante, y siempre fallé que caía el plomo y hilo á
un punto.

Por cosa nueva tengo yo esto, y podrá ser que será tenida que en
poco espacio haga tanta diferencia el cielo.

Yo siempre lei que el mundo, tierra é agua era esférico é las au-

already described, that I have come to another conclusion
respecting the earth, namely, that it is not round as they
describe, but of the form of a pear, which is very round except where the stalk grows, at which part it is most promi-
nent; or like a round ball, upon one part of which is a pro-
minence like a woman's nipple, this protrusion being the
highest and nearest the sky, situated under the equinoctial
line, and at the eastern extremity of this sea,—I call that the
eastern extremity, where the land and the islands end. In
confirmation of my opinion, I revert to the arguments which
I have above detailed respecting the line, which passes from
north to south, a hundred leagues westward of the Azores;
for in sailing thence westward, the ships went on rising
smoothly towards the sky, and then the weather was felt to
be milder, on account of which mildness, the needle shifted
one point of the compass; the further we went, the more the
needle moved to the north-west, this elevation producing the
variation of the circle, which the north star describes with its
satellites; and the nearer I approached the equinoctial line,

---

toridades y esperencias que Tolomeo y todos los otros escribieron de
este sitio, daban é amostraban para ello así por eclipses de la luna
y otras demostraciones que hacen de Oriente fasta Occidente, como
de la elevacion del polo de Septentrion en Austro. Agora ví tanta
disformidad, como ya dije, y por esto me puse á tener esto del mundo,
y fallé que no era redondo en la forma que escriben; salvo que es de
la forma de una pera que sea toda muy redonda, salvo allí donde
tiene el pezon que allí tiene mas alto, ó como quien tiene una pelota
muy redonda, y en un lugar della fuese como una teta de muger allí
puesta, y que esta parte deste pezon sea la mas alta é mas propinca
al cielo, y sea debajo la línea equinocial, y en esta mar Océana en
fin del Oriente, llamo yo fin 'de Oriente, adonde acaba toda la
tierra é islas, é para esto allego todas las razones sobre-escriptas de la raya que pasa al Occidente delas islas de los Azores
cien leguas de Septentrion en Austro, que en pasando de allí
al Poniente ya van los navíos alzándose hácia el cielo suave-
mente, y entonces se goza de mas suave temperancia y se muda

the more they rose, and the greater was the difference between these stars and their circles. Ptolemy and the other
philosophers, who have written upon the globe, thought that
it was spherical, believing that this hemisphere was round as
well as that in which they themselves dwelt, the centre of
which was in the island of Arin,[21] which is under the equinoctial
line between the Arabian Gulf and the Gulf of Persia; and
the circle passes over Cape St. Vincent, in Portugal, westward, and eastward, by Cangara and the Seras,[22] in which
hemisphere I make no difficulty as to its being a perfect
sphere as they describe; but this western half of the world,
I maintain, is like the half of a very round pear, having a
raised projection for the stalk, as I have already described, or
like a woman's nipple on a round ball. Ptolemy and the
others who have written upon the globe, had no information
respecting this part of the world, which was then unexplored;
they only established their arguments with respect to their
own hemisphere, which, as I have already said, is half of a

---

el aguja del marear por causa de la suavidad desa cuarta de
viento, y cuanto mas va adelante e alzándose mas noruestes, y esta
altura causa el desvariar del circulo que escribe la estrella del Norte
con las guardas, y cuanto mas pasare junto con la línea equinocial,
mas se subirán en alto, y mas diferencia habrá en las dichas estrellas, y en los circulos dellas. Y Tolomeo y los otros sabios que escribieron de este mundo, creyeron que era esférico, creyendo queste
hemisferio que fuese redondo como aquel de allá donde ellos estaban, el cual tiene el centro en la Isla de Arin, qués debajo la linea
equinocial entre el sino Arabico y aquel de Persia, y el círculo pasa
sobre el Cabo de S. Vicente en Portugal por el Poniente, y pasa en
Oriente por Cangara y por las Seras, en el cual hemisferio no hago
yo que hay ninguna dificultad, salvo que sea esférico redondo como
ellos dicen : mas este otro digo que es como sería la mitad de la pera
bien redonda, la cual toviese el pezon alto como yo dije, ó como una
teta de muger en una pelota redonda, así que desta media parte non
hobo noticia Tolomeo ni los otros quo escribieron del mundo por

[21] It is difficult to conjecture what island he alludes to.
[22] Japan and China.

perfect sphere. And now that your Highnesses have commissioned me to make this voyage of discovery, the truths which I have stated are evidently proved, because in this voyage, when I was off the island of Hargin,[23] and its vicinity, which is twenty degrees to the north of the equinoctial line, I found the people are black, and the land very much burnt; and when after that I went to the Cape Verde islands, I found the people there much darker still, and the more southward we went, the more they approach the extreme of blackness; so that when I reached the parallel of Sierra Leone, where, as night came on, the north star rose five degrees, the people there were excessively black; and as I sailed westward, the heat became extreme. But after I had passed the meridian, or line which I have already described, I found the climate become gradually more temperate; so that when I reached the island of Trinidad, where the north star rose five degrees as night came on, there, and in the land of Gracia, I found the temperature exceedingly mild; the fields and the foliage likewise were remarkably fresh and green, and as beautiful as the

---

ser muy ignoto; solamente hicieron raiz sobre el hemisferio, adonde ellos estaban ques redondo esférico, como arriba dije. Y agora que vuestras Altezas lo han mandado navegar y buscar y descobrir, se amuestra evidentísimo, porque estando yo en este viage al Septentrion veinte grados de la línea equinocial, allí era en derecho de Hargin, é de aquellas tierras: é allí es la gente negra é la tierra muy quemada, y despues que fuí á las Islas de Cabo Verde, allí en aquellas tierras es la gente mucho mas negra, y cuanto mas bajo se van al Austro tanto mas llegan al extremo, en manera que allí en derecho donde yo estaba, qués la Sierra Leoa, adonde se me alzaba la estrella del Norte en anocheciendo cinco grados, allí es la gente negra en extrema cantidad, y despues que de allí navegue al Occidente tan extremos calores; y pasada la raya de que yo dije fallé multiplicar la temperancia, andando en tanta cantidad que cuando yo llegué á la isla de la Trinidad, adonde la estrella del Norte en anocheciendo tambien se me alzaba cinco grados, allí y

[23] Arguin, off the west coast of Africa.

gardens of Valencia in April. The people there are very graceful in form, less dark than those whom I had before seen in the Indies, and wear their hair long and smooth; they are also more shrewd, intelligent, and courageous. The sun was then in the sign of Virgo, over our heads and theirs; therefore, all this must proceed from the extreme blandness of the temperature, which arises, as I have said, from this country being the most elevated in the world, and the nearest to the sky. On these grounds, therefore, I affirm, that the globe is not spherical, but that there is the difference in its form which I have described; the which is to be found in this hemisphere, at the point where the Indies meet the ocean, the extremity of the hemisphere being below the equinoctial line. And a great confirmation of this is, that when our Lord made the sun, the first light appeared in the first point of the east, where the most elevated point of the globe is; and although it was the opinion of Aristotle, that the antarctic pole, or the land which is below it, was the highest part of the world, and the nearest to the heavens, other philosophers oppose him, and say, that the highest part was below

---

en la tierra de Gracia hallé temperancia suavísima, y las tierras y árboles muy verdes, y tan hermosos como en Abril en las huertas de Valencia; y la gente de allí de muy linda estatura, y blancos mas que otros que haya visto en las Indias, é los cabellos muy largos é llanos, é gente mas astuta é de mayor ingenio, é no cobardes. Entonces era el sol en Virgen encima de nuestras cabezas é suyas, ansí que todo esto procede por la suavísima temperancia que allí es, la cual procede por estar mas alto en el mundo mas cerca del aire que cuento; y así me afirmo quel mundo no es esférico, salvo que tiene esta diferencia que ya dije: la cual es en este hemisferio adonde caen las Indias é la mar Oceana, y el extremo dello es debajo la línea equinocial, y ayuda mucho á esto que sea ansí, porque el sol cuando nuestro Señor lo hizo fue en el primer punto de Oriente, ó la primera luz fue aquí en Oriente, allí donde es el extremo de la altura deste mundo; y bien quel parecer de Aristotel fuese que el Polo antártico ó la tierra ques debajo dél sea la mas alta parte en el

the arctic pole, by which reasoning it appears, that they understood, that one part of the world ought to be loftier, and
nearer the sky, than the other; but it never struck them that
it might be under the equinoctial, in the way that I have said,
which is not to be wondered at, because they had no certain
knowledge respecting this hemisphere, but merely vague
suppositions, for no one has ever gone or been sent to inves-
tigate the matter, until your Highnesses sent me to explore
both the sea and the land. I found that between the two
straits, which, as I have said, face each other in a line from
north to south, is a distance of twenty-six leagues; and there
can be no mistake in this calculation, because it was made
with the quadrant. I also find, that from these two straits on
the west up to the above-mentioned gulf, to which I gave the
name of the Gulf of Pearls,[24] there are sixty-eight leagues
of four miles to the league, which is the reckoning we are
accustomed to make at sea; from this gulf the water runs
constantly with great impetuosity towards the east, and this
is the cause why, in these two straits, there is so fierce a tur-

---

mundo, y mas propincua al cielo, otros sabios le impugnan diciendo
que es esta ques debajo del ártico, por las cuales razones parece que
entendian que una parte deste mundo debia de ser mas propincua y noble al cielo que otra, y no cayeron en esto que sea
debajo del equinocial por la forma que ye dijo, y no es maravilla
porque deste hemisferio non se hobiese noticia cierta, salvo muy
liviana y por argumento, porque nadie nunca lo ha andado ni enviado á buscar, hasta agora que vuestras Altezas le mandaron explorar
é descubrir la mar y la tierra.

Fallo que de allí de estas dos bocas, las cuales como yo dije estan
frontero por línea de Septentrion en Austro, que haya de la una á
la otra veinte y seis leguas, y no pudo haber en ello yerro porque
se midieron con cuadrante, y destas dos bocas de occidente fasta el
golfo que yo dije, al cual llamé de las Perlas, que son sesenta é
ocho leguas de cuatro millas dada una como acostumbramos en la
mar, y que de allá de este golfo corre de contino el agua muy fuerte

[24] The innermost gulf within the Gulf of Paria.

moil from the fresh water encountering the water of the sea. In the southern strait, which I named the Serpent's Mouth, I found that towards evening the polar star was nearly at five degrees elevation; and in the northern, which I called the Dragon's Mouth, it was at an elevation of nearly seven degrees. The before-mentioned Gulf of Pearls is to the west of the[25]   of Ptolemy, nearly three thousand nine hundred miles, which make nearly seventy equinoctial degrees, reckoning fifty-six miles and two thirds to a degree. The Holy Scriptures record, that our Lord made the earthly paradise, and planted in it the tree of life, and thence springs a fountain from which the four principal rivers in the world take their source; namely, the Ganges in India, the Tigris, and Euphrates in[26]   which rivers divide a chain of mountains, and forming Mesopotamia, flow thence into Persia,—and the Nile, which rises in Ethiopia, and falls into the sea at Alexandria.

---

hácia el oriente; y que por esto tienen aquel combate estas dos bocas con la salada. En esta boca de Austro, á que yo llamé de la Sierpe, fallé en anocheciendo que yo tenia la estrella del Norte alta cuasi cinco grados, y en aquella otra del Septentrion, á que yo llamé del Drago, eran cuasi siete, y fallo quel dicho Golfo de las Perlas está occidental al Occidente de el   de Tolomeo cuasi tres mil é novecientas millas, que son cuasi setenta grados equinociales, contando por cada uno cincuenta y seis millas é dos tercios.

La Sacra Escriptura testifica que nuestro Señor hizo al Paraiso terrenal, y en él puso el Arbol de la vida, y del sale una fuente de donde resultan en este mundo cuatro rios principales: Ganges en India, Tigris y Eufrates en   los cuales apartan la sierra y hacen la Mesopotamia y van á tener en Persia, y el Nilo que nace en Etiopa y va en la mar en Alejandría.

[25] A similar gap in the original. In all probability "first meridian" or some such words, are omitted.

[26] A similar gap in the original, which would seem to want the words "Asiatic Turkey."

I do not find, nor have ever found, any account by the
Romans or Greeks, which fixes in a positive manner the
site of the terrestrial paradise, neither have I seen it given
in any mappe-monde, laid down from authentic sources.
Some placed it in Ethiopia, at the sources of the Nile,
but others, traversing all these countries, found neither
the temperature nor the altitude of the sun correspond with
their ideas respecting it; nor did it appear that the overwhelming waters of the deluge had been there.   Some pagans
pretended to adduce arguments to establish that it was in the
Fortunate Islands, now called the Canaries, etc.

St. Isidore, Bede, Strabo,[27] and the master of scholastic
history,[28] with St. Ambrose, and Scotus, and all the learned
theologians, agree that the earthly paradise is in the east, etc.

I have already described my ideas concerning this hemisphere and its form, and I have no doubt, that if I could
pass below the equinoctial line, after reaching the highest
point of which I have spoken, I should find a much milder

Yo no hallo ni jamas he hallado escriptura de Latinos ni de
Griegos que certificadamente diga el sitio en este mundo del Paraiso
terrenal, ni visto en ningun mapamundo, salvo, situado con autoridad de argumento.   Algunos le ponian allí donde son las fuentes
del Nilo en Etiopia ; mas otros anduvieron todas estas tierras y no
hallaron conformidad dello en la temperancia del cielo, en la altura
hácia el cielo, porque se pudiese comprehender que el era allí, ni
que las aguas del diluvio hobiesen llegado allí, las cuales subieron
encima, &c.   Algunos gentiles quisieron decir por argumentos, que
el era en las islas Fortunatas que son las Canarias, &c.

S. Isidro y Beda y Strabo, y el Maestro de la historia escolástica, y San Ambrosio, y Scoto, y todos los sanos teólogos conciertan
quel Paraiso terrenal es en el Oriente, &c.

Ya dije lo que yo hallaba deste hemisferio y de la hechura, y
creo que si yo pasara por debajo de la línea equinocial que en
llegando allí en esto mas alto que fallara muy mayor temperancia,

[27] Walafried Strabus, Abbé of Reichenau, in Baden.
[28] Petrus Comestor, who wrote the " Historia Scholastica."

temperature, and a variation in the stars and in the water; not that I suppose that elevated point to be navigable, nor even that there is water there; indeed, I believe it is impossible to ascend thither, because I am convinced that it is the spot of the earthly paradise, whither no one can go but by God's permission; but this land which your Highnesses have now sent me to explore, is very extensive, and I think there are many other countries in the south, of which the world has never had any knowledge.

I do not suppose that the earthly paradise is in the form of a rugged mountain, as the descriptions of it have made it appear, but that it is on the summit of the spot, which I have described as being in the form of the stalk of a pear; the approach to it from a distance must be by a constant and gradual ascent; but I believe that, as I have already said, no one could ever reach the top; I think also, that the water I have described may proceed from it, though it be far off, and that stopping at the place which I have just left, it forms this lake. There are great indications of this being the terrestrial paradise, for its site coincides with the opinion of the holy and wise theologians whom I have mentioned;

---

y diversidad en las estrellas y en las aguas; no porque yo crea que alli donde es el altura del extremo sea navegable ni agua, ni que se pueda subir allá, porque creo que allí es el Paraiso terrenal adonde no puede llegar nadie, salvo por voluntad Divina; y creo que esta tierra que agora mandaron descubrir vuestras Altezas sea grandísima y haya otras muchas en el Austro de que jamas se hobo noticia.

Yo no tomo quel Paraise terrenal sea en forma de montaña aspera como el escrebir dello nos amuestra, salvo quel sea en el colmo allí donde dije la figura del pezon de la pera, y que poco á poco andando hácia allí desde muy lejos se va subiendo á él; y creo que nadie no podria llegar al colmo como yo dije, y creo que pueda salir de allí esa agua, bien que sea lejos y venga á parar allí donde yo vengo, y faga este lago. Grandes indicios son estos del Paraiso terrenal, porquel sitio es conforme á la opinion de estos santos é

and moreover, the other evidences agree with the supposition, for I have never either read or heard of fresh water coming in so large a quantity, in close conjunction with the water of the sea; the idea is also corroborated by the blandness of the temperature; and if the water of which I speak, does not proceed from the earthly paradise, it appears to be still more marvellous, for I do not believe that there is any river in the world so large or so deep.

When I left the Dragon's Mouth, which is the northernmost of the two straits which I have described, and which I so named on the day of our Lady of August, I found that the sea ran so strongly to the westward, that between the hour of mass, when I weighed anchor, and the hour of complines, I made sixty-five leagues of four miles each; and not only was the wind not violent, but on the contrary very gentle, which confirmed me in the conclnsion, that in sailing southward, there is a continuous ascent, while there is a corresponding descent towards the north.

I hold it for certain, that the waters of the sea move from east to west with the sky, and that in passing this track, they

---

sanos teólogos, y asimismo las señales son muy conformes, que yo jamas leí ni oí que tanta cantidad de agua dulce fuese así adentro é vecina con la salada ; y en ello ayuda asimismo la suavísima temperancia, y si de allí del Paraiso no sale, parece aun mayor maravilla, porque no creo que se scpa en el mundo de rio tan grande y tan fondo.

Despues que yo salí de la boca del Dragon, ques la una de las dos aquella del Septentriun, á la cual así puse nombre, el dia siguiente, que fue dia de Nuestra Señora de Agosto, fallé que corria tanto la mar al Poniente, que despues de hora de misa que entré en camino, anduve fasta hora de completas sesenta y cinco leguas de cuatro millas cada una, y el viento no era demasiado, salvo muy suave ; y esto ayuda el cognoscimiento que de allí yendo al Austro se va mas alto, y andando hácia el Septentrion, como entonces, se va descendiendo.

Muy conoscido tengo que las aguas de la mar llevan su curso de

hold a more rapid course, and have thus carried away large tracts of land, and that from hence has resulted this great number of islands; indeed, these islands themselves afford an additional proof of it, for all of them, without exception, run lengthwise from west to east, and from the north west to the south east, which is in a directly contrary direction to the said winds; furthermore, that these islands should possess the most costly productions, is to be accounted for by the mild temperature, which comes to them from heaven, since these are the most elevated parts of the world. It is true, that in some parts, the waters do not appear to take this course, but this occurs in certain spots, where they are obstructed by land, and hence they appear to take different directions.

Pliny writes that the sea and land together form a sphere, but that the ocean forms the greatest mass, and lies uppermost, while the earth is below and supports the ocean, and that the two afford a mutual support to each other, as the kernel of a nut is confined by its shell. The master of scholastic history, in commenting upon Genesis, says, that the waters are not very extensive; and that although

---

Oriente á Occidente con los cielos, y que allí en esta comarca cuando pasan llevan mas veloce camino, y por esto han comido tanta parte de la tierra, porque por eso son acá tantas islas, y ellas mismas hacen desto testimonio, porque todas á una mano son largas de Poniente á Levante, y Norueste é Sueste ques un poco mas alto é bajo, y angostas de Norte á Sur, y Nordeste Sudueste, que son en contrario de los otros dichos vientos, y aquí en ellas todas nascen cosas preciosas por la suave temperancia que les procede del cielo por estar hácia el mas alto del mundo. Verdad es que parece en algunos lugares que las aguas no hagan este curso; mas esto no es, salvo particularmente en algunos lugares donde alguna tierra le está al encuentro, y hace parecer que andan diversos caminos.

Plinio escribe que la mar é la tierra hace todo una esfera, y pone questa mar Oceana sea la mayor cantidad del agua, y está hácia el cielo, y que la tierra sea debajo y que le sostenga, y mezclado es uno con otro como el amago de la nuez con una tela gorda que va abra-

when they were first created they covered the earth, they were yet vaporous like a cloud, and that afterwards they became condensed, and occupied but small space, and in this notion Nicolas de Lira agrees. Aristotle says that the world is small, and the water very limited in extent, and that it is easy to pass from Spain to the Indies; and this is confirmed by Avenruyz,[29] and by the Cardinal Pedro de Aliaco, who, in supporting this opinion, shows that it agrees with that of Seneca, and says that Aristotle had been enabled to gain information respecting the world by means of Alexander the Great, and Seneca by means of Nero, and Pliny through the Romans; all of them having expended large sums of money, and employed a vast number of people, in diligent inquiry concerning the secrets of the world, and in spreading abroad the knowledge thus obtained. The said cardinal allows to these writers greater authority than to Ptolemy, and other Greeks and Arabs; and in confirmation of their opinion concerning the small quantity of water on the surface of the globe,

---

zado en ello. El Maestro de la Historia escolástica sobre el Genesis dice que las aguas son muy pocas, que bien que cuando fueron criadas que cobijasen toda la tierra que entonces eran vaporables en manera de niebla, y que despues que fueron sólidas é juntadas que ocuparon muy poco lugar, y en esto concierta Nicolao de Lira. El Aristotel dice que este mundo es pequeño y es el agua muy poca, y que facilmente se puede pasar de España á las Indias, y esto confirma el Avenruyz y le alega el Cardenal Pedro de Aliaco, autorizando este decir y aquel de Séneca, el cual conforma con estos diciendo que Aristoteles pudo saber muchos secretos del mundo á causa de Alejandro Magno, y Séneca á causa de Cesar Nero y Plinio por respecto de los Romanos, los cuales todos gastaron dineros é gente, y pusieron mucha diligencia en saber los secretos del mundo y darlos á entender á los pueblos ; el cual Cardenal da á estos grande autoridad mas que á Tolomeo ni á otros Griegos ni Arabes, y á confirmacion de decir quel agua sea poca y quel cubi-

---

[29] Averrhóes, an Arabian philosopher of the twelfth century.

and the limited amount of land covered by that water, in comparison of what had been related on the authority of Ptolemy and his disciples, he finds a passage in the third book of Esdras, where that sacred writer says, that of seven parts of the world six are discovered, and the other is covered with water. The authority of the third and fourth books of Esdras is also confirmed by holy persons, such as St. Augustin, and St. Ambrose in his *Exameron,* where he says,—" Here my son Jesus shall first come, and here my son Christ shall die !" These holy men say that Esdras was a prophet as well as Zacharias, the father of St. John, and *El Braso*[30] Simon; authorities which are also quoted by Francis de Mairones.[31] With respect to the dryness of the land, experience has shown that it is greater than is commonly believed; and this is no wonder, for the further one goes the more one learns. I now return to my subject of the land of Gracia, and of the river and lake found there, which latter might more properly be called a sea; for a lake is but a small expanse of water, which,

---

erto del mundo della sea poco, al rcopooto do lo que se decia por autoridad de Tolomeo y de sus secuaces : á esto trae una autoridad de Esdras del 3°. libro suyo, adonde dice que de siete partes del mundo las seis son descubiertas y la una es cubierta de agua, la cual autoridad es aprobada por Santos, los cuales dan autoridad al 3°. é 4°· libro de Esdras, ansí como es S. Agustin é S. Ambrosio en su exameron, adonde alega allí vendrá mi hijo Jesus é morira mi hijo Cristo, y dicen que Esdrás fue Profeta, y asimismo Zacarías, padre de S. Juan, y el braso Simon ; las cuales autoridades tambien alega Francisco de Mairones: en cuanto en esto del enjuto de la tierra mucho se ha experimentado ques mucho mas de lo quel vulgo crea; y no es maravilla, porque andando mas mas se sabe.

Torno á mi propósito de la tierra de Gracia y rio y lago que allí fallé, atan grande que mas se le puede llamar mar que lago, porque

[30] This expression is described by the ancient copyist of the letter as being " badly written."

[31] A Scotist of the fourteenth century, surnamed " Doctor illuminatus et acutus."

when it becomes great, deserves the name of a sea, just as we speak of the Sea of Galilee and the Dead Sea; and I think that if the river mentioned does not proceed from the terrestrial paradise, it comes from an immense tract of land situated in the south, of which no knowledge has been hitherto obtained. But the more I reason on the subject, the more satisfied I become that the terrestrial paradise is situated in the spot I have described; and I ground my opinion upon the arguments and authorities already quoted. May it please the Lord to grant your Highnesses a long life, and health and peace to follow out so noble an investigation; in which I think our Lord will receive great service, Spain considerable increase of its greatness, and all Christians much consolation and pleasure, because by this means the name of our Lord will be published abroad.

In all the countries visited by your Highnesses' ships, I have caused a high cross to be fixed upon every headland, and have proclaimed, to every nation that I have discovered, the lofty estate of your Hignesses, and of your court in Spain. I also tell them all I can respecting our holy faith and of the belief in the holy mother Church, which has its members in

---

lago es lugar de agua, y en seyendo grande se dice mar, como se dijo á la mar de Galilea y al mar Muerto, y digo que sino procede del Paraiso terrenal que viene este rio y procede de tierra infinita pues al Austro, de la cual fasta agora no se ha habido noticia, mas yo muy asentado tengo en el anima que allí adonde dije es el Paraiso terrenal, y descanso sobre las razones y autoridades sobre-escriptas.

Plega á nuestro Señor de dar mucha vida y salud y descanso á vuestras Altezas para que puedan proseguir esta tan noble empresa, en la cual me parece que rescibe nuestro Señor mucho servicio, y la España crece de mucha grandeza, y todos los Cristianos mucha consolacion y placer, porque aquí se divulgará el nombre de nuestro Señor ; y en todas las tierras adonde los navíos de vuestras Altezas van, y en todo cabo mando plantar una alta cruz, y á toda la gente que hallo notifico el estado de vuestras Altezas y como su asiento es en España, y les digo de nuestra santa fe todo lo que yo puedo, y

all the world; and I speak to them also of the courtesy and nobleness of all Christians, and of the faith they have in the Holy Trinity. May it please the Lord to forgive those who have calumniated and still calumniate this excellent enterprise, and oppose and have opposed its advancement, without considering how much glory and greatness will accrue from it to your Highnesses throughout all the world. They cannot state anything in disparagement of it, except its expense, and that I have not immediately sent back the ships loaded with gold. They speak this without considering the shortness of the time, and how many difficulties there are to contend with; and that every year there are individuals who singly earn by their deserts out of your Majesties' own household, more revenue than would cover the whole of this expense. Nor do they remember that the princes of Spain have never gained possession of any land out of their own country, until now that your Highnesses have become the masters of another world, where our holy faith may become so much increased, and whence such stores of wealth may be derived; for although we have not sent home ships laden with gold, we have, nevertheless,

---

de la creencia de la Santa Madre Iglesia, la cual tiene sus miembros en todo el mundo, y les digo la policía y nobleza de todos los Cristianos, y la fe que en la Santa Trinidad tienen; y plega á nuestro Señor de tirar de memoria á las personas que han impugnado y impugnan tan excelente empresa, y impiden y impidieron porque no vaya adelante, sin considerar cuanta honra y grandeza es del Real Estado da vuestras Altezas en todo el mundo; no saben que entreponer á maldecir de esto, salvo que se hace gasto en ello, y porque luego no enviaron los navíos cargados de oro sin considerar la brevedad del tiempo y tantos inconvenientes como acá se han habido, y no considerar que en Castilla en casa de vuestras Altezas salen cada año personas que por su merecimiento ganaron en ella mas de renta cada uno dellos mas de lo ques necesario que se gaste en esto; ansimesmo sin considerar que ningunos Príncipes de España jamas ganaron tierra alguna fuera della, salvo agora que vuestras Altezas tienen acá otro mundo, de adonde puede ser tan

sent satisfactory samples, both of gold and of other valuable commodities, by which it may be judged that in a short time large profit may be derived. Neither do they take into consideration the noble spirit of the princes of Portugal, who so long ago carried into execution the exploration of Guinea, and still follow it up along the coast of Africa, in which one-half of the population of the country has been employed, and yet the King is more determined on the enterprise than ever. The Lord grant all that I have said, and lead them to think deeply upon what I have written; which is not the thousandth part of what might be written of the deeds of princes who have set their minds upon gaining knowledge, and upon obtaining territory and keeping it.

I say all this, not because I doubt the inclination of your Highnesses to pursue the enterprise while you live,—for I rely confidently on the answers your Highnesses once gave me by word of mouth,—nor because I have seen any change in your Highnesses, but from the fear of what I have heard from those of whom I have been speaking; for I know that water dropping on a stone will at length make a hole.   Your

---

acrescentada nuestra santa fe, y de donde se podrán sacar tantos provechos, que bien que no se hayan enviado los navíos cargados de oro, se han enviado suficientes muestras dello y de otras cosas de valor, por donde se puede juzgar que en breve tiempo se podrá haber mucho provecho, y sin mirar el gran corazon de los Príncipes de Portugal que há tanto tiempo que prosiguen la impresa de Guinea, y prosiguen aquella de Africa, adonde han gastado la mitad de la gente de su Reino, y agora está el Rey mas determinado á ello que nunca.   Nuestro Señor provea en esto como yo dije, y les ponga en memoria de considerar de todo esto que va escripto, que no es de mil partes la una de lo que yo podria escrebir de cosas de Príncipes que se ocuparon á saber y conquistar y sostener.

Todo esto dije, y no porque crea que la voluntad de vuestras Altezas sea salvo proseguir en ello en cuanto vivan, y tengo por muy firme lo que me respondió vuestras Altezas una vez que por palabra le decir desto, no porque yo hobiese visto mudamiento nin-

Highnesses responded to me with that nobleness of feeling which all the world knows you to possess, and told me to pay no attention to these calumniations; for that your intention was to follow up and support the undertaking, even if nothing were gained by it but stones and sand. Your Highnesses also desired me to be in no way anxious about the expense, for that much greater cost had been incurred on much more trifling matters, and that you considered all the past and future expense as well laid out; for that your Highnesses believed that our holy faith would be increased, and your royal dignity enhanced, and that they were no friends of the royal estate who spoke ill of the enterprise.

And now, during the despatch of the information respecting these lands which I have recently discovered, and where I believe in my soul that the earthly paradise is situated, the "Adelantado" will proceed with three ships, well stocked with provisions, on a further investigation, and will make all the discoveries he can about these parts. Meanwhile, I shall send your Highnesses this letter, accompanied by a drawing

---

guno en vuestras Altezas salvo por temor de lo que yo oia destos que yo digo, y tanto da una gotera de agua en una piedra que le hace un agujero ; y vuestras Altezas me respondió con aquel corazon que se sabe en todo el mundo que tienen, y me dijo que no curase de nada de eso, porque su voluntad era de proseguir esta empresa y sostenerla, aunque no fuese sino piedras y peñas, y quel gasto que en ello se hacia que lo tenia en nada, que en otras cosas no tan grandes gastaban mucho mas, y que lo tenian todo por muy bien gastado lo del pasado y lo que se gastase en adelante, porque creian que nuestra santa fe seria acrecentada y su Real Señorío ensanchado, y que no eran amigos de su Real Estado aquellos que les maldecian de esta empresa : y agora entre tanto que vengan á noticia desto destas tierras que agora nuevamente he descubierto, en que tengo asentado en el ánima que allí es el Paraiso terrenal, irá el Adelantado con tres navíos bien ataviados para ello á ver mas adelante, y descubrirán todo lo que pudieren haciá aquellas partes. Entretanto yo enviaré á vuestras Altezas esta escriptura y la pin-

of the country, and your Majesties will determine on what is to be done, and give your orders as to how it is your pleasure that I should proceed: the which, by the aid of the Holy Trinity, shall be carried into execution with all possible diligence, in the faithful service and to the entire satisfaction of your Majesties. Deo Gratias.

---

tura de la tierra, y acordarán lo que en ello se deba facer, y me enviarán á mandar, y se cumplirá con ayuda de la Santa Trinidad con toda diligencia en manera que vuestras Altezas sean servidos y hayan placer. Deo gracias.

LETTER

Of the Admiral to the (quondam) nurse[1] of the Prince John, written near the end of the year 1500.

MOST virtuous lady : Although it is a novelty for me to complain of the ill-usage of the world, it is, nevertheless, no novelty for the world to practise ill-usage. Innumerable are the contests which I have had with it, and I have resisted all its attacks until now, when I find, that neither strength nor prudence is of any avail to me : it has cruelly reduced me to the lowest ebb. Hope in Him who has created us all is my support : His assistance I have always found near at hand. On one occasion, not long since, He supported me with His Divine arm, saying : " O man of little faith, arise, it is I, be

---

CARTA

Del Almirante al ama (que habia sido) del Principe D. Juan, escrita hacia fines del año 1500.

MUY virtuosa Señora : Si mi queja del mundo es nueva, su uso de maltratar es de muy antiguo. Mil combates me ha dado y á todos resistí fasta agora que no me aprovechó armas ni avisos. Con crueldad me tiene echado al fondo. La esperanza de aquel que crio á todos me sostiene : su socorro fue siempre muy presto. Otra vez, y no de lejos estando yo mas bajo, me levantó con su brazo divino, diciendo : *ó hombre de poca fe, levantate que yo soy, no hayas miedo.* Yo vine con amor tan entrañable á servir á estos Principes, y hé

---

[1] Although Zuñiga says that Doña Maria de Guzman was appointed nurse by Queen Isabella at the birth of Prince John, it is nevertheless certain, that this letter was addressed by Columbus to Doña Juana de la Torres, a great favourite of the queen, sister of Antonio de Torres, who was with the admiral in the second voyage, and who bore the memorial to their Highnesses.

not afraid."[2] I offered myself with such earnest devotion to
the service of these princes, and I have served them with a
fidelity hitherto unequalled and unheard of. God made me
the messenger of the new heaven and the new earth, of which
He spoke in the Apocalypse by St. John, after having spoken
of it by the mouth of Isaiah; and He showed me the spot
where to find it. All proved incredulous; except the Queen
my mistress, to whom the Lord gave the spirit of intelligence
and the necessary courage, and made her the heiress of all,
as a dear and well beloved daughter. I went to take possession of it in her royal name. All wished to cover the
ignorance in which they were sunk, by enumerating the in-
conveniences and expense of the proposed enterprise. Her
Highness held the contrary opinion, and supported it with all
her power. Seven years passed away in deliberations, and
nine have been spent in accomplishing things truly memora-
ble, and worthy of being preserved in the history of man.

I have now reached that point, that there is no man so vile
but thinks it his right to insult me. The day will come when

---

servido de servicio de que jamas se oyó ni vido. Del nuevo cielo
y tierra que decia nuestro Señor por S. Juan en el Apocalipse,
despues de dicho por boca de Isaías, me hizo dello mensagero, y
amostró en cual parte. En todos hobo incredulidad, y á la Reina
mi Señora dió dello el espíritu de inteligencia y esfuerzo grande, y
lo hizo de todo heredera como á cara y muy amada hija. La posesion de todo esto fuí yo á tomar en su Real nombre. La igno-
rancia en que habian estado todos quisieron enmendallo traspasando
el poco saber á fablar en inconvenientes y gastos. Su Alteza lo
aprobaba al contrario, y lo sostuvo fasta que pudo. Siete años se
pasaron en la platica y nueve ejecutando cosas muy señaladas y
dignas de memoria se pasaron en este tiempo : de todo no se fizo
concepto. Llegué yo y estoy que non ha nadie tan vil que no pi_

[2] This is related by his son Don Ferdinand, in cap. 84 of his history,
and is more amply described in the letter addressed by Columbus to the
sovereigns, describing his fourth voyage. It took place the day after
Christmas day, 1499.

the world will reckon it a virtue to him who has not given his consent to their abuse. If I had plundered the Indies, even to the country where is the fabled altar of St. Peter's, and had given them all to the Moors, they could not have shown towards me more bitter enmity than they have done in Spain. Who would believe such things in a country where there has always been so much magnanimity? I desire earnestly to clear myself of this affair, if only I had the means of doing so face to face with my queen. The support which I have found in our Lord, and in her Highness, has made me persevere; and I would fain cause her to forget a little the griefs which death has occasioned her.[3] I undertook another voyage to the new heavens and new earth, which had been hidden hitherto; and if these are not appreciated in Spain, like the other parts of the Indies, it is not at all wonderful, since it is to my labours that they are indebted for them. The Holy Spirit encompassed St. Peter, and the rest of the twelve, who all had conflicts here below; they wrought many

---

ense de ultrajarme. Por virtud se contará en el mundo á quien puede no consentillo. Si yo robara las Indias ó tierra que san face* en ello de que agora es la fabla del altar de S. Pedro, y las diera á los moros, no pudieran en España amostrarme mayor enemiga. Quién creyera tal adonde hobo siempre tanta nobleza ? Yo mucho quisiera despedir del negocio si fuera honesto para con mi Reina : el esfuerzo de nuestro Señor y de su Alteza fizo que yo continuase, y por aliviarle algo de los enojos en que á causa de la muerte estaba, cometi viaje nuevo al nuevo cielo é mundo, que fasta entonces estaba en oculto, y sino es tenido allí en estima, así como los otros de las Indias, no es maravilla porque salió á parecer de mi industria. A S. Pedro abrasó el Espíritu Santo y con él otros doce, y todos combatieron acá, y los trabajos y fatigas fueron muchas ; en fin de

* There is no sense in this expression, nor as it is given in the "Codice Colombo Americano", where it stands thus : " que jaz hase ellas de que," etc.

3 He refers to the death of Prince John, which occurred in Salamanca, on the fourth of October 1497.

works, they suffered great fatigues, but at last they obtained the victory. I·believed that this voyage to Paria would in some degree pacify them, because of the pearls, and the discovery of gold in the island of Española. I left orders for the people to fish for pearls, and collect them together, and made an agreement with them that I should return for them; and I was given to understand that the supply would be abundant.

If I have not written respecting this to their Highnesses, it is because I wished first to render an equally favourable account of the gold; but it has happened with this as with many other things; I should not have lost them, and with them my honour, if I had been only occupied about my own private interests, and had suffered Española to be lost, or even if they had respected my privileges and the treaties. I say the same with regard to the gold which I had then collected, and which I have brought in safety, by Divine grace, after so much loss of life and such excessive fatigues.

In the voyage which I made by way of Paria, I found nearly half the colonists of Española in a state of revolt, and they have made war upon me until now as if I had been a Moor;[4]

---

todo llevaron la victoria. Este viaje de Paria creí que apaciguara algo por las perlas y la fallada del oro en la Española. Las perlas mandé yo ayuntar y pescar á la gente con quien quedó el concierto de mi vuelta por ellas, y á mi comprender á medida de fanega : si yo non lo escribí á SS. AA. fue porque así quisiera haber fecho del oro antes. Esto me salió como otras cosas muchas ; no las perdiera ni mi honra si buscara yo mi bien propio y dejara perder la Española, ó se guardaran mis previlegios é asientos. Y otro tanto digo del oro que yo tenia agora junto, que con tantas muertés y trabajos, por virtud divinal, he llegado á perfecto. Cuando yo fuí á Paria fallé cuasi la mitad de la gente en la Española alzados, y me han guerreado fasta agora como á moro, y los indios por otro cabo gra-

[4] After the admiral had discovered the island of Trinidad, he sailed along the coast of Paria, discovered the island of Margarita, and entered the harbour of San Domingo the thirtieth of August 1498, where he found the colony in rebellion, and the Spaniards embroiled in quarrels, both with each other and with the Indians.

while on the other side, I had to contend with the no less cruel Indians. Then arrived Hojeda,[5] and he attempted to put the seal to all these disorders ; he said that their Highnesses had sent him, with promises of presents, of immunities, and treaties ; he collected a numerous band, for in the whole island of Española, there were few men who were not vagabonds, and there were none who had either wife or children. This Hojeda troubled me much, but he was obliged to retreat, and at his departure he said, that he would return with more ships and men, and reported also, that he had left the queen at the point of death.[6] In the meanwhile, Vincent Yañez came with four caravels ; and there were some tumults and suspicions, but no further evil. The Indians reported many other caravels to the cannibals, and in Paria ; and afterwards spread the news of the arrival of six other caravels, commanded by a brother of the alcalde ; but this was from pure malice ; when at last the hope was lost that their Highnesses would send any more ships to the Indies, and we no longer expected them, and when it

---

vemente. En esto vino Hojeda y probó á echar el sello, y dijo que sus Altezas lo enviaban con promesas de dádivas y franquezas y paga : allegó gran cuadrilla, que en toda la Española muy pocos hay, salvo vagabundos y ninguno con muger y fijos. Este Hojeda me trabajó harto y fuele necesario de se ir, y dejó dicho que luego seria de vuelta con mas navíos y gente, y que dejaba la Real persona de la Reina á la muerte. En esto llegó Viceinte Yañez con cuatro carabelas : hobo alboroto y sospechas, mas no daño. Los indios dijeron de otras muchas á los canibales y en Paria, y despues una nueva de seis otras carabelas que traía un hermano del Alcalde, mas fue con malicia, y esto fue ya á la postre cuando ya estaba muy rota la esperanza que sus Altezas hobiesen jamas de enviar navíos á las Indias, ni nos esperarlos, y que vulgarmente decian que su

5 Alonzo de Hojeda reached Española on the fifth of September 1498.

6 Roldan was by this time reconciled to the Admiral, and the rebellion was allayed, when Hojeda arrived, making great boast of his favour with bishop Fonseca, Columbus' enemy, and endeavoured to excite fresh animosity against him; but he had to leave Española completely.

was said openly that her Highness (the queen) was dead. At
this time, one Adrian attempted a new revolt, as he had done
before;[7] but our Lord did not permit his evil designs to succeed. I had determined not to inflict punishment on any person, but his ingratitude obliged me, however regretfully, to
abandon this resolution. I should not have acted otherwise
with my own brother, if he had sought to assassinate me, and
to rob me of the lordship which my sovereigns had given to
my keeping. This Adrian, as is now evident, had sent Don
Ferdinand to Xaragua, to assemble some of his partisans, and
had some discussions with the alcalde, which ended in violence, but all without any good. The alcalde seized him and
a part of his band; and in fact, executed justice without my
having ordered it. While they were in prison, they were
expecting a caravel, in which they hoped to embark; but the
news of what had happened to Hojeda, and which I told them,
deprived them of the hope that he would arrive in this ship.
It is now six months that I have been ready to leave, to bring
to their Highnesses the good news of the gold, and to give up
the government of these dissolute people, who fear neither

Alteza era muerta. Un Adrian en este tiempo probó alzarse otra
vez como de antes, mas nuestro Señor no quiso que llegase á efecto
su mal propósito. Yo tenia propuesto en mi de no tocar el cabello
á nadie, y á este por su ingratitud con lágrimas no se pudo guardar,
así como yo lo tenia pensado. A mi hermano no hiciera menos si
me quisiera matar y robar el señorío que mi Rey é Reina me tenian
dado en guarda. Este Adrian, segun se muestra, tenia enviado á
D. Fernando á Jaragua á allegar á algunos sus secuaces, y allá
hobo debate con el Alcalde, adonde nació discordia de muerte;
mas no llegó á efecto. El Alcalde le prendió y á parte de su
cuadrilla; y el caso era que él los justiciaba sin que yo lo prove-
yere : estovieren presos esperando carabela en que se fuesen : las
nuevas de Hojeda que yo dije ficieron perder la esperanza que ya
no venia. Seis meses habia que yo estaba despachado para venir
á sus Altezas con las buenas nuevas del oro y fuir de gobernar

[7] Adrian Mogica, who had been one of the rebels with Roldan.

their king nor queen, but are full of imbecility and malice. I should have been able to pay every one with six hundred thousand maravedis, and for this purpose there were four millions and more of the tithes, without reckoning the third part of the gold.

Before my departure (from Spain) I have often entreated their Highnesses to send to these parts, at my expense, some one charged to administer justice; and since, when I found the alcalde in a state of revolt, I have besought them afresh to send at least one of their servants with letters, because I myself have had so strange a character given to me, that if I were to build churches or hospitals, they would call them caves for robbers. Their Highnesses provided for this at last, but in a manner quite unequal to the urgency of the circumstances; however, let that point rest, since such is their good pleasure. I remained two years in Spain without being able to obtain anything for myself, or those who came with me,[8] but this man has gained for himself a full purse: God knows

---

gente disoluta que no temo á Dios ni á su Rey ni Reina, llena de achaques y de malicias. A la gente acabara yo de pagar con seiscientos mil maravedises : y para ello habia cuatro cuentos de diezmos é alguno sin el tercio del oro. Antes de mi partida supliqué tantas veces á sus Altezas que enviasen allá á mi costa á quien tuviese cargo de la justicia, y despues que fallé alzado al Alcalde se lo supliqué de nuevo ó por alguna gente, ó al menos algun criado con cartas, porque mi fama es tal que aunque yo faga iglesias y hospitales siempre serán dichas espeluncas para latrones. Proveyeron ya al fin, y fue muy al contrario de lo que la negociacion demandaba : vaya en buena hora, pues que es á su grado. Yo estuve allá dos años sin poder ganar una provision de favor para mí ni por los que allá fuesen, y este llevó una arca llena : si pararán todas á su servicio Dios lo sabe. Ya por comienzos hay franquezas por

---

[8] Columbus returned to Cadiz from his second voyage, on the 11th of June, 1496. He was well received by the sovereigns, and they gave orders for preparing the requisites for a third voyage; but the fulfilment of these orders was delayed by Bishop Fonseca until the 30th of May, 1498.

if all will be employed for His service. Already, to begin
with, there is a revenue for twenty years, which is, according
to man's calculation, an age; and they gather gold in such
abundance, that there are people who, in four hours, have
found the equivalent of five marks; but I will speak on this
subject more fully hereafter.   If their Highnesses would condescend to silence the popular rumours, which have gained
credence among those who know what fatigues I have sus-
tained, it would be a real charity; for calumny has done me
more injury than the services which I have rendered to their
Highnesses, and the care with which I have preserved their
property and their government, have done me good; and, by
their so doing, I should be re-established in reputation, and
spoken of throughout the universe: for the things which I
have accomplished are such, that they must gain, day by day,
in the estimation of mankind.

In the meanwhile, the commander Bobadilla arrived at
St. Domingo,[9] at which time I was at La Vega, and the Adelantado at Xaragua, where this Adrian had made his attempt;
but by that time everything was quiet, the land was thriv-
ing, and the people at peace.   The second day of his arrival he declared himself governor, created magistrates, or-

---

veinte años, que es la edad de un hombre, y se coge el oro, que hobo
persona de cinco marcos en cuatro horas, de que diré despues mas
largo.   Si pluguiese á sus Altezas de desfacer un vulgo de los que
saben mis fatigas, que mayor daño me ha hecho el mal decir de las
gentes que no me ha aprovechado el mucho servir y guardar su
facienda y señorío, seria limosna, é yo restituido en mi honra, é se
fablaria dello en todo el mundo, porquel negocio es de calidad que
cada dia ha de ser mas sonado y en alta estima.   En esto vino el
Comendador Bobadilla á Santo Domingo, yo estaba en la Vega y el
Adelantado en Jaragua, donde este Adrian habia hecho cabeza,
mas ya todo era llano y la tierra rica, y en paz toda.   El segundo
dia que llegó se crió Gobernador y fizo oficiales y ejecuciones, y

[9] Francesco de Bobadilla, commander of the order of Calatrava, reached
San Domingo on the 23rd of August, 1500.

dered executions, published immunities from the collection
of gold and from the paying of tithes; and, in fine, an-
nounced a general franchise for twenty years, which is, as I
have said, the calculation of an age. He also gave out that
he was going to pay every one, although they had not even
done the service which was due up to that day; and he
further proclaimed, with respect to me, that he would send
me back loaded with chains, and my brother also (this he has
accomplished);[10] and that neither I, nor any of my family,
should return for ever to these lands: and, in addition to
this, he made innumerable unjust and disgraceful charges
against me. All this took place, as I have said, on the very
day after his arrival, at which time I was absent at a secure
distance, thinking neither of him nor of his coming. Some
letters of their Highnesses, of which he brought a considerable number signed in blank, he filled up with exaggerated
language, and sent round to the alcalde and his myrmidons,
accompanying them with compliments and flattery. To me
he never sent either a letter or a messenger, nor has he done
so to this day. Reflect upon this, madam! what could any
man in my situation think? That honour and favour should

---

apregonó franquezas del oro y diezmos, y generalmente de toda otra
cosa por veinte años, que como digo es la edad de un hombre, y que
venia para pagar á todos, bien que no habian servido llenamente
hasta ese dia, y publicó que á mi me habia de enviar en fierros, y
á mis hermanos, así como lo ha fecho, y que nunca yo volveria mas
allí ni otro de mi linage, diciendo de mi mil deshonestidades y des-
corteses cosas. Esto todo fue el segundo dia quel llegó, como dije,
y estando yo lejos absente sin saber dello ni de su venida. Unas
cartas de sus Altezas firmadas en blanco, de que él llevaba una cantidad, hinchó y envió al Alcalde y á su compañía con favores y en-
comiendas. A mi nunca me envió carta ni mensagero, ni me ha
dado fasta hoy. Piense vuestra merced qué pensaria quien tuviera

[10] This expression of the Admiral's, makes it appear that he wrote
this letter when he was near reaching Cadiz, on the 25th of November,
1500.

be granted to him who had given his sanction to plundering their Highnesses of their sovereignty, and who had done so much injury and caused so much mischief?—that he who had defended and preserved their cause through so many dangers, should be dragged through the mire?   When I heard this, I thought he must be like Hojeda, or one of the other rebels; but I held my peace, when I learned for certain from the friars, that he had been sent by their Highnesses.   I wrote to him, to salute him on his arrival, to let him know that I was ready to set out to go to court, and that I had put up to sale all that I possessed.   I entreated him not to be in haste on the subject of the immunities; and I assured him that I would shortly yield this, and everything else connected with the government, implicitly into his charge.   I wrote the same thing to the ecclesiastics, but I received no answer either from the one or the other.   On the contrary, he took a hostile position, and obliged those who went to his residence to acknowledge him for governor, as I have been told, for twenty years.   As soon as I knew what he had done with regard to the immunities, I believed it needful to repair so great an

---

mi cargo ? honrar y favorecer á quien probó á robar á sus Altezas el señorío, y ha fecho tanto mal y daño ? y arrastrar á quien con tantos peligros se lo sostuvo ?   Cuando supe esto, creí que esto seria como lo de Hojeda, ó uno de los otros : templóme que supe de los frailes de cierto que sus Altezas lo enviaban.   Escrebile yo que su venida fuese en buena hora, y que yo estaba despachado para ir á la corte, y fecho almoneda de cuanto yo tenia, y que en esto de las franquezas que no se acelerase, que esto y el gobierno yo se lo daria luego tan llano como la palma, y así lo escribí á los religiosos. Ni él ni ellos me dieron respuesta, antes se puso él en son de guerra, y apremiaba á cuantos allí iban que le jurasen por Gobernador, dijeronme que por veinte años.   Luego que yo supe de estas franquezas pensé de adobar un yerro tan grande, y que él seria contento, las cuales dió sin necesidad y causa de cosa tan gruesa y á gente vagabunda, que fuera demasiado para quien trujera muger y hijos.   Publiqué por palabra y por cartas que él no podia usar de

error, and I thought he would himself be glad of it; because
he had, without any reason or necessity, bestowed upon vagabonds privileges of such importance, that they would have
been excessive even for men with wives and children. I
published verbally, and by writings, that he could not make
use of these grants, because mine had still more power, and
I showed the immunities brought by Juan Aguado. All this
I did for the purpose of gaining time, that their Highnesses
might be informed as to the state of things, and that they
might have opportunity to give fresh orders upon everything
touching their interests. It is useless to publish such grants
in the Indies,—all is in favour of the settlers who have taken
up their abode there, because the best lands are given up to
them; and, at a low estimate, they are worth two hundred
thousand maravedis a head for the four years, at which they
are taken, without their having given one stroke of the spade
or the mattock. I should not say so much if these people
were married men; but there are not six among them all,
whose purpose is not to amass all they can, and then decamp
with it. It would be well to send people from Spain, and

---

sus provisiones, porque las mias eran las mas fuertes, y les mostré
las franquezas que llevó Juan Aguado. Todo esto que yo fice era
por dilatar, porque sus Altezas fuesen sabidores del estado de la
tierra, y hobiesen lugar de tornar á mandar en ello lo que fuese su
servicio. Tales franquezas escusado es de las apregonar en las Indias. Los vecinos que han tomado vecindad es logro, porque se les
dan las mejores tierras y á poco valer valerán docientos mil maravedis al cabo de los cuatro años que la vecindad se acaba, sin que den
una azadonada en ellas. No diria yo así si los vecinos fuesen casados, mas no hay seis entre todos que no esten sobre el aviso de
ayunta lo que pudieren y se ir en buena hora. De Castilla seria
bien que fuesen, y aun saber quién y cómo, y se poblase de gente
honrada. Yo tenia asentado con estos vecinos que pagarian el tercio del oro y los diezmos, y esto á su ruego, y lo recibieron en
grande merced de sus Altezas. Reprendiles cuando yo oí que se
dejaban dello, y esperaban quél conmigo faria otro tanto, mas fue el

only to send such as are well known, that the country may be peopled with honest men. I had agreed with these settlers that they should pay the third of the gold and of the tithes; and this they not only assented to, but were very grateful to their Highnesses. I reproached them when I heard they had afterwards refused it; they expected, however, to deal with me on the same terms as with the commander, but I would not consent to it. He meanwhile irritated them against me, saying, that I wished to deprive them of that which their Highnesses had given them; and strove to make me appear their enemy, in which he succeeded to the full. He induced them to write to their Highnesses, that they should send me no more commissioned as governor (truly, I do not desire it any more for myself, or for any who belong to me, while the people remain unchanged); and to conciliate them, he ordered inquiries to be made respecting me with reference to imputed misdeeds, such as were never invented in hell. But God is above, who with so much wisdom and power rescued Daniel and the three children, and who, if he please, can rescue me with a similar manifestation of his power, and to the advancement of his own cause. I should have known well enough how to find a remedy for the evils which I now describe and have been describing as having happened to

---

contrario. Indignólos contra mí diciendo, que yo les queria quitar lo que sus Altezas les daban, y trabajo de me los echar acuestas, y lo hizo, y que escribiesen á sus Altezas que no me enviasen mas al cargo, y así se lo suplico yo por mí y por toda cosa mia, en cuanto no haya otro pueblo, y me ordenó él con ellos pesquisas de maldades que al infierno nunca se supo de las semejantes. Allí está nuestro Señor que escapó á Daniel y á los tres muchachos con tanto saber y fuerza como tenia, y con tanto aparejo si le pluguiere como con su gana. Supiera yo remediar todo esto y lo otro que está dicho y ha pasado despues que estoy en las Indias, si me consintiera la voluntad á procurar por mi bien propio y me fuera honesto. Mas el sostener de la justicia y acrecentar el señorío de sus Altezas fasta agora, me tiene al fondo. Hoy en dia que se falla tanto oro

me since I came to the Indies, if I had had the wish or had thought it decent, to busy myself about my personal interest; but now I find myself shipwrecked, because until now, I have maintained the justice and augmented the territorial dominions of their Highnesses. Now that so much gold is found, these people stop to consider whether they can obtain the greatest quantity of it by theft, or by going to the mines. For one woman they give a hundred castellanos,[11] as for a farm; and this sort of trading is very common, and there are already a great number of merchants who go in search of girls; there are at this moment from nine or ten on sale; they fetch a good price, let their age be what it will. In saying that the commander could not confer immunities, I did what he desired, although I told him, that it was in order to gain time until their Highnesses had received information respecting the country, and had given their orders as to the regulations best calculated to advance their interest. I say that the calumnies of injurious men have done me more harm, than my services have done me good : which is a bad example for the present as well as for the future. I aver, that a great number of men have been to the Indies, who did not deserve

---

hay division en que haya mas ganancia, ir robando ó ir á las minas. Por una muger tambien se fallan cien castellanos como por una labranza, y es mucho en uso, y ha ya fartos mercaderes que andan buscando muchacha: de nueve á diez son agora en precio : de todas edades ha de tener un bueno. Digo que en decir yo que el Comendador no podia dar franquezas que hice yo lo que él deseaba ; bien que yo á él dijese que era para dilatar fasta que sus Altezas toviesen el aviso de la tierra y tornasen á ver y mandar lo que fuese su servicio. Digo que la fuerza del maldecir de desconcertados me ha hecho mas daño que mis servicios fecho provecho : mal ejemplo es por lo presente y por lo futuro. Fago juramento que cantidad de hombres han ido á las Indias que no merescian el agua para con Dios y con el mundo, y agora vuelven allá. Enemistólos á ellos

[11] An ancient gold coin, varying in value under different kings.

baptism in the eyes of God or men, and who are now returning thither. The governor has made every one hostile to me; and it appears, from the manner of his acting, and the plans that he has adopted, that he was already my enemy, and very virulent against me when he arrived; and it is said, that he has been at great expense to obtain this office : but I know nothing about the matter except what I have heard. I never before heard of any one who was commissioned to make an inquiry, assembling the rebels, and taking as evidence against their governor, wretches without faith, and who are unworthy of belief. If their Highnesses would cause a general inquiry to be made throughout the land, I assure you they would be astonished, that the island has not been swallowed up. I believe that you will recollect, that when I was driven by a tempest into the port of Lisbon (having lost my sails), I was falsely accused of having put in thither with the intention of giving the Indies to the sovereign of that country. Since then, their Highnesses have learned the contrary, and that the report was produced by the malice of certain people. Although I am an ignorant man, I do not imagine that any one supposed me so stupid as not to be aware, that even if the Indies had

---

todos conmigo, y él parece, segun se hobo y segun sus formas, que ya lo venia y bien encendido, ó es que se dice que ha gastado mucho por venir á este negocio ; no se dello mas de lo que oyo. Yo nunca oí que el pesquisidor allegase los rebeldes y los tomase por testigos contra aquel que gobierna á ellos y á otros sin fe, ni dignos della. Si sus Altezas mandasen hacer una pesquisa general allí vos digo yo que verian por gran maravilla como la isla no sé funde. Yo creo que se acordará vuestra merced cuando lo tormenta sin velas me echó en Lisbona, que fuí acusado falsamente que habia ido ya allá al Rey para darle las Indias. Despues supieron sus Altezas al contrario, y que todo fue con malicia. Bien que yo sepa poco : no sé quien me tenga por tan torpe que yo no conozca que aunque las Indias fuesen mias, que yo no me pudiera sostener sin ayuda de Príncipe. Si esto es así adónde pudiera yo tener mejor arrimo y seguridad de no ser echado dellas del todo que en el Rey

belonged to me, I could not support myself without the assistance of some prince. Since it is thus, where should I find better support, or more security against expulsion, than in the king and queen our sovereigns? who, from nothing, have raised me to so great an elevation, and who are the greatest princes of the world, on the land and on the sea. These princes know how I have served them, and they uphold my privileges and rewards; and if any one violates them, their Highnesses augment them by ordering great favour to be shown me, and ordain me many honours, as was shown in the affair of Juan Aguado. Yes, as I have said, their Highnesses have received some services from me, and have taken my son into their household, which would not have happened with another prince, because where there is no attachment, all other considerations prove of little weight. If I have now spoken severely of a malicious slander, it is against my will, for it is a subject I would not willingly recall even in my dreams. The governor Bobadilla has maliciously exhibited in open day his character and conduct in this affair; but I will prove without difficulty, that his ignorance, his laziness, and his inordinate cupidity, have frustrated all his undertakings. I have already said that I wrote to him, as well as to the monks, and

---

é Reina nuestros Señores, que de nada me han puesto en tanta honra y son los mas altos Príncipes por la mar y por la tierra del mundo? los cuales tienen que yo les haya servido, é me guardan mis privilegios y mercedes, y si alguien me los quebranta sus Altezas me los acrescientan con aventaja, como se vido en lo de Juan Aguado, y me mandar hacer mucha honra, y como dije ya sus Altezas rescibieron de mí servicios y tienen mis hijos sus criados, lo que en ninguna manera pudiera esto llegar con otro Príncipe, porque adonde no hay amor todo lo otro cesa. Dije yo agora ansi contra un maldecir con malicia y contra mi voluntad, porque es cosa que ni en sueños debiera allegar á memoria, porque las formas y fechos del Comendador Bobadilla, con malicia las quiere alumbrar en esto: mas yo le faré ver con el brazo izquierdo que su poco saber y gran cobardiá con desordenada cudicia le ha fecho caer

I set out almost alone, all our people being with the Adelantado and elsewhere, to remove suspicion; when he heard this, he caused D. Diego to be loaded with irons, and thrown into a caravel; he acted in the same manner towards myself, and towards the Adelantado when he arrived. I have never spoken with him, and to this day he has not permitted any one to hold converse with me, and I make oath that I have no conception for what cause I am made prisoner. His first care was to take the gold that I had, and that without measuring or weighing it, although I was absent; he said he would pay those to whom it was owing, and if I am to believe that which has been reported to me, he reserved to himself the greater part, and sent for strangers to make the bargains. I had put aside certain specimens of this gold, as large as the eggs of a goose or a fowl, and many other sizes, which had been collected in a short space of time, in order to please their Highnesses, and that they might be impressed with the importance of the affair, when they saw a great number of large stones loaded with gold. This gold was the first that, after he had feathered his own nest (which he was in great haste to do), his malice suggested to give away, in order that their Highnesses might have a low

---

en ello. Ya dije como yo le escrebí y á los frailes, y luego partí así como le dije muy solo, porque toda la gente estaba con el Adelantado, y tambien por le quitar de sospecha : él cuando lo supo echó á D. Diego preso en una carabela cargado de fierros, y á mi en llegando fizo otro tanto, y despues al Adelantado cuando vino. Ni le fablé mas á él ni consintió que hasta hoy nadie me haya fablado, y fago juramento que no puedo pensar por qué sea yo preso. La primera diligencia que fizo fue á tomar el oro, el cual hobo sin medida ni peso, é yo absente dijo que queria él pagar dello á la gente, y segun oí para si fizo la primera parte, y enviar por resgate resgatadores nuevos. Deste oro tenia yo apartado ciertas muestras, granos muy gruesos como huevos como de ánsar, de gallina y de pollas, y de otras muchas fechuras, que algunas personas tenian cogido en breve espacio, con que se alegrasen sus Altezas, y por ello comprendiesen el negocio con una cantidad de piedras grandes llenas

opinion of the whole affair: the gold which required melting, diminished at the fire, and a chain, weighing nearly twenty marks, disappeared altogether. I have been yet more concerned respecting the affair of the pearls, that I have not brought them to their Highnesses. In every thing that could add to my annoyance, the governor has always shown himself ready to bestir himself. Thus, as I have said, with six hundred thousand maravedis, I should have paid every one, without occasioning loss to any; and I had more than four millions of tithes and constabulary dues, without touching the gold. He made the most absurd gifts, although I believe he began by awarding them to the stronger party; their Highnesses will be able to ascertain the truth on this subject when they demand the account to be rendered them, especially if I may assist at the examination. He is continually saying, that there is a considerable sum owing, while it is only what I have already reported, and even less. I have been wounded extremely by the thought, that a man should have been sent out to make inquiry into my conduct, who knew, that if he sent home a very aggravated account of the result of his investigation, he would remain at the head of the government. Would

---

de oro. Este fue el primero á se dar con malicia, porque sus Altezas no tuviesen este negocio en algo fasta quel tenga fecho el nido de que se dá buena priesa. El oro que está por fundir mengua al fuego: una cadena que pesaria fasta veinte marcos nunca se ha visto. Yo he sido muy agraviado en esto del oro mas aun que de las perlas, porque no las he traido á sus Altezas. El Comendador en todo lo que le pareció que me dañaria luego fue puesto en obra. Ya dije, con seiscientos mil maravedises pagara á todos sin robar á nadie y habia mas de cuatro cuentos de diezmos y alguacilazgo sin tocar en el oro. Hizo unas larguezas que son de risa, bien que creo que encomenzó en sí la primera parte: allá lo sabran sus Altezas cuando le mandaren tomar cuenta, en especial si yo estuviese á ella. El no face sino decir que se debe gran suma, y es la que yo dije y no tanto. Yo he sido muy mucho agraviado en que se haya enviado pesquisidor sobre mí, que sepa que si la pesquisa

to God, their Highnesses had sent either him or some other
person two years ago, for then I know that I should have had
no cause to fear either scandal or disgrace; they could not
then have taken away my honour, and I could not have been
in the position to have lost it.   God is just, and He will in due
time make known all that has taken place and why it has taken
place.   I am judged in Spain, as a governor who had been sent
to a province, or city, under regular government, and where
the laws could be executed without fear of endangering the
public weal; and in this I receive enormous wrong.   I ought
to be judged as a captain sent from Spain to the Indies, to
conquer a nation numerous and warlike, with customs and
religion altogether different to ours; a people who dwell in
the mountains, without regular habitations for themselves or
for us; and where, by the Divine will, I have subdued another
world to the dominion of the King and Queen, our sovereigns; in consequence of which, Spain, that used to be called
poor, is now the most wealthy of kingdoms.   I ought to be
judged as a captain, who for so many years has borne arms,
never quitting them for an instant.   I ought to be judged
by cavaliers who have themselves won the meed of victory;[12]

---

que él enviare fuere muy grave que él quedará en el gobierno.—
Pluguiera á nuestro Señor que sus Altezas le enviaran á él ó á otro
dos años há, porque sé que yo fuera ya libre de escándalo y de in-
famia, y no se me quitara mi honra ni la perdiera: Dios es justo, y
ha de hacer que se sepa por que y cómo.   Allí me juzgan como
Gobernador que fue á Cecilia ó ciudad ó villa puesta en regimiento
y adonde las leyes se pueden guardar por entero sin temor de que
se pierda todo, y rescibo grande agravio.   Yo debo ser juzgado como
Capitan que fue de España á conquistar fasta las Indias á gente
belicosa y mucha, y de costumbres y seta á nos muy contraria : los
cuales viven por sierras y montes, sin pueblo asentado ni nosotros ;
y adonde por voluntad Divina he puesto só el señorio del Rey é
de la Reina nuestros Señores otro mundo ; y por donde la España,

[12] The old Spaniards used to give the name of "*caballero de conquista*,"
to each of the conquerors, among whom the conquered lands were divided.

by gentlemen indeed, and not by the lawyers; as least so it would have been among the Greeks and Romans, or any modern nation in which exists so much nobility as in Spain; for under any other judgment I receive great injury, because in the Indies there is neither civil right nor judgment seat.

Already the road is opened to the gold and pearls, and it may surely be hoped that precious stones, spices, and a thousand other things, will also be found. Would to God that it were as certain that I should suffer no greater wrongs than I have already experienced, as it is that I would, in the name of our Lord, again undertake my first voyage; and that I would undertake to go to Arabia Felix as far as Mecca, as I have said in the letter that I sent to their Highnesses by Antonio de Torres, in answer to the division of the sea and land between Spain and the Portuguese; and I would go afterwards to the North Pole, as I have said and given in writing to the monastery of the Mejorada.

The tidings of the gold which I said I would give, are, that on Christmas-day, being greatly afflicted and tormented by the wicked Spaniards and the Indians, at the moment

---

que era dicha pobre, es la mas rica. Yo debo ser juzgado como Capitan que de tanto tiempo fasta hoy trae las armas á cuestas sin las dejar una hora, y de Caballeros de conquistas y del uso, y no de letras, salvo si fuesen de Griegos ó de Romanos, ó de otros modernos de que hay tantos y tan nobles en España, ca de otra guisa rescibo grande agravio porque en las Indias no hay pueblo ni asiento. Del oro y perlas ya está abierta la puerta y cantidad de todo piedras preciosas y especería, y de otras mil cosas se pueden esperar firmemente ; y nunca mas mal me viniese como con el nombre de Nuestro Señor le daria el primer viage, así como diera la negociacion del Arabia feliz fasta la Meca, como yo escribí á sus Altezas con Antonio de Torres en la respuesta de la reparticion del mar é tierra con los Portogueses : y despues viniera á lo de polo artico, así como lo dije y dí por escripto en el monesterio de la Mejorada. Las nuevas del oro que yo dije que daria son que dia de Navidad, estando yo muy afligido guerreado de los malos Cristianos y de

of leaving all to save my life if possible, our Lord comforted
me miraculously, saying to me, "Take courage, do not abandon thyself to sadness and fear, I will provide for all; the
seven years, the term of the gold, are not yet passed; and in
this, as in the rest, I will redress thee." I learned, that same
day, that there were twenty-four leagues of land where they
found mines at every step, which appear now to form but
one. Some of the people collected a hundred and twenty castellanos' worth in one day, others ninety; and there have been
those who have gathered the equivalent of nearly two hundred
and fifty castellanos. They consider it a good day's work
when they collect from fifty to seventy, or even from twenty
to fifty, and many continue searching; the mean day's work
is from six to twelve, and those who get less are very dis-
satisfied. It appears that these mines, like all others, do not
yield equally every day; the mines are new, and those who
collect their produce inexperienced. According to the judgment of everybody here, it seems that, if all Spain were to come
over, every individual, however inexpert he might be, would
gain the equivalent of at least one or two castellanos in a day;
and so it is up to the present time. It is certain that any

Indios, en términos de dejar todo y escapar si pudiese la vida; me con-
soló nuestro Señor milagrosamente y dijo: "Esfuerza, no desmayes
ni temas : yo proveeré en todo ; los siete años del término del oro
no son pasados, y en ello y en lo otro te daré remedio." Ese dia
supe que habia ochenta leguas de tierra, y en todo cabo dellas minas ; el parecer agora es que se toda una. Algunos han cogido
ciento y veinte castellanos en un dia, otros noventa, y se ha llegado
fasta docientos y cincuenta. De cincuenta fasta setenta, y otros
muchos de veínte fasta cincuenta, es tenido por buen jornal y muchos lo continuaban : el comun es seis fasta doce, y quien de aquí
abaja no es contento. Parece tambien que estas minas son como
las otras que responden en los dias no igualmente ; las minas son
nuevas y los cogedores. El parecer de todos es que aunque vaya
allá toda Castilla, que por torpe que sea la persona, que no abajará
de un castellano ó dos cada dia, y agora es esto así en fresco. Es

man who has an Indian to work for him, collects as much, but the working of the traffic depends upon the Spaniard. See, now, what discernment was shown by Bobadilla when he gave up everything for nothing, and four millions of tithes without any reason, and even without being asked to do so, and without first giving notice to their Highnesses of his intention; and this is not the only evil which he has caused. I know, assuredly, that the errors which I may have fallen into, have been done without the intention to do wrong, and I think that their Highnesses will believe me when I say so; but I know and see that they show mercy towards those who intentionally do injury to their service. I, however, feel very certain that the day will come when they will treat me much better; since, if I have been in error, it has been innocently and under the force of circumstances, as they will shortly understand beyond all doubt: I, who am their creature, and whose services and usefulness they will every day be more willing to acknowledge. They will weigh all in the balance, even as, according to the Holy Scripture, it will be with the evil and the good at the day of judgment. If, nevertheless, their Highnesses ordain me another judge, which I hope will not be

---

verdad que el que tiene algun indio coge esto, mas el negocio consiste en el Cristiano. Ved que discrecion fue de Bobadilla dar todo por ninguno y cuatro cuentos de diezmos sin causa ni ser requerido, sin primero lo notificar á sus Altezas; y el daño no es este solo. Yo sé que mis yerros no han sido con fin de facer mal, y creo que sus Altezas lo creen así como yo lo digo; y sé y veo que usan de misericordia con quien maliciosamente los desirve. Yo creo y tengo por muy cierto que muy mejor y mas piedad harán conmigo que caí en ello con inocencia y forzosamente, como sabran despues por entero, y el cual soy su fechura, y mirirán á mis servicios, y cognoscerán de cada dia que son muy aventajados. Todo pornan en una balanza, así como nos cuenta la Santa Escritura que será el bien con el mal en el dia del juicio. Si todavía mandan que otro me juzgue, lo cual no espero, y que sea por pesquisa de las Indias, humilmente les suplico que envien allá dos personas de consciencia

the case, and if my examination is to be holden in the Indies, I humbly beseech them to send over two conscientious and respectable persons at my expense, who would readily acknowledge that, at this time, five marks of gold may be found in four hours: be it however as it may, it is highly necessary that their Highnesses should have this matter inquired into. The governor, on his arrival at St. Domingo, took up his abode in my house, and appropriated to himself all that was therein. Well and good; perhaps he was in want of it: but even a pirate does not behave in this manner towards the merchants that he plunders. That which grieved me most was the seizure of my papers, of which I have never been able to recover one; and those that would have been most useful to me in proving my innocence, are precisely those which he has kept most carefully concealed. Behold the just and honest inquisitor! I am told that he does not at all confine himself to the bounds of justice, but that he acts in all things despotically. God our Saviour retains His power and wisdom as of old; and, above all things, He punishes ingratitude.

---

y honrados á mi costa, los cuales fallaran de ligero agora que se halla el oro cinco marcos en cuatro horas, con esto é sin ello es muy necesario que lo provean. El Comendador en llegando á Santo Domingo se aposentó en mi casa ; así como la falló así dió todo por suyo : vaya en buena hora, quizá lo habia menester : cosario nunca tal usó con mercader. De mis escripturas tengo yo mayor queja que así me las haya tomado, que jamas se le pudo sacar una, y aquellas que mas me habian de aprovechar en mi disculpa esas tenia mas ocultas. Ved que justo y honesto pesquisidor. Cosa de cuantas él haya hecho me dicen que haya seido con término de justicia, salvo absolutamente. Dios nuestro Señor está con sus fuerzas y saber, como solia, y castiga en todo cabo, en especial la ingratitud de injurias.

FOURTH VOYAGE OF COLUMBUS.

A Letter written by Don Christopher Columbus, Viceroy and Admiral of the Indies, to the most Christian and mighty Sovereigns, the King and Queen of Spain, in which are described the events of his voyage, and the countries, provinces, cities, rivers and other marvellous matters therein discovered, as well as the places where gold and other substances of great richness and value are to be found.

Most Serene, and very high and mighty Princes, the King and Queen our Sovereigns:—My passage from Cadiz to the Canary occupied four days, and thence to the Indies, from which I wrote, sixteen days. My intention was to expedite my voyage as much as possible while I had good vessels, good crews and stores, and because Jamaica was the place to which I was bound. I wrote this in Dominica: and until now my time has been occupied in gaining information.

Up to the period of my reaching these shores I experienced

CUARTO VIAGE DE COLON.

Que escribió D. Cristóbal Colon, Virey y Almirante de las Indias, á los Cristianísimos y muy poderosos Rey y Reina de España, nuestros Señores, en que les notifica cuanto le ha acontecido en su viage; y las tierras, provincias, ciudades, rios y otras cosas maravillosas, y donde hay minas de oro en mucha cantidad, y otras cosas de gran riqueza y valor.

Serenísimos y muy altos y poderosos Príncipes Rey é Reina, nuestros Señores: De Caliz pasé á Canaria en cuatro dias, y dende á las Indias en diez y seis dias, donde escribia. Mi intencion era dar prisar á mi viage en cuanto yo tenia los navíos buenos, la gente y los bastimentos, y que mi derrota era en la Isla Jamaica ; y en la Isla Dominica escribí esto : fasta allí truje el tiempo á pedir por la boca.

most excellent weather, but the night of my arrival came on
with a dreadful tempest, and the same bad weather has continued ever since.   On reaching the island of Española I
despatched a packet of letters, by which I begged as a favour
that a ship should be supplied me at my own cost in lieu of
one of those that I had brought with me, which had become
un-seaworthy, and could no longer carry sail.   The letters
were taken, and your Highnesses will know if a reply has
been given to them.   For my part I was forbidden to go on
shore; the hearts of my people failed them lest I should take
them further, and they said that if any danger were to befall
them, they should receive no succour, but, on the contrary,
in all probability have some great affront offered them.
Moreover every man had it in his power to tell me that the
new Governor would have the superintendance of the countries that I might acquire.

The tempest was terrible throughout the night, all the
ships were separated, and each one driven to the last extremity, without hope of anything but death; each of them
also looked upon the loss of the rest as a matter of certainty.
What man was ever born, not even excepting Job, who would
not have been ready to die of despair at finding himself as I

Esa noche que alli entré fué con tormenta y grande, y me persiguió
despues siempre. Cuando llegué sobre la Española invié el envoltorio
de cartas, y á pedir por merced un navío por mis dineros, porque otro
que yo llevaba era inavegable y no sufria velas. Las cartas tomaron,
y sabrán si se las dieron la respuesta. Para mí fue mandarme de
parte de ahí, que yo no pasase ni llegase á la tierra: cayó el corazon á la gente que iba conmigo, por temor de los llevar yo lejos,
diciendo que si algun caso de peligro les viniese que no serian re-
mediados allí, antes les sería fecha alguna grande afrenta.   Tambien á quien plugo dijo que el Comendador habia de proveer las
tierras que yo ganase.   La tormenta era terrible, y en aquella noche
me desmembró los navíos: á cada uno llevó por su cabo sin espe-
ranzas, salvo de muerte : cada uno de ellos tenia por cierto que los
otros eran perdidos.   ¿ Quién nasció, sin quitar á Job, que no mu-

then was, in anxious fear for my own safety, and that of my
son, my brother and my friends, and yet refused permission
either to land or to put into harbour on the shores which by
God's mercy I had gained for Spain with so much toil and
danger?

But to return to the ships: although the tempest had so
completely separated them from me as to leave me single,
yet the Lord restored them to me in His own good time. The
ship which we had the greatest fear for, had put out to sea
for safety, and reached the island of Gallega, having lost her
boat and a great part of her provisions, which latter loss indeed all the ships suffered. The vessel in which I was, though
dreadfully buffeted, was saved by our Lord's mercy from any
injury whatever; my brother went in the ship that was un-
sound, and he under God was the cause of its being saved.
With this tempest I struggled on till I reached Jamaica, and
there the sea became calm, but there was a strong current
which carried me as far as the Queen's Garden without seeing
land.   Hence as opportunity afforded I pushed on for terra
firma, in spite of the wind and a fearful contrary current,
against which I contended for sixty days, and during that time

---

riera desesperado? que por mi salvacion y de mi fijo, hermano y
amigos me fuese en tal tiempo defendida la tierra y los puertos que
yo, por la voluntad de Dios, gané á España sudando sangre?   E
torno á los navíos que así me habia llevado la tormenta y dejado á
mí solo.   Deparómelos nuestro Señor cuando le plugo.   El navío
Sospechoso habia echado á la mar, por escapar, fasta la isola la
Gallega; perdió la barca, y todas gran parte de los bastimentos:
en el que yo iba, abalumado á maravilla, nuestro Señor le salvó
que no hubo daño de una paja.   En el Sospechoso iba mi hermano;
y él, despues de Dios, fue su remedio.   E con esta tormenta, así á
gatas, me llegué á Jamaica: allí se mudó de mar alta en calmería
y grande corriente, y me llevó fasta el Jardin de la Reina sin ver
tierra.   De allí, cuando pude, navegué á la tierra firme; adonde
me salió el viento y corriente terrible al opósito: combatí con ellos
sesenta dias, y en fin no le pude ganar mas de setenta leguas.   En

only made seventy leagues.   All this time I was unable to
get into harbour, nor was there any cessation of the tempest,
which was one continuation of rain, thunder and lightning;
indeed it seemed as if it were the end of the world.   I at
length reached the Cape of Gracias a Dios, and after that the
Lord granted me fair wind and tide; this was on the twelfth
of September.   Eighty-eight days did this fearful tempest
continue, during which I was at sea, and saw neither sun nor
stars; my ships lay exposed, with sails torn, and anchors,
rigging, cables, boats and a great quantity of provisions lost;
my people were very weak and humbled in spirit, many of
them promising to lead a religious life, and all making vows
and promising to perform pilgrimages, while some of them
would frequently go to their messmates to make confession.
Other tempests have been experienced, but never of so long
a duration or so fearful as this: many whom we looked upon
as brave men, on several occasions showed considerable tre-
pidation; but the distress of my son who was with me grieved
me to the soul, and the more when I considered his tender
age, for he was but thirteen years old, and he enduring so
much toil for so long a time.   Our Lord, however, gave him

---

todo este tiempo no entré puerto, ni pude, ni me dejó tormenta del
cielo, agua y trombones y relámpagos de continuo, que parecia el
fin del mundo.   Llegué al cabo de Gracias á Dios, y de allí me dió
nuestro Señor próspero el viento y corriente.   Esto fue á doce de Setiembre.   Ochenta y ocho dias habia que no me habia dejado espantable
tormenta, á tanto que no vide el sol ni estrellas por mar ; que á los
navíos tenia yo abiertos, á las velas rotas, y perdidas anclas y jarcia,
cables, con las barcas y muchos bastimentos, la gente muy enferma, y
todos contritos, y muchos con promesa de religion, y no ninguno sin
otros votos y romerías.   Muchas veces habian llegado á se confesar los
unos á los otros.   Otras tormentas se han visto, mas no durár tanto
ni con tanto espanto.   Muchos esmorecieron, harto y hartas veces,
que teniamos por esforzados.   El dolor del fijo que yo tenia allí me
arrancaba el ánima, y mas por verle de tan nueva edad de trece
años en tanta fatiga, y durar en ello tanto : nuestro Señor le dió tal

strength even to enable him to encourage the rest, and he worked as if he had been eighty years at sea, and all this was a consolation to me. I myself had fallen sick, and was many times at the point of death, but from a little cabin that I had caused to be constructed on deck, I directed our course. My brother was in the ship that was in the worst condition and the most exposed to danger; and my grief on this account was the greater that I brought him with me against his will.

Such is my fate, that the twenty years of service through which I have passed with so much toil and danger, have profited me nothing, and at this very day I do not possess a roof in Spain that I can call my own; if I wish to eat or sleep, I have nowhere to go but to the inn or tavern, and most times lack wherewith to pay the bill. Another anxiety wrung my very heartstrings, which was the thought of my son Diego, whom I had left an orphan in Spain, and stripped of the honour and property which were due to him on my account, although I had looked upon it as a certainty, that your Majesties, as just and grateful Princes, would restore it to him in all respects with increase. I reached the land of Cariay, where I stopped to repair my vessels and take in pro-

---

esfuerzo que él avivaba á los otros, y en las obras hacia él como si hubiera navegado ochenta años, y él me consolaba. Yo habia adolescido y llegado fartas veces á la muerte. De una camarilla, que yo mandé facer sobre cubierta, mandaba la via. Mi hermano estaba en el peor navío y mas peligroso. Gran dolor era mio, y mayor porque lo truje contra su grado ; porque por mi dicha, poco me han aprovechado veinte años de servicio que yo he servido con tantos trabajos y peligros, que hoy dia no tengo en Castilla una teja ; si quiero comer ó dormir no tengo, salvo al meson ó taberna, y las mas de las veces falta parar pagar el escote. Otra lastima me arrancaba el corazon por las espaldas, y era de D. Diego mi hijo, que yo dejé en España tan huérfano y desposesionado de mi honra é hacienda ; bien que tenia por cierto que allá como justos y agradecidos Príncipes le restituirian con acrescentamiento en todo. Llegué á tierra

visions, as well as to afford relaxation to the men, who had become very weak. I myself (who, as I said before, had been several times at the point of death) gained information respecting the gold mines of which I was in search, in the province of Ciamba; and two Indians conducted me to Carambaru, where the people (who go naked) wear golden mirrors round their necks, which they will neither sell, give, nor part with for any consideration. They named to me many places on the sea-coast where there were both gold and mines. The last that they mentioned was Veragua, which was five-and-twenty leagues distant from the place where we then were. I started with the intention of visiting all of them, but when I had reached the middle of my journey I learned that there were other mines at so short a distance that they might be reached in two days. I determined on sending to see them. It was on the eve of St. Simon and St. Jude, which was the day fixed for our departure; but that night there arose so violent a storm, that we were forced to go wherever it drove us, and the Indian who was to conduct us to the mines was with us all the time. As I had found every thing true that had been told me in the different places which I had visited,

---

de Cariay, adonde me detuve á remediar los navíos y bastimentos, y dar aliento á la gente, que venia muy enferma. Yo que, como dije, habia llegado muchas veces á la muerte, allí supe de las minas del oro de la provincia de Ciamba, que yo buscaba. Dos indios me llevaron á Carambaru, adonde la gente anda desnuda y al cuello un espejo de oro, mas no le querian vender ni dar á trueque. Nombraronme muchos lugares en la costa de la mar, adonde decian que habia oro y minas ; el postrero era Veragua, y lejos de allí obra de veinte y cinco leguas : partí con intencion de los tentar á todos, y llegado ya el medio supe que habia minas á dos jornadas de andadura : acorde de inviarlas á ver vispera de San Simon y Judas, que habia de ser la partida : en esa noche se levantó tanta mar y viento, que fue necesario de correr hácia adonde él quiso ; é el indio adalid de las minas siempre conmigo. En todos estos lugares, adonde yo habia estado, fallé verdad todo ly que yo habia oido : esto me

I felt satisfied it would be the same with respect to Ciguare, which according to their account, is nine days journey across the country westward: they tell me there is a great quantity of gold there, and that the inhabitants wear coral ornaments on their heads, and very large coral bracelets and anklets, with which article also they adorn and inlay their seats, boxes and tables. They also said that the women there wore necklaces hanging down to their shoulders. All the people agree in the report I now repeat, and their account is so favourable that I should be content with the tithe of the advantages that their description holds out. They are all likewise acquainted with the pepper-plant; according to the account of these people, the inhabitants of Ciguare are accustomed to hold fairs and markets for carrying on their commerce, and they showed me also the mode and form in which they transact their various exchanges; others assert that their ships carry guns, and that the men go clothed and use bows and arrows, swords and cuirasses, and that on shore they have horses which they use in battle, and that they wear rich clothes and have most excellent houses.[1] They also say that the sea sur-

certifico que es así de la provincia de Ciguare, que segun ellos, es descrita nueve jornadas de andadura por tierra al Poniente: allí dicen que hay infinito oro, y que traen corales en las cabezas, manillas á los pies y á los brazos dello, y bien gordas; y dél sillas, arcas, y mesas las guarnecen y enforran. Tambien dijeron que las mugeres de allí traian collares colgados de la cabeza á las espaldas. En esto que yo digo, la gente toda de estos lugares conciertan en ello, y dicen tanto que yo seria contento con el diezmo. Tambien todos conocieron la pimienta. En Ciguare usan tratar en ferias y mercaderías: esta gente así lo cuentan, y me amostraban el modo y forma que tienen en la barata. Otrosi dicen que las naos traen bombardas, arcos y flechas, espadas y corazas, y andan vestidos, y en la tierra hay caballos, y usan la guerra, y traen ricas vestiduras, y tienen buenas cosas. Tambien dicen que la mar boxa á Ci-

[1] The word " cosas" has been replaced on conjecture by " casas," such being the idea entertained in the Italian translation, republished by Morelli.

rounds Ciguare, and that at ten days' journey from thence is
the river Ganges; these lands appear to hold the same relation
to Veragua, as Tortosa to Fontarabia, or Pisa to Venice.
When I left Carambaru and reached the places in its neighbourhood, which I have above-mentioned as being spoken of
by the Indians, I found the customs of the people correspond
with the accounts that had been given of them, except as regarded the golden mirrors: any man who had one of them
would willingly part with it for three hawk's-bells, although
they were equivalent in weight to ten or fifteen ducats. These
people resemble the natives of Española in all their habits.
They have various modes of collecting the gold, none of which
will bear comparison with the plans adopted by the Christians.

All that I have here stated is from hearsay. This, however, I know, that in the year ninety-four I sailed twenty-
four degrees to the westward in nine hours, and there can be
no mistake upon the subject, because there was an eclipse;
the sun was in Libra and the moon in Aries. What I had
learned by the mouth of these people I already knew in detail
from books. Ptolemy thought that he had satisfactorily cor-
rected Marinus, and yet this latter appears to have come very

---

guare, y de allí á diez jornadas es el rio de Gangues.   Parece que
estas tierras estan con Veragua, como Tortosa con Fuenterabía, ó
Pisa con Venecia.   Cuando yo partí de Carambaru y llegué á esos
lugares que dije, fallé la gente en aquel mismo uso, salvo que los
espejos del oro : quien los tenia los daba por tres cascabeles d♂
gabilan por el uno, bien que pesasen diez ó quince ducados de peso.
En todos sus usos son como los de la Española.   El oro cogen con
otras artes, bien que todos son nada con los de los Cristianos.   Esto
que yo he dicho es lo que oyo.   Lo que yo sé es que el año de
noventa y cuatro navegué en veinte y cuatro grados al Poniente
en término de nueve horas, y no pudo haber yerro porque hubo
eclipses : el sol estaba en Libra y la luna en Ariete.   Tambien
esto que yo supe por palabra habialo yo sabido largo por escrito.
Tolomeo creyó de haber bien remedado á Marino, y ahora se falla
su escritura bien propincua al cierto.   Tolomeo asienta Catigara á

near to the truth. Ptolemy places Catigara at a distance of twelve lines to the west of his meridian,[2] which he fixes at two degrees and a third above Cape St. Vincent, in Portugal. Marinus comprises the earth and its limits in fifteen lines, and the same author describes the Indus in Ethiopia as being more than four-and-twenty degrees from the equinoctial line, and now that the Portuguese have sailed there they find it correct. Ptolemy says also that the most southern land is the first boundary, and that it does not go lower down than fifteen degrees and a third. The world is but small; out of seven divisions of it the dry part occupies six, and the seventh is entirely covered by water.[3] Experience has shown it, and I have written it with quotations from the Holy Scripture, in other letters, where I have treated of the situation of the terrestrial paradise, as approved by the Holy Church ; and I say that the world is not so large as vulgar opinion makes it, and that one degree from the equinoctial line measures fifty-six

doce lineas lejos de su Occidente, que él asentró sobre el cabo de San Vicente en Portugal dos grados y un tercio. Marino en quince lineas constituyó la tierra é términos. Marino en Etiopia escribe al Indo la línea equinocial mas de veinte y cuatro grados, y ahora que los Portugueses le navegan le fallan cierto. Tolomeo diz que la tierra mas austral es el plazo primero, y que no abaja mas de quince grados y un tercio. E el mundo es poco : el enjuto de ello es seis partes, la séptima solamente cubierta de agua : la experiencia ya está vista, y la escribí por otras letras y con adornamiento de la Sacra Escriptura, con el sitio del Paraiso terrenal, que la santa Iglesia aprueba : digo que el mundo no es tan grande como dice el vulgo, y que un grado de la equinoccial está cincuenta

[2] The " line" of Columbus implies fifty degrees, or one hour of longitude ; and the twelve lines which describe the distance of Catigara from the meridian of Ptolemy, equal one hundred and eighty degrees. Marinus of Tyre, reckoned two hundred and twenty-five degrees to the same space, which is equivalent to the fifteen degrees of Columbus.

[3] Every one will immediately see the incorrectness of this notion ; as instead of the land bearing a proportion of six-sevenths to the water, the water bears a proportion of about two-thirds to the land.

miles and two-thirds; and this may be proved to a nicety. But I leave this subject, which it is not my intention now to treat upon, but simply to give a narrative of my laborious and painful voyage, although of all my voyages it is the most honourable and advantageous. I have said that on the eve of St. Simon and St. Jude I ran before the wind wherever it took me, without power to resist it; at length I found shelter for ten days from the roughness of the sea and the tempest overhead, and resolved not to attempt to go back to the mines, which I regarded as already in our possession. When I started in pursuance of my voyage it was under a heavy rain, and reaching the harbour of Bastimentos I put in, though much against my will. The storm and a rapid current kept me in for fourteen days, when I again set sail, but not with favourable weather. After I had made fifteen leagues with great exertions, the wind and the current drove me back again with great fury, but in again making for the port which I had quitted, I found on the way another port, which I named Retrete, where I put in for shelter with as much risk as regret, the ships being in sad condition, and my crews and myself exceedingly fatigued. I remained there fifteen days, kept in

---

y seis millas y dos tercios : pero esto se tocará con el dedo. Dejo esto, por cuanto no es mi propósito de fablar en aquella materia, salvo de dar cuenta de mi duro y trabajoso viage, bien que él sea el mas noble y provechoso. Digo que víspera de San Simon y Judas corrí donde el viento me llevaba, sin poder resistirle. En un puerto excusé diez dias de gran fortuna de la mar y del cielo : allí acordé de no volver atras á las minas, y dejelas ya por ganadas. Partí, por seguir mi viage, lloviendo : llegué á puerto de Basti- mentos, adonde entré y no de grado : la tormenta y gran corriente me entró allí catorce dias ; y despues partí, y no con buen tiempo. Cuando yo hube andado quince leguas forzosamente, me reposó atras el viento y corriente con furia : volviendo yo al puerto de donde habia salido fallé en el camino al Retrete, adonde me retruje con harto peligro y enojo y bien fatigado yo y los navíos y la gente : detúveme allí quince dias, que así lo quiso el cruel tiempo ; y

by stress of weather, and when I fancied my troubles were at an end, I found them only begun. It was then that I changed my resolution with respect to proceeding to the mines, and proposed doing something in the interim, until the weather should prove more favourable for my voyage. I had already made four leagues when the storm recommenced, and wearied me to such a degree that I absolutely knew not what to do; my wound reopened, and for nine days my life was despaired of; never was the sea so high, so terrific, and so covered with foam; not only did the wind oppose our proceeding onward, but it also rendered it highly dangerous to run in for any headland, and kept me in that sea which seemed to me as a sea of blood, seething like a cauldron on a mighty fire. Never did the sky look more fearful; during one day and one night it burned like a furnace, and every instant I looked to see if my masts and my sails were not destroyed; for the lightnings flashed with such alarming fury that we all thought the ships must have been consumed. All this time the waters from heaven never ceased descending, not to say that it rained, for it was like a repetition of the deluge. The men were at this time so crushed in spirit that they longed for death as a

---

cuando creí de haber acabado me fallé de comienzo : allí mudé de sentencia de volver á las minas, y hacer algo fasta que me viniese tiempo para mi viage y marear ; y llegado con cuatro leguas revino la tormenta, y me fatigó tanto á tanto que ya no sabia de mi parte. Allí se me refrescó del mal la llaga ; nueve dias anduve perdido sin esperanza de vida : ojos nunca vieron la mar tan alta, fea y hecha espuma. El viento no era para ir adelante, ni daba lugar para correr hácia algun cabo. Allí me detenia en aquella mar fecha sangre, herbiendo como caldera por gran fuego. El cielo jamas fue visto tan espantoso : un dia con la noche ardió como forno ; y así echaba la llama con los rayos, que cada vez miraba yo si me habia llevado los masteles y velas ; venian con tanta furia espantables que todos creiamos que me habian de fundir los navíos. En todo este tiempo jamas cesó agua del cielo, y no para decir que llovia, salvo que resegundaba otro diluvio. La gente estaba ya tan

deliverance from so many martyrdoms. Twice already had the ships suffered loss in boats, anchors, and rigging, and were now lying bare without sails.

When it pleased our Lord, I returned to Puerto Gordo, where I recruited my condition as well as I could. I then once more attempted the voyage towards Veragua, although I was by no means in a fit state to undertake it. The wind and currents were still contrary. I arrived at nearly the same spot as before, and there again the wind and currents still opposed my progress; and once again I was compelled to put into port, not daring to encounter the opposition of Saturn[4] with such a boisterous sea, and on so formidable a coast; for it almost always brings on a tempest or severe weather. This was on Christmas-day, about the hour of mass. Thus, after all these fatigues, I had once more to return to the spot from whence I started; and when the new year had set in, I returned again to my task: but although I had fine weather for my voyage, the ships were no longer in a sailing condition, and my people were either dying or very sick. On the day of the

---

molida que deseaban la muerte para salir de tantos martirios. Los navíos ya habian perdido dos veces las barcas, anclas, cuerdas, y estaban abiertos, sin velas.

Cuando plugo á nuestro Señor volví á Puerto Gordo, adonde reparé lo mejor que pude. Volví otra vez hácia Veragua para mi viage, aunque yo no estuviera para ello. Todavía era el viento y corrientes contrarios. Llegué casi adonde antes, y allí me salió otra vez el viento y corrientes al encuentro, y volví otra vez al puerto, que no osé esperar la oposicion de Saturno con mares tan desbaratados en costa brava, porque las mas de las veces trae tempestad ó fuerte tiempo. Esto fue dia de Navidad en horas de misa. Volví otra vez adonde yo habia salido con harta fatiga; y pasado año nuevo torné á la porfia, que aunque me hiciera buen tiempo para mi viage, ya tenia los navíos innavegables, y la gente muerta y enferma.

[4] Morelli has given this passage thus: "la opposizion de Saturno con Marte." The adjective "desbaratados," however, sufficiently proves this reading to be incorrect. The sentence is here literally translated without any random guessing at the author's meaning.

Epiphany, I reached Veragua in a state of exhaustion; there, by our Lord's goodness, I found a river and a safe harbour, although at the entrance there were only ten spans of water. I succeeded in making an entry, but with great difficulty; and on the following day the storm recommenced, and had I been still on the outside at that time, I should have been unable to enter on account of the reef.   It rained without ceasing until the fourteenth of February, so that I could find no opportunity of penetrating into the interior, nor of recruiting my condition in any respect whatever; and on the twenty-fourth of January, when I considered myself in perfect safety, the river suddenly rose with great violence to a considerable height, breaking my cables and the supports[5] to which they were fastened, and nearly carrying away my ships altogether, which certainly appeared to me to be in greater danger than ever. Our Lord, however, brought a remedy as He has always done. I do not know if any one else ever suffered greater trials.

On the sixth of February, while it was still raining, I sent seventy men on shore to go into the interior, and, at five leagues' distance they found several mines.   The Indians who

---

Dia de la Epifania llegué á Veragua, ya sin aliento : allí me deparó nuestro Señor un rio y seguro puerto, bien que á la entrada no tenia salvo diez palmos de fondo : metíme en él con pena, y el dia siguiente recordó la fortuna : si me falla fuera, no pudiera entrar á causa del banco.   Llovió sin cesar fasta catorce de Febrero, que nunca hubo lugar de entrar en la tierra, ni de me remediar en nada: y estando ya seguro á veinte y cuatro de Enero, de improviso vino el rio muy alto y fuerte ; quebróme las amarras y proeses, y hubo de llevar los navíos, y cierto los ví en mayor peligro que nunca. Remedio nuestro Señor, como siempre hizo.   No sé si hubo otro con mas martirios.

A seis de Febrero, lloviendo, invié setenta hombres la tierra adentro ; y á las cinco leguas fallaron muchas minas : los Indios que iban con ellos los llevaron á un cerro muy alto, y de allí les mos-

[5] The word *proeses* or *proizes*, answers to our English word bollards— or the posts to which cables are fastened.

went with them, conducted them to a very lofty mountain,
and thence showing them the country all round, as far as the
eye could reach, told them there was gold in every part, and
that, towards the west, the mines extended twenty days' journey; they also recounted the names of the towns and villages
where there was more or less of it.   I afterwards learned that
the cacique Quibian, who had lent these Indians, had ordered
them to show the distant mines, and which belonged to an
enemy of his; but that in his own territory, one man
might, if he would, collect in ten days a great abundance of
gold.[6] I bring with me some Indians, his servants, who
are witnesses of this fact.   The boats went up to the spot
where the dwellings of these people are situated; and, after
four hours, my brother returned with the guides, all of them
bringing back gold which they had collected at that place.
The gold must be abundant, and of good quality, for none of
these men had ever seen mines before; very many of them
had never seen pure gold, and most of them were seamen and
lads.   Having building materials in abundance, I established
a settlement, and made many presents to Quibian, which is

traron hácia toda parte cuanto los ojos alcanzaban, diciendo que en
toda parte habia oro, y que hácia el Poniente llegaban las minas
veinte jornadas, y nombraban las villas y lugares, y adonde habia
de ello mas ó menos.   Despues supe yo que el Quibian que habia
dado estos Indios, les habia mandado que fuesen á mostrar las minas
lejos y de otro su contrario ; y que adentro de su pueblo cogian,
cuando, el queria, un hombre en diez dias una mozada de oro : los
indios sus criados y testigos de esto traigo conmigo.   Adonde él
tiene el pueblo llegan las barcas. Volvió mi hermano con esa gente,
y todos con oro que habian cogido en cuatro horas que fué allá á la
estada.   Lacalidad es grande, porque ninguno de estos jamas habia
visto minas, y los mas oro.   Los mas eran gente de la mar, y casí
todos grumetes.   Yo tenia mucho aparejo para edificar y muchos
bastimentos,   Asenté pueblo, y dí muchas dádivas al Quibian, que

6 " Mozada," probably " mojada," a moistening, and hence the idea of a
" shower," or " great abundance" of gold.

the name they gave to the lord of the country. I plainly saw that harmony would not last long, for the natives are of a very rough disposition, and the Spaniards very encroaching; and, moreover, I had taken possession of land belonging to Quibian. When he saw what we did, and found the traffic increasing, he resolved upon burning the houses, and putting us all to death; but his project did not succeed, for we took him prisoner, together with his wives, his children, and his servants. His captivity, it is true, lasted but a short time, for he eluded the custody of a trustworthy man, into whose charge he had been given, with a guard of men; and his sons escaped from a ship, in which they had been placed under the special charge of the master.

In the month of January the mouth of the river was entirely closed up, and in April the vessels were so eaten with the teredo, that they could scarcely be kept above water. At this time the river forced a channel for itself, by which I managed, with great difficulty, to extricate three of them after I had unloaded them. The boats were then sent back into the river for water and salt, but the sea became so high and furious, that it afforded them no chance of exit; upon which

---

así llaman al Señor de la tierra ; y bien sabia que no habia de durar la concordia : ellos muy rústicos y nuestra gente muy importunos, y me aposesionaba en su término : despues que él vido las cosas fechas y el tráfago tan vivo acordó de las quemar y matarnos á todos : muy al reves salió su propósito : quedó preso él, mugeres y fijos y criados ; bien que su prision duró poco : el Quibian se fuyo á un hombre honrado, á quien se habia entregado con guarda de hombres ; é los hijos se fueron á un Maestre de navío, a quien se dieron en él á buen recaudo.

En Enero se habia cerrado la boca del rio. En Abril los navíos estaban todos comidos de broma, y no los podia sostener sobre agua. En este tiempo hizo el rio una canal, por donde saqué tres dellos vacios con gran pena. Las barcas volvieron adentro por la sal y agua. La mar se puso alta y fea, y no les dejó salir fuera : los Indios fueron muchos y juntos y las combatieron, y en fin los ma-

the Indians collected themselves together in great numbers, and made an attack upon the boats, and at length massacred the men. My brother, and all the rest of our people, were in a ship which remained inside; I was alone, outside, upon that dangerous coast, suffering from a severe fever and worn with fatigue. All hope of escape was gone. I toiled up to the highest part of the ship, and, with a quivering voice and fast-falling tears, I called upon your Highnesses' war-captains from each point of the compass to come to my succour, but there was no reply. At length, groaning with exhaustion, I fell asleep, and heard a compassionate voice address me thus:—
" O fool, and slow to believe and to serve thy God, the God of all! what did He do more for Moses, or for David his servant, than He has done for thee? From thine infancy He has kept thee under His constant and watchful care. When He saw thee arrived at an age which suited His designs respecting thee, He brought wonderful renown to thy name throughout all the land. He gave thee for thine own the Indies, which form so rich a portion of the world, and thou hast divided them as it pleased thee, for He gave thee power to do so. He gave thee also the keys of those barriers of the ocean sea

---

taron. Mi hermano y la otra gente toda estaban en un navío que quedo adentro : yo muy solo de fuera en tan brava costa, con fuerte fiebre, en tanta fatiga : la esperanza de escapar era muerta : subi así trabajando lo mas alto, llamando á voz temerosa, llorando y muy aprisa, los maestros de la guerra de vuestras Altezas, á todos cuatro los vientos, por socorro ; mas nunca me respondieron. Cansado, me'dormecí gimiendo : una voz muy piadosa oí, diciendo : "¡ O estulto y tardo á creer y servir á tu Dios, Dios de todos ! ¿ Que hizo él mas por Moysés ó por David su siervo ? Desque nasciste, siempre él tuvo de tí muy grande cargo. Cuando te vido en edad de que él fue contento, maravillosamente hizo sonar tu nombre en la tierra. Las Indias, que son parte del mundo, tan ricas, te las dió por tuyas : tu las repartiste adonde te plugo, y te dió poder para ello. De los atamientos de la mar océana, que estaban cerrados con cadenas tan fuertes, te dió las llaves ; y fuiste obedescido en

which were closed with such mighty chains; and thou wast
obeyed through many lands, and gained an honourable fame
throughout Christendom. What more did the Most High do
for the people of Israel, when he brought them out of Egypt?
or for David, whom from a shepherd He made to be king in
Judea? Turn to Him, and acknowledge thine error—His
mercy is infinite. Thine old age shall not prevent thee from
accomplishing any great undertaking. He holds under His
sway the greatest possessions. Abraham had exceeded a hundred years of age when he begat Isaac; nor was Sarah young.
Thou criest out for uncertain help: answer, who has afflicted
thee so much and so often, God or the world? The privileges promised by God, He never fails in bestowing; nor does
He ever declare, after a service has been rendered Him, that
such was not agreeable with His intention, or that He had
regarded the matter in another light; nor does he inflict suffering, in order to give effect to the manifestation of His
power. His acts answer to His words; and it is His custom
to perform all his promises with interest. Thus I have told
you what the Creator has done for thee, and what He does
for all men. Even now He partially shows thee the reward of so many toils and dangers incurred by thee in the
service of others."

---

tantas tierras. y de los cristianos cobraste tan honrada fama. ¿ Qué
hizo el mas alto pueblo de Israel cuando le sacó de Egipto? ¿ Ni
por David, que de pastor hizo Rey en Judea? Tórnate á él, y co-
noce ya tu yerro : su misericordia es infinita : tu vejez no impedirá
á toda cosa grande : muchas heredades tiene él grandísimas.
Abrahan pasaba de cien años cuando engendró á Isaac, ¿ ni Sara
era moza? Tú llamas por socorro incierto : responde, ¿ quién te
ha afligido tanto y tantas veces, Dios ó el mundo? Los privilegios
y promesas que dá Dios, no las quebranta, ni dice despues de haber
recibido el servicio, que su intencion no era esta, y que se entiende
de otra manera, ni dá martirios por dar color á la fuerza : él vá al
pie de la letra : todo lo que él promete cumple con acrescentamiento :
¿ esto es uso? Dicho tengo lo que tu Criador ha fecho por tí y

I heard all this, as it were, in a trance; but I had no answer
to give in definite words, and could but weep for my errors.
He who spoke to me, whoever it was, concluded by saying,—
" Fear not, but trust; all these tribulations are recorded on
marble, and not without cause." I arose as soon as I could;
and at the end of nine days there came fine weather, but not
sufficiently so to allow of drawing the vessels out of the river.
I collected the men who were on land, and, in fact, all of them
that I could, because there were not enough to admit of one
party remaining on shore while another stayed on board to
work the vessel. I myself should have remained with my men
to defend the buildings I had constructed, had your Highnesses been cognizant of all the facts; but the doubt whether
any ships would ever reach the spot where we were, as well
as the thought, that while I was asking for succour I might
bring succour to myself, made me decide upon leaving. I
departed, in the name of the Holy Trinity, on Easter night,
with the ships rotten, worn out, and eaten into holes. One
of them I left at Belen, with a supply of necessaries; I did
the same at Belpuerto. I then had only two left, and they in

---

hace con todos. Ahora medio muestra el galardon de estos afanes y
peligros que has pasado sirviendo á otros."

Yo así amortecido oí todo ; mas no tuve yo respuesta á palabras
tan ciertas, salvo llorar por mis yerros. Acabó él de fablar, quien
quiera que fuese, diciendo : " No temas, confia : todas estas tribu-
laciones estan escritas en piedra mármol, y no sin causa."

Levantéme cuando pude : y al cabo de nueve dias hizo bonanza,
mas no para sacar navíos del rio. Recogí la gente que estaba en
tierra, y todo el resto que puede, porque no bastaban para quedar
y para navegar los navíos. Puedara yo á sostener el pueblo con
todos, si vuestras Altezas supieran de ello. El temor que nunca
aportarian alli navíos me determinó á esto, y la cuenta que cuando
se haya de proveer de socorro se proveerá de todo. Partí en nombre de la Santísima Trinidad, la noche de Pascua, con los navíos
podridos, abrumados, todos fechos agujeros. Allí en Belen dejé
uno, y hartas cosas. En Belpuerto hice otro tanto. No me que-

the same state as the others. I was without boats or provisions, and in this condition I had to cross seven thousand miles of sea; or, as an alternative, to die on the passage with my son, my brother, and so many of my people. Let those who are accustomed to slander and aspersion, ask, while they sit in security at home, " Why didst thou not do so and so under such circumstances?" I wish that they were now embarked in this voyage. I verily believe that another journey of another kind awaits them, if there is any reliance to be placed upon our holy faith.

On the thirteenth of May I reached the province of Mago, which is contiguous to that of Cathay, and thence I started for the island of Española. I sailed two days with a good wind, after which it became contrary. The route that I followed called forth all my care to avoid the numerous islands, that I might not be stranded on the shoals that lie in their neighbourhood. The sea was very tempestuous, and I was driven backward under bare poles. I anchored at an island, where I lost, at one stroke, three anchors; and, at midnight, when the weather was such that the world appeared to be coming to an end, the cables of the other ship broke, and

---

daron salvo dos en el estado de los otros, y sin barcas y bastimentos, por haber de pasar siete mil millas de mar y de agua, ó morir en la via con figo y hermano y tanta gente. Respondan ahora los que suelen tachar y reprender, diciendo allá de en salvo : ¿ por qué no haciades esto allí ? Los quisiera yo en esta jornada. Yo bien creo que otra de otro saber los aguarda : á nuestra fe es ninguna. Llegué á trece de Mayo en la provincia de Mago, que parte con aquella del Catayo, y de allí partí para la Española : navegué dos dias con buen tiempo, y despues fue contrario. El camino que yo llevaba era para desechar tanto número de islas, por no me embarazar en los bajos de ellas. La mar brava me hizo fuerza, y hube volver atras sin velas: surgí á una isla adonde de golpe perdí tres anclas, y á la media noche, que parecia que el mundo se ensolvia, se rompieron las amarras al otro navío, y vino sobre mí, que fue maravilla como no nos acabamos de se hacer rajas : el ancla, de

it came down upon my vessel with such force that it was a wonder we were not dashed to pieces; the single anchor that remained to me, was, next to the Lord, our only preservation. After six days, when the weather became calm, I resumed my journey, having already lost all my tackle; my ships were pierced with worm-holes, like a bee-hive, and the crew entirely dispersed and down-hearted. I reached the island a little beyond the point at which I first arrived at it, and there I stayed to recover myself from the effects of the storm; but I afterwards put into a much safer port in the same island. After eight days I put to sea again, and reached Jamaica by the end of June; but always beating against contrary winds, and with the ships in the worst possible condition. With three pumps, and the use of pots and kettles, we could scarcely clear the water that came into the ship, there being no remedy but this for the mischief done by the ship-worm. I steered in such a manner as to come as near as possible to Española, from which we were twenty-eight leagues distant, but I afterwards wished I had not done so, for the other ship which was half under water was obliged to run in for a port. I determined on keeping the sea in spite of the weather, and

---

forma que me quedó, fue ella despues de nuestro Señor, quien me sostuvo. Al cabo de seis dias, que ya era bonanza, volví á mi camino : asi ya perdido del todo de aparejos y con los navíos horadados de gusanos mas que un panal de abejas, y la gente tan acobardada y perdida, pasé algo adelante de donde yo habia llegado denantes : allí me torné á reposar atras la fortuna : paré en la misma isla en mas seguro puerto : al cabo de ocho dias torné á la via y llegué á Jamaica en fin de Junio, siempre con vientos punteros, y los navíos en peor estado : con tres bombas, tinas y calderas no podian con toda la gente vencer el agua que entraba en el navío, ni para este mal de broma hay otra cura. Cometí el camino para me acercar á lo mas cercar de la Española, que son veinte y ocho leguas, y no quisiera haber comenzado. El otro navío corrió á buscar puerto casi anegado. Yo porfié la vuelta de la mar con tormenta. El navio se me anegó, que milagrosamente

my vessel was on the very point of sinking when our Lord miraculously brought us upon land. Who will believe what I now write? I assert that in this letter I have not related one hundredth part of the wonderful events that occurred in this voyage; those who were with the Admiral[7] can bear witness to it. If your Highnesses would be graciously pleased to send to my help a ship of above sixty-four tons, with two hundred quintals of biscuits and other provisions, there would then be sufficient to carry me and my crew from Española to Spain. I have already said that there are not twenty-eight leagues between Jamaica and Española; and I should not have gone there, even if the ships had been in a fit condition for so doing, because your Highnesses ordered me not to land there. God knows if this command has proved of any service. I send this letter by means of and by the hands of Indians; it will be a miracle if it reaches its destination.

This is the account I have to give of my voyage. The men who accompanied me were a hundred and fifty in number, among whom were many calculated for pilots and good sailors, but none of them can explain whither I went nor whence I

---

me trujo nuestro Señor á tierra. ¿ Quién creyera lo que yo aquí escribo ? Digo que de cien partes no he dicho la una en esta letra. Los que fueron con el Almirante lo atestigüen. Si place á vuestras Altezas de me hacer merced de socorro un navío que pase de sesenta y cuatro, con ducientos quintales de bizcocho y algun otro bastimento, abastará para me llevar á mí y á esta gente á España de la Española. En Jamaica ya dije que no hay veinte y ocho leguas á la Española. No fuera yo, bien que los navíos estuvieran para ello. Ya dije que me fue mandado de parte de vuestras Altezas que no llegase á alla. Si este mandar ha aprovechado, Dios lo sabe. Esta carta invio por via y mano de Indios : grande maravilla será si allá llega. De mi viage digo : que fueron ciento y cincuenta personas conmigo, en que hay hartos suficientes para pilotos y grandes marineros : ninguno puede dar razon cierta por donde fuí yo ni vine : la razon es muy presta. Yo partí de sobre

[7] Of course he here speaks of himself.

came ; the reason is very simple : I started from a point above the port of Brazil, and while I was in Española, the storm prevented me from following my intended route, for I was obliged to go wherever the wind drove me ; at the same time I fell very sick, and there was no one who had navigated in these parts before. However, after some days, the wind and sea became tranquil, and the storm was succeeded by a calm, but accompanied with rapid currents. I put into harbour at an island called Isla de las Bocas, and then steered for terra firma ; but it is impossible to give a correct account of all our movements, because I was carried away by the current so many days without seeing land. I ascertained, however, by the compass and by observation, that I moved parallel with the coast of terra firma. No one could tell under what part of the heavens we were, nor at what period I bent my course for the island of Española. The pilots thought we had come to the island of St. John, whereas it was the land of Mango, four hundred leagues to the westward of where they said. Let them answer and say if they know where Veragua is situated. I assert that they can give no other account than that they went to lands, where there was an abundance of gold, and this they

---

el puerto del Brasil : en la Española no me dejó la tormenta ir al camino que yo queria : fue por fuerza correr adonde el veinto quiso. En ese dia caí yo muy enfermo : ninguno habia navegado hácia aquella parte : cesó el viento y mar dende á ciertos dias, y se mudó la tormenta en calmería y grandes corrientes. Fuí á aportar á una isla que se dijo de las Bocas, y de allí a Tierra firme. Ninguno puede dar cuenta verdadera de esto, porque no hay razon que abaste ; porque fue ir con corriente sin ver tierra tanto número de dias. Seguí la costa de la Tierra firme : esta se asentó con compás y arte. Ninguno hay que diga debajo cuál parte del cielo ó cuándo yo partí de ella para venir á la Española. Los pilotos creian venir á parar á la isla de Sanct-Joan ; y fue en tierra de Mango, cuatrocientas leguas mas al Poniente de adonde decian. Respondan, si saben, adónde es el sitio de Veragua. Digo que no pueden dar otra razon ni cuenta, salvo que fueron á unas tierras

can certify surely enough; but they do not know the way to
return thither for such a purpose; they would be obliged to
go on a voyage of discovery as much as if they had never
been there before.   There is a mode of reckoning derived
from astronomy which is sure and safe, and a sufficient guide
to any one who understands it.   This resembles a prophetic
vision.   The Indian vessels do not sail except with the wind
abaft, but this is not because they are badly built or clumsy,
but because the strong currents in those parts, together with
the wind, render it impossible to sail with the bowline,[8] for in
one day they would lose as much way as they might have
made in seven; for the same reason 1 could make no use of
caravels, even though they were Portuguese latteens.   This
is the cause that they do not sail unless with a regular
breeze, and they will sometimes stay in harbour waiting for
this seven or eight months at a time; nor is this anything
wonderful, for the same very often occurs in Spain.   The
nation of which Pope Pius writes has now been found, judging
at least by the situation and other evidences, excepting the
horses with the saddles and poitrels and bridles of gold; but

---

adonde hay mucho oro, y certificarle ; mas para volver á ella el
camino tienen ignoto : seria necesario para ir á ella descubrirla
como de primero.   Una cuenta hay y razon de astrología, y cierta :
quien la entiende esto le abasta.   A vision profética se asemeja
esto.   Las naos de las Indias, sino navegan, salvo á popa, no es
por la mala fechura, ni por ser fuertes ; las grandes corrientes que
allí vienen ; juntamente con el viento hacen que nadie porfie con
bolina, porque en un dia perderian lo que hubiesen ganado en
siete ; ni saco carabela aunque sea latina portuguesa.   Esta razon
hace que no naveguen, salvo con colla, y por esperarle se detienen
á las veces seis y ocho meses en puerto ; ni es maravilla, pues, que
en España muchas veces acaece otro tanto.   La gente de que
escribe Papa Pio, segun el sitio y señas, se ha hallado, mas no los

[8] Bow-lines are ropes employed to keep the windward edges of the principal sails steady, and are only used when the wind is so unfavourable that
the sails must be all braced sideways, or close hauled to the wind.

this is not to be wondered at, for the lands on the sea-coast
are only inhabited by fishermen, and moreover I made no
stay there, because I was in haste to proceed on my voyage.
In Cariay and the neighbouring country there are great en-
chanters of a very fearful character.   They would have given
the world to prevent my remaining there an hour.   When I
arrived they sent me immediately two girls very showily
dressed; the eldest could not be more than eleven years of age
and the other seven, and both exhibited so much immodesty,
that more could not be expected from public women ; they
carried concealed about them a magic powder ; when they
came I gave them some articles to dress themselves out with,
and directly sent them back to the shore.   I saw here, built on
a mountain, a sepulchre as large as a house, and elaborately
sculptured, the body lay uncovered and with the face down-
wards ; they also spoke to me of other very excellent works
of art.   There are many species of animals both small and
large, and very different from those of our country.   I had
at the time two pigs, and an Irish dog who was always in
great dread of them.   An archer had wounded an animal like
an ape, except that it was larger, and had a face like a

---

caballos, pretales y frenos de oro, ni es maravilla, porque allí las
tierras de la costa de la mar no requieren, salvo pescadores, ni yo
me detuve porque andaba á prisa.   En Cariay, y en esas tierras de
su comarca, son grandes fechiceros y muy medrosos.   Dieran el
mundo porque no me detuviera allí una hora.   Cuando llegué allí
luego me inviaron dos muchachas muy ataviadas : la mas vieja no
seria de once años y la otra de siete ; ambas con tanta desenvoltura
que no serian mas unas putas : traian polvos de hechizos escondi-
dos: en llegando las mandé adornar de nuestras cosas y las invié
luego á tierra : allí vide una sepultura en el monte, grande como
una casa y labrada, y el cuerpo descubierto y mirando en ella.   De
otras artes me dijeron y mas excelentes.   Animalias menudas y
grandes hay hartas y muy diversas de las nuestras.   Dos puercos
hube yo en presente, y un perro de Irlanda no osaba esperarlos.
Un ballestero habia herido una animalia, que se parece á gato paul,

man's; the arrow had pierced it from the neck to the tail, which made it so fierce that they were obliged to disable it by cutting off one of its arms and a leg; one of the pigs grew wild on seeing this and fled; upon which I ordered the *begare* (as the inhabitants called him) to be thrown to the pig, and though the animal was nearly dead, and the arrow had passed quite through his body, yet he threw his tail round the snout of the pig, and then holding him firmly, seized him by the nape of the neck with his remaining hand, as if he were engaged with an enemy. This action was so novel and so extraordinary, that I have thought it worth while to describe it here. There is a great variety of animals here, but they all die of the barra.[9] I saw some very large fowls (the feathers of which resemble wool), lions, stags, fallow-deer and birds.

When we were so harassed with our troubles at sea, some of our men imagined that we were under the influence of sorcery, and even to this day entertain the same notion. Some of the people whom I discovered were cannibals, as was evidenced by the brutality of their countenances. They

---

salvo que es mucho mas grande, y el rostro de hombre: teniale atravesado con una saeta desde los pechos á la cola, y porque era feroz le hubo de cortar un brazo y una pierna: el puerco en viéndole se le encrespó y se fue huyendo: yo cuando esto ví mandé echarle *begare*, que así se llama adonde estaba: en llegando á él, así estando á la muerte y la saeta siempre en el cuerpo, le echó la cola por el hocico y se la amarró muy fuerte, y con la mano que le quedaba le arrebató por el copete como á enemigo. El auto tan nuevo y hermosa montería me hizo escribir esto. De muchas maneras de animalias se hubo, mas todas mueren de barra. Gallinas muy grandes y la pluma como lana vide hartas. Leones, ciervos, corzos, otro tanto, y así aves.

Cuando yo andaba por aquella mar en fatiga en algunos se puso heregía que estabamos enfechizados, que hoy dia estan en ello. Otra gente fallé que comian hombres: la desformidad de su gesto lo dice.

[9] This is a malady undefined in any dictionary.

say that there are great mines of copper in the country, of which they make hatchets and other elaborate articles both cast and soldered; they also make of it forges, with all the apparatus of the goldsmith, and crucibles. The inhabitants go clothed; and in that province I saw some large sheets of cotton very elaborately and cleverly worked, and others very delicately pencilled in colours. They tell me that more inland towards Cathay they have them interwoven with gold. For want of an interpreter we were able to learn but very little respecting these countries, or what they contain. Although the country is very thickly peopled, yet each nation has a very different language; indeed so much so, that they can no more understand each other than we understand the Arabs. I think, however, that this applies to the barbarians on the sea-coast, and not to the people who live more inland. When I discovered the Indies, I said that they composed the richest lordship in the world; I spoke of gold and pearls and precious stones, of spices and the traffic that might be carried on in them; and because all these things were not forthcoming at once I was abused. This punishment causes me to refrain from relating anything but what the natives tell me. One

---

Allí dicen qué hay grandes mineros de cobre : hachas de ello, otras cosas labradas, fundidas, soldadas hube, y fraguas con todo su aparejo de platero y los crisoles. Allí van vestidos; y en aquella provincia vide sábanas grandes de algodon, labradas de muy sotiles labores; otras pintadas muy sútilmente á colores con pinceles. Dicen que en la tierra adentro hácia el Catayo las hay tejidas de oro. De todas estas tierras y de lo que hay en ellas, faila de lengua, no se saben tan presto. Los pueblos, bien que sean espesos, cada uno tiene diferenciada lengua, y es en tanto que no se entienden los unos con los otros, mas que nos con los de Arabia. Yo creo que esto sea en esta gente salvage de la costa de lar mar, mas no en la tierra dentro. Cuando yo descubrí las Indias dije que eran el mayor señorío rico que hay en el mundo. Yo dije del oro, perlas, piedras preciosas, especerías, con los tratos y ferias, y porque no pareció todo tan presto fuí escandalizado. Este castigo me hace agora que no diga salvo lo que yo oigo de los naturales de la tierra.

thing I can venture upon stating, because there are so many witnesses of it, viz., that in this land of Veragua I saw more signs of gold in the two first days than I saw in Española during four years, and that there is not a more fertile or better cultivated country in all the world, nor one whose inhabitants are more timid; added to which there is a good harbour, a beautiful river, and the whole place is capable of being easily put into a state of defence. All this tends to the security of the Christians and the permanency of their sovereignty, while it affords the hope of great increase and honour to the Christian religion; moreover the road hither will be as short as that to Española, because there is a certainty of a fair wind for the passage. Your Highnesses are as much lords of this country as of Xerez or Toledo, and your ships that may come here will do so with the same freedom as if they were going to your own royal palace. From hence they will obtain gold, and whereas if they should wish to become masters of the products of other lands, they will have to take them by force or retire empty-handed; in this country they will simply have to trust their persons in the hands of a savage.

I have already explained my reason for refraining to treat

De una oso decir, porque hay tantos testigos, y es que yo vide en esta tierra de Veragua mayor señal de oro en dos dias primeros que en la Española en cuatro años, y que las tierras de la comarca no pueden ser mas fermosas, ni mas labradas, ni la gente mas cobarde, y buen puerto, y fermoso rio, y defensible al mundo. Todo esto es seguridad de los cristianos y certeza de señorío, con grande esperanza de la honra y acrescentamiento de la religion cristiana ; y el camino allí será tan breve como á la Española, porque ha de ser con viento. Tan señores son vuestras Altezas de esto como de Jerez ó Toledo : sus navíos que fueren allí van á su casa. De allí sacarán oro : en otras tierras, para haber de lo que hay en ellas, conviene que se lo lleven, ó se volverán vacíos ; y en la tierra es necesario que fien sus personas de un salvage. Del otro que yo dejo de decir, ya dije por qué me encerré : no digo así, ni que yo

of other subjects respecting which I might speak. I do not state as certain, nor do I confirm even the sixth part of all that I have said or written, nor do I pretend to be at the fountain-head of the information. The Genoese, Venetians, and all other nations that possess pearls, precious stones, and other articles of value, take them to the ends of the world to exchange them for gold. Gold is the most precious of all commodities ; gold constitutes treasure, and he who possesses it has all he needs in this world, as also the means of rescuing souls from purgatory, and restoring them to the enjoyment of paradise. They say that when one of the lords of the country of Veragua dies, they bury all the gold he possessed with his body. There were brought to Solomon at one journey six hundred and sixty-six quintals of gold, besides what the merchants and sailors brought, and that which was paid in Arabia. Of this gold he made two hundred lances and three hundred shields, and the entablature which was above them was also of gold, and ornamented with precious stones : many other things he made likewise of gold, and a great number of vessels of great size, which he enriched with precious stones. This is related by Josephus in his Chronicle de " Antiquita-

---

me afime en el tres doble en todo lo que yo haya jamas dicho ni escrito, y que yo estó á la fuente. Genoveses, Venecianos y toda gente que tenga perlas, piedras preciosas y otras cosas de valor, todos las llevan hasta el cabo del mundo para las trocar, convertir en oro : el oro es excelentísimo : del oro se hace, tesoro, y con él, quien lo tiene, hace cuanto quiere en el mundo, y llega á que echa las animas al paraiso. Los señores de aquellas tierras de la comarca Veragua cuando mueren entierran el oro que tienen con el cuerpo, así lo dicen : á Salomon llevaron de un camino seiscientos y sesenta y seis quintales de oro, allende lo que llevaron los mercaderes y marineros, y allende lo que se pagó en Arabia. De este oro fizo doscientas lanzas y trescientos escudos, y fizo el tablado que habia de estar arriba dellas de oro y adornado de piedras preciosas, y fizo otras muchas cosas de oro, y vasos muchas y muy grandes y ricos de piedras preciosas. Josefo en su corónica de Antiquitatibus

tibus"; mention is also made of it in the Chronicles and in
the Book of Kings. Josephus thinks that this gold was found
in the Aurea; if it were so, I contend that these mines of
the Aurea are identical with those of Veragua, which, as I
have said before, extends westward twenty days' journey, at
an equal distance from the Pole and the Line. Solomon
bought all of it,—gold, precious stones, and silver,—but your
Majesties need only send to seek them to have them at your
pleasure. David, in his will, left three thousand quintals of
Indian gold to Solomon, to assist in building the Temple;
and, according to Josephus, it came from these lands. Jerusalem and Mount Sion are to be rebuilt by the hands of
Christians, as God has declared by the mouth of His prophet
in the fourteenth Psalm. The Abbé Joaquim said that he
who should do this was to come from Spain; Saint Jerome
showed the holy woman the way to accomplish it; and the
emperor of China has, some time since, sent for wise men to
instruct him in the faith of Christ. Who will offer himself
for this work? Should any one do so, I pledge myself, in
the name of God, to convey him safely thither, provided the

---

lo escribe. En el Paralipomenon y en el libro de los Reyes se
cuenta de esto. Josefo quiere que este oro se hobiese en la Aurea:
si así fuese digo que aquellas minas de la Aurea son unas y se con-
vienen con estas de Veragua, que como yo dije arriba se alarga al
Poniente veinte jornadas, y son en una distancia lejos del polo y de
la línea. Salomon compró todo aquello, oro, piedras y plata, é
allí le pueden mandar á coger si les aplace. David en su testamento dejó tres mil quintales de oro de las Indías á Salomon para
ayuda de edificar el templo, y segun Josefo era el destas mismas
tierras. Hierusalem y el monte Sion ha de ser reedificado por
mano de cristianos : quien ha de ser, Dios por boca del Profeta en
el décimo cuarto salmo lo dice. El Abad Joaquin dijo que este
habia de salir de España. San Gerónimo á la santa muger le mostró el camino para ello. El Emperador del Catayo ha dias que
mandó sabios que le enseñen en la fé de Cristo. ¿ Quién será que
se ofrezca á esto ? Si nuestro Señor me lleva á España, yo me

Lord permits me to return to Spain.   The people who have
sailed with me have passed through incredible toil and danger,
and I beseech your Highnesses, since they are poor, to pay
them promptly, and to be gracious to each of them according
to their respective merits; for I can safely assert, that to my
belief they are the bearers of the best news that ever were
carried to Spain.   With respect to the gold which belongs to
Quibian, the cacique of Veragua, and other chiefs in the
neighbouring country, although it appears by the accounts
we have received of it to be very abundant, I do not think it
would be well or desirable, on the part of your Highnesses,
to take possession of it in the way of plunder; by fair dealing,
scandal and disrepute will be avoided, and all the gold will
thus reach your Highnesses' treasury without the loss of a
grain.   With one month of fair weather I shall complete my
voyage.   As I was deficient in ships, I did not persist in de-
laying my course; but in everything that concerns your
Highnesses' service, I trust in Him who made me, and I hope
also that my health will be re-established.   I think your
Highnesses will remember that I had intended to build some
ships in a new manner, but the shortness of the time did not

---

obligo de llevarle, con el nombre de Dios, en salvo.   Esta gente
que vino conmigo han pasado increibles peligros y trabajos.   Suplico á V. A., porque son pobres, que les mande pagar luego, y les
haga mercedes á cada uno segun la calidad de la persona, que les
certifico que á mi creer les traen las mejores nuevas que nunca
fueron á España.   El oro que tiene el Quibian de Veragua y los
otros de la comarca, bien que segun informacion él sea mucho, no
me paresció bien ni servicio de vuestras Altezas de se le tomar por
via de robo : la buena orden evitará escándalo y mala fama, y hará
que todo ello venga· al tesoro, que no quede un grano.   Con un
mes de buen tiempo yo acabára todo mi viage : por falta de los
navíos no porfié á esperarle para tornar á ello, y para toda cosa de
su servicio espero en aquel que me hizo, y estaré bueno.   Yo creo
que V. A. se acordará que yo queria mandar hacer los navíos de
nueva manera : la brevedad del tiempo no dió lugar á ello, y cierto

permit it. I had certainly foreseen how things would be. I think more of this opening for commerce, and of the lordship over such extensive mines, than of all that has been done in the Indies. This is not a child to be left to the care of a step-mother.

I never think of Española, and Paria, and the other countries, without shedding tears. I thought that what had occurred there would have been an example for others ; on the contrary, these settlements are now in a languid state, although not dead, and the malady is incurable, or at least very extensive : let him who brought the evil come now and cure it, if he knows the remedy, or how to apply it; but when a disturbance is on foot, every one is ready to take the lead. It used to be the custom to give thanks and promotion to him who placed his person in jeopardy ; but there is no justice in allowing the man who opposed this undertaking, to enjoy the fruits of it with his children. Those who left the Indies, avoiding the toils consequent upon the enterprise, and speaking evil of it and me, have since returned with official appointments,—such is the case now in Veragua : it is an evil example, and profitless both as regards the business in which we

---

yo habia caido en lo que cumplia. Yo tengo en mas esta negociacion y minas con esta escala y señorio, que todo lo otro que está hecho en las Indias. No es este hijo para dar á criar á madrastra. De la Española, de Paria y de las otras tierras no me acuerdo de ellas, que yo no llore : creia yo que el ejemplo dellas hobiese de ser por estotras al contrario : ellas estan boca á yuso, bien que no mueren : la enfermedad es incurable, ó muy larga : quien las llegó á esto venga agora con el remedio si puede ó sabe : al descomponer cada uno es maestro. Las gracias y acrescentamiento siempre fue uso de las dar á quien puso su cuerpo á peligro. No es razon que quien ha sido tan contrario á esta negociacion le goce ni sus fijos. Los que se fueron de las Indias fuyendo los trabajos y diciendo mal dellas y de mí, volvieron con cargos : así se ordenaba agora en Veragua : malo ejemplo, y sin provecho del negocio y para la justicia del mundo : este temor con otros casos hartos que yo veia

are embarked, and as respects the general maintenance of justice. The fear of this, with other sufficient considerations, which I clearly foresaw, caused me to beg your Highnesses, previously to my coming to discover these islands and terra firma, to grant me permission to govern in your royal name. Your Highnesses granted my request; and it was a privilege and treaty granted under the royal seal and oath, by which I was nominated viceroy, and admiral, and governor-general of all: and your Highnesses limited the extent of my government to a hundred leagues beyond the Azores and Cape Verde islands, by a line passing from one pole to the other, and gave me ample power over all that I might discover beyond this line; all which is more fully described in the official document.

But the most important affair of all, and that which cries most loudly for redress, remains inexplicable to this moment. For seven years was I at your royal court, where every one to whom the enterprise was mentioned, treated it as ridiculous; but now there is not a man, down to the very tailors, who does not beg to be allowed to become a discoverer. There is reason to believe, that they make the voyage only for plunder, and

---

claro, me hizo suplicar á V. A. antes que yo viniese á descubrir esas islas y tierra firme, que me las dejasen gobernar en su Real nombre : plúgoles : fue por privilegio y asiento, y con sello y juramento, y me intitularon de Viso-Rey y Almirante y Gobernador general de todo ; y aseñalaron el término sobre las islas de los Azores cien leguas, y aquellas del Cabo Verde por línea que pasa de polo á polo, y desto y de todo que mas se descubriese, y me dieron poder largo : la escritura á mas largamente lo dice. El otro negocio famosísimo está con los brazos abiertos llamando : extrangero ha sido fasta ahora. Siete años estuve yo en su Real corte, que á cuantos se fabló de esta empresa todos á una dijeron que era burla : agora fasta los sastres suplican por descubrir. Es de creer que van á saltear, y se les otorga, que cobran con mucho perjuicio de mi honra y tanto daño del negocio. Bueno es de dar á Dios lo suyo y acetar lo que le pertenece. Esta es justa sentencia, y de

that they are permitted to do so, to the great disparagement
of my honour, and the detriment of the undertaking itself.
It is right to give God His due,—and to receive that which
belongs to one's self. This is a just sentiment, and proceeds
from just feelings. The lands in this part of the world, which
are now under your Highnesses' sway, are richer and more extensive than those of any other Christian power, and yet, after
that I had, by the Divine will, placed them under your high
and royal sovereignty, and was on the point of bringing your
majesties into the receipt of a very great and unexpected
revenue; and while I was waiting for ships, to convey me in
safety, and with a heart full of joy, to your royal presence,
victoriously to announce the news of the gold that I had discovered, I was arrested and thrown, with my two brothers,
loaded with irons, into a ship, stripped, and very ill-treated,
without being allowed any appeal to justice. Who could
believe, that a poor foreigner would have risen against your
Highnesses, in such a place, without any motive or argument
on his side; without even the assistance of any other prince
upon which to rely; but on the contrary, amongst your own
vassals and natural subjects, and with my sons staying at your
royal court? I was twenty-eight years old when I came into
your Highnesses' service, and now I have not a hair upon me

---

justo. Las tierras que acá obedecen á V. A. son mas que todas las
otras de cristianos y ricas. Despues que yo, por voluntad divina,
las hube puestas debajo de su Real y alto señorío, y en filo para
haber grandísima renta, de improviso, esperando navíos para venir
á su alto conspecto con victoria y grandes nuevas del oro, muy seguro y alegre, fuí preso y echado con dos hermanos en un navío,
cargados de fierros, desnudo en cuerpo, con muy mal tratamiento,
sin ser llamado ni vencido por justicia: ¿ quién creerá que un pobre extrangero se hobiese de alzar en tal lugar contra V. A. sin
causa, ni sin brazo de otro Príncipe, y estando solo entre sus vasallos y naturales, y teniendo todos mis fijos en su Real corte ? Yo
vine á servir de veinte y ocho años, y agora no tengo cabello en mi
persona que no sea cano y el cuerpo enfermo, y gastado cuanto me

that is not grey; my body is infirm, and all that was left to me, as well as to my brothers, has been taken away and sold, even to the frock that I wore, to my great dishonour.   I cannot but believe that this was done without your royal permission.   The restitution of my honour, the reparation of my losses, and the punishment of those who have inflicted them, will redound to the honour of your royal character; a similar punishment also is due to those who plundered me of my pearls, and who have brought a disparagement upon the privileges of my admiralty.   Great and unexampled will be the glory and fame of your Highnesses, if you do this; and the memory of your Highnesses, as just and grateful sovereigns, will survive as a bright example to Spain in future ages.   The honest devotedness I have always shown to your majesties' service, and the so unmerited outrage with which it has been repaid, will not allow my soul to keep silence, however much I may wish it : I implore your Highnesses to forgive my complaints.   I am indeed in as ruined a condition as I have related ; hitherto I have wept over others ;—may Heaven now have mercy upon me, and may the earth weep for me.   With regard to temporal things, I have not even a blanca for an offering ; and in spiritual things, I have ceased here in the

---

quedó de aquellos, y me fue tomado y vendido, y á mis hermanos fasta el sayo, sin ser oido ni visto, con gran deshonor mio.   Es de creer que esto no se hizo por su Real mandado.   La restitucion de mi honra y daños, y el castigo en quien lo fizo, fará sonar su Real nobleza ; y otro tanto en quien me robó las perlas, y de quien ha fecho daño en ese almirantado.   Grandísima virtud, fama con ejemplo será si hacen esto, y quedará á la España gloriosa memoria con la de vuestras Altezas de agradecidos y justos Príncipes.   La intencion tan sana que yo siempre tuve al servicio de vuestras Altezas, y la afrenta tan desigual, no da lugar al anima que calle, bien que yo quiera : suplico á vuestras Altezas me perdonen.   Yo estoy tan perdido como dije : yo he llorado fasta aquí á otros : haya misericordia agora el Cielo, y llore por mi la tierra.   En el temporal no tengo solamente una blanca para el oferta : en el

Indies from observing the prescribed forms of religion. Solitary in my trouble, sick, and in daily expectation of death, surrounded by millions of hostile savages full of cruelty, and thus separated from the blessed sacraments of our holy Church, how will my soul be forgotten if it be separated from the body in this foreign land ? Weep for me, whoever has charity, truth, and justice ! I did not come out on this voyage to gain to myself honour or wealth ; this is a certain fact, for at that time all hope of such a thing was dead. I do not lie when I say, that I went to your Highnesses with honest purpose of heart, and sincere zeal in your cause. I humbly beseech your Highnesses, that if it please God to rescue me from this place, you will graciously sanction my pilgrimage to Rome and other holy places. May the Holy Trinity protect your Highnesses' lives, and add to the prosperity of your exalted position.

Done in the Indies, in the island of Jamaica, on the seventh of July, in the year one thousand five hundred and three.

---

espiritual he parado aquí en las Indias de la forma que está dicho : aislado en esta pena, enfermo, aguardando cada dia por la muerte, y cercado de un cuento de salvages y llenos de crueldad y enemigos nuestros, y tan apartado de los Santos Sacramentos de la Santa Iglesia, que se olvidará desta anima si se aparta acá del cuerpo. Llore por mí quien tiene caridad, verdad y justicia. Yo no vine este viage á navegar por ganar honra ni hacienda : esto es cierto, porque estaba ya la esperanza de todo en ella muerta. Yo vine á V. A. con sana intencion y buen zelo, y no miento. Suplico humildemente á V. A. que si á Dios place de me sacar de aquí, que haya por bien mi ida á Roma y otros romerías. Cuya vida y alto estado la Santa Trinidad guarde y acresciente. Fecha en las Indias en la Isla de Jamaica á siete de Julio de mil quinientos y tres años.

AN ACCOUNT

*Given by Diego Mendez in his will of some events that oc-
curred in the last voyage of the Admiral Don Christopher Columbus.*

DIEGO MENDEZ, citizen of St. Domingo, in the island of
Española, being in the city of Valladolid, where the Court
of their most sacred Majesties was at the time staying,
made his will on the sixth day of June, of the year one
thousand five hundred and thirty-six, before Fernando
Perez, their Majesties' scrivener, and notary public in that
their Court, and in all their Kingdoms and Lordships, the
witnesses to the same being Diego de Arana, Juan Diez
Miranda de la Cuadra, Martin de Orduña, Lucas Fernandez,
Alonzo de Angulo, Francisco de Hinojosa and Diego de
Aguilar, all servants of my Lady the Vicequeen of the Indies.[10]
And among other chapters of the said will there is one which
runs literally as follows ·—

RELACION

*Hecha por Diego Mendez, de algunos acontecimientos del último viage
del Almirante Don Cristóbal Colon.*

DIEGO Mendez, vecino de la ciudad de Santo Domingo de la Isla
Española, hallándose en la villa de Valladolid, donde á la sazon estaba la Corte de SS. MM., otorgó testamento en seis dias del mes
de Junio del año de mil quinientos treinta y seis, por testimonio de
Fernan Perez, escribano de SS. MM., y su notario público en la su
Corte y en todos los sus Reinos y Señoríos ; siendo testigos al otor-
gamiento Diego de Arana, Juan Diez Miranda de la Cuadra, Martin de Orduña, Lucas Fernandez, Alonso de Angulo, Francísco de
Hinojosa y Diego de Aguilar, todos criados de la Señora Vireina
de las Indias.   Y entre otros capítulos del mencionado testamento
hay uno que á la letra dice así.

[10] Donna Maria de Toledo, widow of Diego Columbus.

Clause of the will, Item : The very illustrious gentlemen, the admiral Don Christopher Columbus, of glorious memory, and his son the admiral Don Diego Columbus, and his grandson the admiral Don Louis, (whom may God long preserve), and through them my Lady, the Vicequeen, as tutress and guardian of the latter, are in debt to me, for many and great services that I have rendered them, in as much as I have spent and worn out the best part of my life even to its close in their service ; especially did I serve the admiral Don Christopher, going with his Lordship to the discovery of the islands and terra firma, and often putting myself in danger of death in order to save his life and the lives of those who were with him, more particularly when we were shut in at the mouth of the river Belen or Yebra, through the violence of the sea and the winds which drove up the sand, and raised such a mountain of it as to close up the entrance of the port. His Lordship being there greatly afflicted, a multitude of Indians collected together on shore to burn the ships, and kill us all, pretending that they were going to make war against other Indians of the province of Cabrara Aurira,

---

Cláusula del testamento. Item: Los muy ilustres Señores, el Almirante D. Cristobal Colon, de gloriosa memoria, y su hijo el Almirante D. Diego Colon, y su nieto el Almirante D. Luis, á quien Dios dé largos dias de vida, y por ellos la Vireina mi Señora, como su tutriz y curadora, me son en cargo de muchos y grandes servicios que yo les hice, en que consumí y gasté todo lo mejor de mi vida hasta acaballa en su servicio ; especialmente serví al gran Almirante D. Cristóbal andando con su Señoria descubriendo Islas y Tierra firme, en que puse muchas veces mi persona á peligro de muerte por salvar su vida y de los que con él iban y estaban ; mayormente cuando se nos cerró el puerto del rio de Belen ó Yebra donde estábamos con la fuerza de las tempestades de la mar y de los vientos que acarrearon y amontonaron la arena en cantidad con que cegaron la entrada del puerto. Y estando su Señoria allí muy congojado, juntóse gran multitud de Indios de la tierra para venir á quemarnos los navios y matarnos á todos, con color que decian que

with whom they were at enmity. Though many of them passed by that port where our ships were lying, none of the fleet took notice of the matter except myself, who went to the admiral and said to him, "Sir, these people who have passed by in order of battle, say that they go to unite themselves with the people of Veragua, to attack the people of Cobrara Aurira: I do not believe it, but, on the contrary, I think that they are collected together to burn our ships and kill all of us,"—as in fact was the case. The admiral then asked me what were the best means of preventing this, and I proposed to his Lordship that I should go with a boat along the coast towards Veragua, to see where the royal court sat. I had not proceeded on my errand half a league when I found nearly a thousand men of war with great stores of provisions of all kinds, and I went on shore alone amongst them, leaving my boat at sea; I then spoke with them, making them understand me as well as I could, and offered to go with them to the battle with that armed boat; but this they strongly refused, saying there was no need of such a thing. After that I returned to the boat, and

---

iban á hacer guerra a otros Indios de las provincias de Cobrava Aurira, con quien tenian guerra: y como pasaron muchos dellos por aquel puerto en que teniamos nosotros las naos, ninguno de la armada caia en el negocio sino yo, que fuí al Almirante y le dije: " Señor, estas gentes que por aquí han pasado en orden de guerra dicen que se han de juntar con los de Veragoa para ir contra los de Cobrava Aurira: yo no lo creo sino el contrario, y es que se juntan para quemarnos los navíos y matarnos á todos," como de hecho lo era. Y diciendome el Almirante cómo se remediaria, yo dije á su Señoría que saldria con una barca é iría por la costa hácia Veragoa, para ver donde asentaban el real. Y no hube andado media legua cuando halle al pie de mil hombres de guerra con muchas vituallas y brevages, y salté en tierra solo entre ellos, dejando mi barca puesta en flota: y hablé con ellos segun pude entender, y ofrecíme que queria ir con ellos á la guerra con aquella barca armada, y ellos se escusaron reciamente diciendo que no le habian

remained there in sight of them all that night, so that they
could not go to the ships to burn or destroy them, according
to their previous arrangements, without my seeing them,
upon which they changed their plan, and on that same night
they all returned to Veragua. I then went back to the
ships, and related all this to his Lordship, who thought no
little of what I had done, and upon his consulting me as to
the best manner of proceeding so as clearly to ascertain what
was the intention of the people, I offered to go to them with
one single companion; and this task I undertook, though
more certain of death than of life in the result.

After journeying along the beach up to the river of Veragua, I found two canoes of strange Indians, who related
to me more in detail, that these people were indeed collected
together to burn our ships and kill us all, and that they had
forsaken their purpose in consequence of the boat which had
come up to the spot, but that they intended to return after
two days to make the attempt once more. I then asked them
to carry me in their canoes to the upper part of the river,
offering to remunerate them if they would do so; but they

---

menester : y como yo me volviese á la barca y estuviese allí á
vista dellos toda la noche, vieron que no podian ir á las naos para
quemallas y destruillas, segun tenian acordado, sin que yo lo viese,
y mudaron propósito ; y aquella noche se volvieron todos á Veragoa, y yo me volví á las naos y hice relacion de todo á su Señoría,
é no lo tuvo en poco. Y platicando conmigo sobrello sobre que
manera se ternia para saber claramente el intento de aquella gente,
yo me ofrecí de ir allá con un solo compañero, y lo puse por obra,
yendo mas cierto de la muerte que de la vida : y habiendo cami-
nado por la playa hasta el rio de Veragoa hallé dos canoas de Indios extrangeros que me contaron muy á la clara como aquellas
gentes iban para quemar las naos y matarnos á todos, y que lo dejaron de hacer por la barca que allí sobrevino, y questaban todavia
de propósito de volver á hacello dende á dos dias, é yo les rogué
que me llevasen en sus canoas el rio arriba, y que gelo pa-
garia ; y ellos se escusaban aconsejándome que en ninguna manera

excused themselves, and advised me by no means to go, for that both myself and my companion would certainly be killed.   At length, in spite of their advice, I prevailed upon them to take me in their canoes to the upper part of the river, until I reached the villages of the Indians, whom I had found in order of battle.   They, however, would not, at first, allow me to go to the principal residence of the cacique, till I pretended that I was come as a surgeon to cure him of a wound that he had in his leg; then, after making them some presents, they suffered me to proceed to the seat of royalty, which was situated on the top of a hillock, surmounted by a plain, with a large square surrounded by three hundred heads of the enemies he had slain in battle. When I had passed through the square, and reached the royal house, there was a great clamour of women and children at the gate, who ran into the palace screaming.   Upon this, one of the chief's sons came out in a high passion, uttering angry words in his own language; and, laying hands upon me, with one push he thrust me far away from him.   In order to appease him, I told him that I was come to cure the wound in

---

fuese, porque fuese cierto que en llegando me matarian á mí y al compañero que llevaba.   E sin embargo de sus consejos hice que me llevasen en sus canaos el rio arriba hasta llegar á los pueblos de los Indios, los cuales hallé todos puestos en orden de guerra, que no me querian dejar ir al asiento principal del Cacique ; y yo fingiendo que le iba á curar como cirujano de una llaga que tenia en una pierna, y con dádivas que les dí me dejaron ir hasta el asiento Real, que estaba encima de un cerro llano con una plaza grande, rodeada de trescientas cabezas de muertos que habian ellos muerto en una batalla : y como yo hubiese pasado toda la plaza y llegado á la Casa Real hubo grande alboroto de mugeres y muchachos que estaban á la puerta, que entraron gritando dentro en el palacio. Y salió de él un hijo del Señor muy enojado diciendo palabras recias en su lenguage, é puso las manos en mí y de un empellon me desvió muy lejos de sí : diciéndole yo por amansarle como iba á curar á su padre de la pierna, y mostrándole cierto unguento que

his father's leg, and showed him an ointment that I had brought for that purpose; but he replied, that on no account whatever should I go in to the place where his father was. When I saw that I had no chance of appeasing him in that way, I took out a comb, a pair of scissors, and a mirror, and caused Escobar, my companion, to comb my hair and then cut it off. When the Indian, and those who were with him, saw this, they stood in astonishment; upon which I prevailed on him to suffer his own hair to be combed and cut by Escobar; I then made him a present of the scissors, with the comb and the mirror, and thus he became appeased. After this, I begged him to allow some food to be brought, which was soon done, and we ate and drank in love and good fellowship, like very good friends. I then left him and returned to the ships, and related all this to my lord the Admiral, who was not a little pleased when he heard all these circumstances, and the things that had happened to me. He ordered a large stock of provisions to be put into the ships, and into certain straw houses that we had built there, with a view that I should remain, with some of the men, to examine and ascertain the secrets of the country. The next morning his lordship called me to ask my

---

para ello llevaba, dijo que en ninguna manera habia de entrar donde estaba su padre. Y visto por mí que por aquella via no podia amansarle, saqué un peine y unas tijeras y un espejo, y hice que Escobar mi compañero me peinase y cortase el cabello. Lo cual visto por él y por los que allí estaban quedaban espantados ; y yo entonces hice que Escobar le peinase á él y le cortase el cabello con las tijeras, y díselas y el peine y el espejo, y con esto se amansó ; y yo pedí que trajesen algo de comer, y luego lo trajeron, y comimos y bebimos en amor y compaña, y quedamos amigos ; y despedime dél y vine á las naos, y hice relacion de todo esto al Almirante mi Señor, el cual no poco holgó en saber todas estas circunstancias y cosas acaecidas por mi ; y mandó poner gran recabdo en las naos y en ciertas casas de paja, que teniamos hechas allí en la playa con intencion que habia yo de quedar allí con cierta gente para calar y saber los secretos de la tierra.

advice as to what ought to be done : my opinion was that we
ought to seize that chief and all his captains; because, when
they were taken, great numbers of the people would submit.
His lordship was of the same opinion.   I then submitted the
stratagem and plan by which this might be accomplished; and
his lordship ordered that the Adelantado, his brother, and I,
accompanied by eighty men, should go to put it into execution.   We went, and our Lord gave us such good fortune,
that we took the cacique and most of his captains, his wives,
sons, and grandsons, with all the princes of his race; but in
sending them to the ships, thus captured, the cacique extri-
cated himself from the too slight grasp of the man who held
him, a circumstance which afterwards caused us much injury.
At this moment it pleased God to cause it to rain very heavily,
occasioning a great flood, by which the mouth of the harbour
was opened and the Admiral enabled to draw out the ships to
sea, in order to proceed to Spain; I, meanwhile, remaining
on land as Accountant of his Highness, with seventy men, and
the greater part of the provisions of biscuit, wine, oil, and
vinegar being left with me.

Otro dia de mañana su Señoría me llamó para tomar parecer conmigo de lo que sobre ello se debia hacer, y fue mi parecer que de-
biamos prender aquel Señor y todos sus Capitanes, porque presos
aquellos se sojuzgaria la gente menuda ; y su Señoria fue del mismo parecer : é yo di el ardid y la manera con que se debia hacer,
y su Señoría mandó que el Señor Adelantado, su hermano, y yo
con él fuesemos á poner en efecto lo sobredicho con ochenta hombres.
Y fuimos, y diónos Nuestro Señor tan buena dicha que prendimos
el Cacique y los mas de sus Capitanes y mugeres y hijos y nietos
con todos los principales de su generacion ; y enviándolos á las
naos ansí presos, soltóse el Cacique al que le llevaba por su mal
recabdo, el cual despues nos hizo mucho daño.   En este instante
plugó á Dios que llovió mucho, y con la gran avenida abriósenos
el puerto, y el Almirante sacó los navíos á la mar para venirse á
Castilla, quedando yo en tierra para haber de quedar en ella por
Contador de su Alteza con setenta hombres, y quedábame allí la

The Admiral had scarcely got to sea (while I stayed on shore with about twenty men, for the others had gone to assist the Admiral), when suddenly more than four hundred natives, armed with cross-bows and arrows, came down upon me, extending themselves along the face of the mountain; they then gave a shriek, then another, and another, and these repeated cries, by the goodness of God, gave me opportunity to prepare for the engagement. While I was on the shore among the huts which we had built, and they were collected on the mountain at about the distance of an arrow's flight, they began to shoot their arrows and hurl their darts, as if they had been attacking a bull. The arrows and cross-bow shots came down thick as hail, and some of the Indians then separated themselves from the rest, for the purpose of attacking us with clubs; none of them, however, returned, for with our swords we cut off their arms and legs, and killed them on the spot; upon which the rest took such fright, that they fled, after having killed in the contest seven out of twenty of our men; while, on their side, they lost nine or ten of those who advanced the most boldly towards us. This contest lasted three long

---

mayor parte de los mantenimientos de bizcocho y vino y aceite y vinagre.

Acabado de salir el Almirante á la mar, y quedando yo en tierra con obra de veinte hombres porque los otros se habian salido con el Almirante á despedir, subitamente sobrevino sobre mi mucha gente de la tierra, que serian mas de cuatrocientos hombres armados con sus varas y flechas y tiraderos, y tendierónse por el monte en haz y dieron una grita y otra y luego otra, con las cuales plugo á Dios me apercibieron á la pelea y defensa de ellos : y estando yo en la playa entre los bohios que tenia hechos, y ellos en el monte á trecho de tiro de dardo, comenzaron á flechar y á garrochar como quien agarrocha toro, y eran las flechas y tiraderas tantas y tan continuas como granizo ; y algunos dellos se desmandaban para venirnos á dar con las machadasnas ; pero ninguno dellos volvian porque quedaban allí cortados brazos y piernas y muertos á espada : de lo cual cobraron tanto miedo que se retiraron atras, habiéndonos muerto siete

hours, and our Lord gave us the victory in a marvellous manner, we being so few and they so numerous. After this fight was over, the captain, Diego Tristan, came with the boats from the ships to ascend the river, in order to take in water for the voyage; and, notwithstanding I advised and warned him not to go, he would not trust me, but, against my wish, went up the river with two boats and twelve men; upon which the natives attacked him, and killed him and all the men that he took with him, except one who escaped by swimming, and from whom we heard the news. The Indians then took the boats and broke them to pieces, which caused us great vexation; for the Admiral was at sea with his ships without boats, while we were on shore deprived of the means of going to him. Besides this, the Indians came continually to assail us; every instant playing trumpets and kettle-drums, and uttering loud cries in the belief that they had conquered us. The only means of defending ourselves against these people, were two very good brass falconets and plenty of powder and ball, with

---

hombres en la pelea de veinte que eramos, y de ellos murieron diez ó nueve de los que se venian á nosotros mas arriscados. Duró esta pelea tres horas grandes, y Nuestro Señor nos dió la vitoria milagrosamente, siendo nosotros tan poquitos y ellos tanta muchedumbre.

Acabada esta pelea vino de las naos el Capitan Diego Tristan con las barcas para subir el rio arriba á tomar agua para su viage; y no embargante que yo le aconsejé y amonesté que no subiese el rio arriba no me quiso creer, y contra mi grado subió con las dos barcas y doce hombres el rio arriba, donde le toparon aquella gente y pelearon con él, y le mataron á él y todos los que llevaba, que no escapó sino uno á nado que trujo la nueva; y tomaron las barcas y hiciéronlas pedazos, de que quedamos en gran fatiga, ansí el Almirante en la mar con sus naos sin barcas como nosotros en tierra sin tener con que poder ir á él. Y á todo esto no cesaban los Indios de venirnos á cometer cada rato tañiendo bocinas y atabales, y dando alaridos pensando que nos tenian vencidos.   El remedio contra esta gente que teniamos eran dos tiros falconetes

which we frightened them so that they did not dare approach us. This lasted for the space of four days, during which time I caused several bags to be made out of the sails of one of the vessels which we had remaining on shore, and into them I put all our biscuit. I then took two canoes, and secured them together with sticks across the tops, and, after loading them with the biscuit, the pipes of wine, and the oil and vinegar, I fastened them together with a rope, and had them towed along the sea while it was calm, so that in seven trips we contrived to get all of it to the ships, and the people were also carried over by few at a time. Meanwhile I remained with five men to the last, and at night I put to sea with the last boatful. The Admiral thought very highly of this conduct of mine, and did not content himself with embracing me and kissing me on the cheeks for having performed so great a service, but asked me take the captaincy of the ship *Capitana*, with the government of all the crew, and, in fact, of the entire voyage; which I accepted in order to oblige him, as it was a service of great responsibility.

---

de fruslera, muy buenos, y mucha pólvora y pelotas con que los ojeábamos que no osaban llegar á nosotros. Y esto duró por espacio de cuatro dias, en los cuales yo hice cosar muchos costales de las velas de una nao que nos quedaba, y en aquellos puse todo el bizcocho que teniamos, y tomé dos canoas y até la una con la otra parejas, con unos palos atravesados por encima, y en estos cargué el bizcocho todo en viages, y las pipas de vino y azeite y vinagre atadas en una guindaleja y á jorno por la mar, tirando por ellas las canoas, abonanzando la mar, en siete caminos que hicieron lo llevaron todo á las naos, y la gente que conmigo estaba poco á poco la llevaron, é yo quedé con cinco hombres á la postre siendo de noche, y en la postrera barcada me embarqué : lo cual el Almirante tuvo á mucho, y no se hartaba de me abrazar y besar en los carrillos por tan gran servicio como allí le hice, y me rogó tomase la capitanía de la nao Capitana y el regimiento de toda la gente y del viage, lo cual yo acepté por le hacer servicio en ello por ser, como era, cosa de gran trabajo.

On the last day of April, in the year fifteen hundred and three we left Veragua, with three ships, intending to make our passage homeward to Spain, but as the ships were all pierced and eaten by the teredo, we could not keep them above water; we abandoned one of them after we had proceeded thirty leagues; the two which remained were even in a worse condition than that,[11] so that all the hands were not sufficient with the use of pumps and kettles and pans to draw off the water that came through the holes made by the worms. In this state with the utmost toil and danger we sailed for thirty-five days, thinking to reach Spain, and at the end of this time we arrived at the lowest point of the island of Cuba, at the province of Homo, where the city of Trinidad now stands, so that we were three hundred leagues further from Spain than when we left Veragua for the purpose of proceeding thither; and this, as I have said, with the vessels in very bad condition, unfit to encounter the sea, and our provisions nearly gone. It pleased God that we were enabled to reach the island of Jamaica, where we drove the two ships on shore, and

---

Postrero de Abril de mil quinientos y tres partimos de Veragoa con tres navíos, pensando venir la vuelta de Castilla : y como los navíos estaban todos abujerados y comidos de gusanos no los podiamos tener sobre agua ; y andadas treinta leguas dejamos el uno, quedándonos otros dos peor acondicionados que aquel, que toda la gente no bastaba con las bombas y calderas y vasijas á sacar el agua que se nos entraba por los abujeros de la broma : y de esta manera, no sin grandísimo trabajo y peligro, pensando venir á Castilla navegamos treinta y cinco dias, y en cabo dellos llegamos á la isla de Cuba á lo mas bajo della, á la provincia de Homo, allá donde agora está el pueblo de la Trinidad ; de manera que estábamos mas lejos de Castilla trescientas leguas que cuando partimos de Veragoa para ir á ella ; y como digo los navíos mal acondicionados, innavegables, y las vituallas que se nos acababan. Plugo á Dios Nuestro Señor que pudimos llegar á la isla de Jamaica, donde zabordamos

[11] Possibly the ship they abandoned was inferior in size, or in some other respect.

made of them two cabins thatched with straw, in which we took up our dwelling, not however without considerable danger from the natives, who were not yet subdued, and who might easily set fire to our habitation in the night, in spite of the greatest watchfulness. It was there that I gave out the last ration of biscuit and wine; I then took a sword in my hand, three men only accompanying me, and advanced into the island; for no one else dared go to seek food for the admiral and those who were with him. It pleased God that I found some people who were very gentle and did us no harm, but received us cheerfully, and gave us food with hearty good will. I then made a stipulation with the Indians who lived in a village called Aguacadiba, and with their cacique, that they should make cassava bread, and that they should hunt and fish to supply the admiral every day with a sufficient quantity of provisions, which they were to bring to the ships, where I promised there should be a person ready to pay them in blue beads, combs and knives, hawks-bells and fish-hooks, and other such articles which we had with us for that purpose. With this understanding I despatched one of the

---

los dos navíos en tierra, y hicimos de ellos dos casas pajizas, en que estabamos no sin gran peligro de la gente de aquella isla, que no estaba domada ni conquistada, nos pusiesen fuego de noche, que fácilmente lo podian hacer por mas que nosotros velabamos.

Aquí acabe de dar la postrera racion de bizcocho y vino, y tomé una espada en la mano y tres hombres conmigo, y fuíme por esa isla adelante, porque ninguno osaba ir á buscar de comer para el Almirante y los que con él estaban : y plugo á Dios que hallaba la gente tan mansa que no me hacian mal, antes se holgaban conmigo y me daban de comer de buena voluntad. Y en un pueblo que se llama Aguacadiba, concerté con los Indios y Cacique que harian pan cazabe, y que cazarian y pescarian, y que darian de todas las vituallas al Almirante cierta cuantía cada dia, y lo llevarian á las naos, con que estuviese allí persona que ge lo pagase en cuentas azules y peines y cuchillos y cascabeles y anzuelos y otros rescates que para ello llevabamos : y con este concierto despaché uno de los

Spaniards whom I had brought with me to the admiral, in
order that he might send a person to pay for the provisions,
and secure their being sent. From thence I went to another
village, at three leagues distance from the former, and made
a similar agreement with the natives and their cacique, and
then despatched another Spaniard to the admiral, begging him
to send another person with a similar object to this village.
After this I went further on, and came to a great cacique
named Huareo, living in a place which is now called Melilla,
thirteen leagues from where the ships lay. I was very well
received by him; he gave me plenty to eat, and ordered all
his subjects to bring together in the course of three days a
great quantity of provisions, which they did, and laid them
before him, whereupon I paid him for them to his full satisfaction. I stipulated with him that they should furnish a
constant supply, and engaged that there should be a person
appointed to pay them; having made this arrangement I sent
the other Spaniard to the admiral with the provisions they
had given me, and then begged the cacique to allow me two
Indians to go with me to the extremity of the island, one to

---

dos cristianos que conmigo traía al Almirante, para que enviase
persona que tuviese cargo de pagar aquellas vituallas y enviarlas.

Y de allí fuí á otro pueblo que estaba tres leguas de este y hice
el mismo concierto con el Cacique y Indios de él, y envié otro
cristiano al Almirante para que enviase allí otra persona al mismo
cargo.

Y de allí pasé adelante y llegué á un gran Cacique que se llamaba Huareo, donde agora dicen Melilla, que es trece leguas de las
naos, del cual fuí muy bien recebido, que me dió muy bien de comer, y mandó que todos sus vasallos trajiesen dende á tres dias
muchas vituallas, que le presentaron, é yo ge las pagué de manera
que fueron contentos : y concerté que ordinariamente las traerian,
habiendo allí persona que ge las pagase, y con este concierto envié
el otro cristiano con los mantenimientos que allá me dieron al
Almirante, y pedí al Cacique que me diese dos Indios que fuesen
conmigo fasta el cabo de la isla, que el uno me llevaba la hamaca

carry the hammock in which I slept, and the other carrying the food.

In this manner I journeyed eastward to the end of the island, and came to a cacique who was named Ameyro, with whom I entered into close friendship. I gave him my name and took his, which amongst these people is regarded as an evidence of brotherly attachment. I bought of him a very good canoe, and gave him in exchange an excellent brass helmet that I carried in a bag, a frock, and one of the two shirts that I had with me; I then put out to sea in this canoe, in search of the place that I had left, the cacique having given me six Indians to assist in guiding the canoe. When I reached the spot to which I had dispatched the provisions, I found there the Spaniards whom the admiral had sent, and I loaded them with the victuals that I had brought with me, and went myself to the admiral, who gave me a very cordial reception. He was not satisfied with seeing and embracing me, but asked me respecting everything that had occurred in the voyage, and offered up thanks to God for having delivered me in safety from so barbarous a people. The men rejoiced

---

en que dormia é el otro la comida. Y desta manera camine hasta el cabo de la isla, á la parte del Oriente, y llegué á un Cacique que se llamaba Ameyro, é hice con él amistades de hermandad, y díle mi nombre y tomé el suyo, que entre ellos se tiene por grande hermandad. Y compréle una canoa muy buena que él tenia, y díle por ella una bacineta de laton muy buena que llevaba en la manga y el sayo y una camisa de dos que llevaba, y embarquéme en aquella canoa, y vine por la mar requiriendo las estancias que habia dejado con seis Indios que el Cacique me dió para que me la ayudasen á navegar, y venido á los lugares donde yo habia proveido, hallé en ellos los cristianos que el Almirante habia enviado, y cargué de todas las vituallas que les hallé, y fuime al Almirante, del cual fuí muy bien recebido, que no se hartaba de verme y abrazarme, y preguntar lo que me habia sucedido en el viage, dando gracias á Dios que me habia llevado y traido á salvamiento libre de tanta gente salvage. Y como el tiempo que yo llegué á las naos no

greatly at my arrival, for there was not a loaf left in the ships
when I returned to them with the means of allaying their
hunger; this, and every day after that, the Indians came to
the ships loaded with provisions from the places where I had
made the agreements; so that there was enough for the two
hundred and thirty people who were with the admiral.   Ten
days after this, the admiral called me aside, and spoke to me
of the great peril he was in, addressing me as follows:—
"Diego Mendez, my son, not one of those whom I have here
with me, has any idea of the great danger in which we stand,
except myself and you; for we are but few in number, and
these wild Indians are numerous and very fickle and capri-
cious: and whenever they may take it into their heads to come
and burn us in our two ships, which we have made into straw-
thatched cabins, they may easily do so by setting fire to them
on the land side, and so destroy us all.   The arrangement
that you have made with them for the supply of food, to which
they agreed with such good-will, may soon prove disagree-
able to them; and it would not be surprising if, on the morrow, they were not to bring us anything at all: in such case

---

habia en ellas un pan que comer, fueron todos muy alegres con mi
venida, porque les maté la hambre en tiempo de tanta necesidad, y
de allí adelante cada dia venian los Indios cargados de vituallas á
las naos de aquellos lugares que yo habia concertado, que bastaban
para doscientas y treinta personas que estaban con el Almirante.
Dende á diez dias el Almirante me llamó á parte y me dijo el gran
peligro en que estaba, deciéndome ansi : "Diego Mendez, hijo :
ninguno de cuantos aquí yo tengo siente el gran peligro en que
estamos sino yo y vos, porque somos muy poquitos, y estos indios
salvages son muchos y muy mudables y antojadizos, y en la hora
que se les antojare de venir y quemarnos aquí donde estamos en
estos dos navios hechos casas pajizas, fácilmente pueden echar
fuego dende tierra y abrasarnos aquí á todos : y el concierto que
vos habeis hecho con ellos del traer los mantenimientos que traen
de tan buena gana, mañana se les antojará otra cosa y no nos traerán
nada, y nosotros no somos parte para tomargelo por fuerza si no

we are not in a position to take it by main force, but shall be compelled to accede to their terms. I have thought of a remedy, if you consider it advisable; which is, that some one should go out in the canoe that you have purchased, and make his way in it to Española, to purchase a vessel with which we may escape from the extremely dangerous position in which we now are. Tell me your opinion." To which I answered:—" My lord, I distinctly see the danger in which we stand, which is much greater than would be readily imagined. With respect to the passage from this island to Española in so small a vessel as a canoe, I look upon it not merely as difficult, but impossible; for I know not who would venture to encounter so terrific a danger as to cross a gulf of forty leagues of sea, and amongst islands where the sea is most impetuous, and scarcely ever at rest." His lordship did not agree with the opinion that I expressed, but adduced strong arguments to show that I was the person to undertake the enterprise. To which I replied:—" My lord, I have many times put my life in danger to save yours, and the lives of all those who are with you, and God has marvellously preserved me : in consequence of this, there have not been wanting murmur-

---

estar á lo que ellos quisieren. Yo he pensado un remedio si á vos os parece : que en esta canoa que comprastes se aventurase alguno á pasar á la Isla Española á comprar una nao en que pudiesen salir de tan gran peligro como este en que estamos. Decidme vuestro parecer." Yo le respondi : " Señor : el peligro en que estamos bien lo veo, que es muy mayor de lo que se puede pensar. El pasar desta Isla á la Isla Española en tan poca vasija como es la canoa, no solamente lo tengo por dificultoso, sino por imposible : porque haber de atravesar un golfo de cuarenta leguas de mar y entre islas donde la mar es mas impetuosa y de menos reposo, no sé quien se ose aventurar á peligro tan notorio. Su Señoría no me replicó, persuadiendome reciamente que yo era el que lo habia de hacer, á lo cual yo respondí : " Señor : muchas veces he puesto mi vida á peligro de muerte por salvar la vuestra y de todos estos que aqui estan, y nuestro Señor milagrosamente me ha guardado y

ers who have said that your lordship entrusts every honourable undertaking to me, while there are others amongst them who would perform them as well as I. My opinion is, therefore, that your lordship would do well to summon all the men, and lay this business before them, to see if, amongst them all, there is one who will volunteer to undertake it, which I certainly doubt; and if all refuse, I will risk my life in your service, as I have done many times already."

On the following day his lordship caused all the men to appear together before him, and then opened the matter to them in the same manner as he had done to me. When they heard it they were all silent, until some said that it was out of the question to speak of such a thing; for it was impossible, in so small a craft, to cross a boisterous and perilous gulf of forty leagues' breadth, and to pass between those two islands, where very strong vessels had been lost in going to make discoveries, not being able to encounter the force and fury of the currents. I then arose, and said:—" My lord, I have but one life, and I am willing to hazard it in the service

---

la vida ; y con todo no han faltado murmuradores que dicen que vuestra Señoria me acomete á mí todas las cosas de honra, habiendo en la compañía otros que las harian tan bien como yo : y por tanto paréceme á mí que vuestra Señoría los haga llamar á todos y los proponga este negocio, para ver si entre todos ellos habrá alguno que lo quiera emprender, lo cual yo dudo ; y euando todos se echen de fuera, yo pondré mi vida á muerte por vuestro servicio, como muchas veces lo he hecho.

Luego el dia siguiente su Señoría los hizo juntar á todos delante sí, y les propuso el negocio de la manera que á mí : é oido, todos enmudecieron, y algunos dijeron que era por demas platicarse en semejante cosa, porque era imposible en tan pequeña vasija pasar tan impetuoso y peligroso golfo de cuarenta leguas como este, entre estas dos islas donde muy recias naos se habian perdido andando á descubrir, sin poder romper ni forzar el ímpetu y furia de las corrientes. Entonces yo me levanté y dije : " Señor : una vida téngo no mas, yo la quiero aventurar por servicio de vuestra

of your lordship, and for the welfare of all those who are here
with us; for I trust in God, that in consideration of the motive which actuates me, he will give me deliverance, as he has
already done on many other occasions." When the admiral
heard my determination, he arose and embraced me, and,
kissing me on the cheek, said,—"Well did I know that there
was no one here but yourself, who would dare to undertake
this enterprise: I trust in God, our Lord, that you will come
out of it victoriously, as you have done in the others which
you have undertaken." On the following day I drew my
canoe on to the shore, fixed a false keel on it, and pitched and
greased it; I then nailed some boards upon the poop and
prow, to prevent the sea from coming in, as it was liable to
do from the lowness of the gunwales; I also fixed a mast in it,
set up a sail, and laid in the necessary provisions for myself,
one Spaniard, and six Indians, making eight in all, which was
as many as the canoe would hold. I then bade farewell to
his lordship, and all the others, and proceeded along the coast
of Jamaica, up to the extremity of the island,[12] which was

Señoría y por el bien de todos los que aquí estan, porque tengo
esperanza en Dios nuestro Señor que vista la intencion con que yo
lo hago me librará, como otras muchas veces lo ha hecho." Oida
por el Almirante mi determinacion levantóse y abrazóme y besóme
en el carrillo, diciendo: "Bien sabia yo que no habia aquí ninguno
que osase tomar esta empresa sino vos: esperanza tengo en Dios
nuestro Señor saldreis della con vitoria como de las otras que habeis
emprendido."

El dia siguiente yo puse mi canoa á monte, y le eché una quilla
postiza, y le dí su brea y sebo, y en la popa y proa clavéle algunas
tablas para defensa de la mar que no se me entrase como hiciera
siendo rasa; y púsele un mástil y su vela, y metí los mantenimientos que pude para mí y para un cristiano y para seis indios, que
éramos ocho personas, y no cabian mas en la canoa: y despedíme
de su Señoría y de todos, y fuime la costa arriba de la Isla de

12 Ferdinand Columbus says that the Indians called this eastern point
of the island Aramaquique, and that it was thirty-four leagues from Maima,
where the admiral was.

thirty-five leagues from the point whence we started. Even
this distance was not traversed without considerable toil and
danger; for on the passage I was taken prisoner by some
Indian pirates, from whom God delivered me in a marvellous
manner. When we had reached the end of the island, and
were remaining there in the hope of the sea becoming sufficiently calm to allow us to continue our voyage across it,
many of the natives collected together with the determination
of killing me, and seizing the canoe with its contents, and they
cast lots for my life, to see which of them should carry their
design into execution.

As soon as I became aware of their project, I betook myself secretly to my canoe, which I had left at three leagues
distance from where I then was, and set sail for the spot
where the admiral was staying, and reached it after an interval of fifteen days from my departure. I related to him all
that had happened, and how God had miraculously rescued
me from the hands of those savages. His lordship was very
joyful at my arrival, and asked me if I would recommence
my voyage; I replied that I would, if I might be allowed to
take some men, to be with me at the extremity of the island

Jamaica, donde estábamos, que hay dende las naos hasta el cabo
della treinta y cinco leguas, las cuales yo navegué con gran peligro
y trabajo, porque fuí preso en el camino de Indios salteadores en
la mar, de que Dios me libró milagrosamente. Y llegado al cabo
de la isla, estando esperando que la mar se amansase para acometer
mi viage, juntáronse muchos Indios y determinaron de matarme y
tomar la canoa y lo que en ella llevaba ; y así juntos jugaron mi
vida á la pelota para ver á cual dellos cabria la ejecucion del
negocio. Lo cual sentido por mí víneme ascondidamente á mi
canoa, que tenia tres leguas de allí, y hícime á la vela y víneme
donde estaba el Almirante, habiendo quince dias que de allí habia
partido : y contele todo lo sucedido, y cómo Dios milagrosamente
me habia librado de las manos de aquellos salvages. Su Señoría
fue muy alegre de mi venida, y preguntóme si volveria al viage.
Yo dije que sí, llevando gente que estuviese conmigo en el cabo de

until I should find a fair opportunity of putting to sea to pro-
secute my voyage. The admiral gave me seventy men, and
with them his brother the Adelantado, to stay with me until
I put to sea, and to remain there for three days after my departure; with this arrangement I returned to the extremity
of the island and waited there four days. Finding the sea
become calm I parted from the rest of the men with much
mutual sorrow; I then commended myself to God and our
Lady of Antigua, and was at sea five days and four nights
without laying down the oar from my hand, but continued
steering the canoe while my companions rowed. It pleased
God that at the end of five days I reached the island of
Española at Cape San Miguel,[13] having been two days without eating or drinking, for our provisions were exhausted. I
brought my canoe up to a very beautiful part of the coast, to
which many of the natives soon came, and brought with them
many articles of food, so that I remained there two days to
take rest. I took six Indians from this place, and leaving those
that I had brought with me, I put off to sea again, moving

---

la isla hasta que yo entrase en la mar á proseguir mi viage. Su
Señoría me dió setenta hombres y con ellos á su hermano le Adelantado, que fuesen y estuviesen conmigo hasta embarcarme, y tres
dias despues. Y desta manera volví al cabo de la isla donde estuve
cuatro dias. Viendo que la mar se amansaba me despedí dellos y
ellos de mí, con hartas lágrimas; y encomendéme á Dios y á
nuestra Señora del Antigua, y navegué cinco dias y cuatro noches
que jamas perdí el remo de la mano gobernando la canoa y los
compañeros remando. Plugo á Dios nuestro Señor que en cabo de
cinco dias yo arribé á la Isla Española, al Cabo de S. Miguel,
habiendo dos dias que no comiamos ni bebiamos por no tenello ; y
entré con mi canoa en una ribera muy hermosa, donde luego vino
mucha gente de la tierra y trajeron muchas cosas de comer, y estuve
allí dos dias descansando. Yo tomé seis Indios de allí, dejados los

---

[13] This cape is since called Cape Tiburon. Mendez does not speak of
his arrival at the little island of Naraza, and other places spoken of by
Ferdinand Columbus and Herrera.

along the coast of Española, for it was a hundred and thirty
leagues from the spot where I landed to the city of St. Domingo, where the Governor dwelt, who was the commander
of Lares.   When I had proceeded eighty leagues along the
coast of the island (not without great toil and danger, for that
part of the island was not yet brought into subjugation), I
reached the province of Azoa, which is twenty-four leagues
from San Domingo, and there I learned from the commander
Gallego, that the governor was gone out to subdue the province of Xuragoa, which was at fifty leagues distance. When
I heard this I left my canoe and took the road for Xuragoa,[14]
where I found the governor, who kept me with him seven
months, until he had burned and hanged eighty-four caciques,
lords of vassals, and with them Nacaona, the sovereign mistress of the island, to whom all rendered service and obe-
dience.   When that expedition was finished I went on foot
to San Domingo, a distance of seventy leagues, and waited in
expectation of the arrival of ships from Spain, it being now
more than a year since any had come.   In this interval it

que llevaba, y comencé á navegar por la costa de la Isla Española,
que hay dende allí hasta la Cibdad de Santo Domingo ciento y
treinta leguas que yo habia de andar, porque estaba allí el Gobernador, que era el Comendador de Lares ; y habiendo andado por la
costa de la isla ochenta leguas, no sin grandes peligros y trabajos,
porque la isla no estaba conquistada ni allanada, llegué á la Provincia de Azoa, que es veinte y cuatro leguas antes de Santo Domingo, y allí supe del Comendador Gallego como el Gobernador
era partido á la Provincia de Xuragoa á allanarla ; la cual estaba
cincuenta leguas de allí.   Y esto sabido dejé mi canoa y tomé el
camino por tierra de Xuragoa, donde hallé el Gobernador, el cual
me detuvo allí siete meses hasta que hizo quemar y ahorcar ochenta
y cuatro Caciques, señores de vasallos, ycon ellos á Nacaona la
mayor señora de la isla, á quien todos ellos obedecian y servian.
Y esto acabado vine de pie á tierra de Santo Domingo, que era
setenta leguas de allí, y estuve esperando que viniesen naos de

[14] This should be Xaragua.

pleased God that three ships arrived, one of which I bought, and loaded it with provisions, bread, wine, meat, hogs, sheep, and fruit, and despatched it to the place where the admiral was staying, in order that he might come over in it with all his people to San Domingo, and from thence sail for Spain. I myself went on in advance with the two other ships, in order to give an account to the king and queen of all that had occurred in this voyage.

I think I should now do well to say somewhat of the events which occurred to the admiral and to his family during the year that they were left on the island. A few days after my departure the Indians became refractory, and refused to bring food as they had hitherto done; the admiral therefore caused all the caciques to be summoned, and expressed to them his surprise that they should not send food as they were wont to do, knowing as they did, and as he had already told them, that he had come there by the command of God. He said that he perceived that God was angry with them, and that He would that very night give tokens of His displeasure by signs that He would cause to appear in the

---

Castilla, que habia mas de un año que no habian venido. Y en este comedio plugo á Dios que vinieron tres naos, de las cuales yo compré la una y la cargué de vituallas, de pan y vino y carne y puercos y carneros y frutas, y la envié adonde estaba el Almirante para en que viniesen él y toda la gente como vinieron allí á Santo Domingo y de allí á Castilla E yo me vine delante en las otras dos naos á hacer relacion al Rey y á la Reina de todo lo sucedido en aquel viage.

Pareceme que será bien que se diga algo de lo acaecido al Almirante y á su familiar en un año que estuvieron perdidos en aquesta isla : y es que dende á pocos dias que yo me partí los Indios se amotinaron y no le querian traer de comer como antes ; y él los hizo llamar á todos los Caciques y les digo que se maravillaba dellos en no traerle la comida como solian, sabiendo como él les habia dicho, que habia venido allí por mandado de Dios, y que Dios estaba enojado dellos, y que él ge lo mostraria aquella noche por

heavens; and as on that night there was to be an almost total
eclipse of the moon, he told them that God caused that appearance, to signify His anger against them for not bringing the
food.   The Indians, believing him, were very frightened, and
promised that they would always bring him food in future;
and so in fact they did, until the arrival of the ship which I
had sent loaded with provisions.   The Admiral, and those who
were with him, felt no small joy at the arrival of this ship;
and his lordship afterwards informed me in Spain, that in no
part of his life did he ever experience so joyful a day, for he
had never hoped to have left that place alive: and in that
same ship he set sail,[15] and went to San Domingo, and thence
to Spain.

I have wished thus to give a succinct account of my troubles, and of my great and important services; which are such
as no man in the world ever rendered to a master, or ever
will again; and I do so in order that my sons may know these
facts, and be encouraged to serve faithfully, and that, at the
same time, his lordship may see that he is bound to make
them a handsome return for such services.   When his lord-

---

señales que haria en el cielo ; y como aquella noche era el eclipse
de la luna que casi toda se escureció, díjoles que Dios hacia aquello
por enojo que tenia dellos porque no le traian de comer, y ellos lo
creyeron y fueron muy espantados, y prometieron que le traerian
siempre de comer, como de hecho lo hicieron, hasta que llegó la
nao con los mantenimientos que yo envié, de que no pequeño gozo
fue en el Almirante y en todos los que con él estaban : que despues
en Castilla me dijo su Señoría que en toda su vida [nunca ?] habia
visto tan alegre dia, y que nunca pensó salir de allí vivo : y en
esta nao se embarcó y vino á Santo Domingo y de alli á Castilla.

He querido poner aqui esta breve suma de mis trabajos y grandes
y señalados servicios, cuales nunca hizo hombre á Señor, ni los
hará de aquí adelante del mundo ; y esto á fin que mis hijos lo

[15] On the twenty-eighth of June 1504 ; he entered the harbour of St.
Domingo on the thirteenth of August, started for Spain on the twelfth
of September, and arrived at San Lucar on Thursday, the seventh of November.

ship came to the court, and while he was at Salamanca, confined to his bed with the gout, and I was left in sole charge
of his affairs, endeavouring to obtain the restitution of his
estate and government for his son Diego, I addressed him
thus: "My lord, your lordship knows how much I have done
in your service, and what trouble I am still taking, night and
day, in the management of your affairs; I beseech your lordship to grant me some recompense for what I have done." He
cheerfully replied that he would do for me whatever I asked,
adding, that there was very great reason for his so doing. I
then specified my wish, and begged his lordship to do me the
favour to grant me the office of principal Alguazil of the island
of Española for life; to which his lordship assented most cor-
dially, saying, that it was but a trifling remuneration for the
great services I had rendered. He also desired me to communicate his wish to his son Diego, who was very glad to hear
of the favour his father had shown me in appointing me to the
said office; and said, that if his father gave it me with one hand,
he, for his part, gave it me with both hands. This promise

---

sepan y se animen á servir, é su Señoria sepa que es obligado á
hacerles muchas mercedes.

Venido su Señoría á la Corte, y estando en Salamanca en la cama
enfermo de gota, andando yo solo entendiendo en sus negocios y en la
restitucion de su estado y de la gobernacion para su hijo D. Diego, yo
le dije ansi: "Señor: ya vuestra Señoría sabe lo mucho que os he
servido y lo mas que trabajo de noche y de dia en vuestros negocios:
suplico á vuestra Señoría' me señale algun galardon para en pago
dello": y él me respondió alegremente que yo lo señalase y él lo
cumpliria, porque era mucha razon. Y entonces yo le señalé y
suplique á su Señoría me hiciese merced del oficio del Alguacilazgo
mayor de la Isla Española para en toda mi vida: y su Señoría dijo que
de muy buena voluntad, y que era poco para lo mucho que yo habia
servido; y mandóme que lo dijese ansi al Sr. D. Diego, su hijo, el
cual fue muy alegre de la merced á mí hecha de dicho oficio, y dijo
que si su padre me lo daba con una mano, él con dos. Y esto es
ansi la verdad para el siglo que á ellos tiene y á mi espera.

holds good as much now as it did then; but when, after I had succeeded, with considerable difficulty, in securing the restitution of the government of the Indies to my lord the Admiral Don Diego, (his father being then dead), I asked him for the provision of the said office, his lordship replied that he had given it to his uncle, the Adelantado, saying, however, that he would give me another post equivalent to it. I told him that he ought to make such a proposition to his uncle, and that he ought to give me that which his father, and he himself, had promised to me. But he did not do so; and thus I remained without any recompense for all my services: while my lord, the Adelantado, without having rendered any service at all, continued in the enjoyment of the dignity which belonged to me, and reaped the reward of all my exertions.

When his lordship arrived at the city of San Domingo, he assumed the reins as governor, and gave the post which he had promised to me, to Francisco de Garay, a servant of the Adelantado, to hold it for him. This took place on the tenth day of July of the year fifteen hundred and ten, and the office was then worth at least a million per annum. My lady, the Vicequeen, as tutress and guardian of my lord the

---

Habiendo yo acabado, no sin grandes trabajos mios, de negociar la restitucion de la gobernacion de las Indias al Almirante D. Diego, mi Señor, siendo su padre fallecido, le pedi la provision del dicho oficio. Su Señoria me respondió que lo tenia dado al Adelantado su tio; pero que él me daria otra cosa equivalente á aquella. Yo dije que aquella diese él á su tio, y á mi me diese lo que su padre y él me habian prometido, lo cual no se hizo; y yo quedé cargado de servicios sin ningun galardon, y el Sr. Adelantado, sin haberlo servido, quedó con mi oficio y con el galardon de todos mis afanes.

Llegado su Señoría á la Cibdad de Santo Domingo por Gobernador tomó las varas y dió este oficio á Francisco dè Garay, criado del Sr. Adelantado, que lo sirviese por él. Esto fue en diez dias del mes de Julio de mil quinientos diez años. Valia entonces el oficio á lo menos un cuento de renta, del cual la Vireina, mi Se-

viceroy, and my lord the viceroy himself, are really charge-able to me for this loss, and are debtors to me for it in justice and on the score of conscience. The post had been given to me by way of recompense, and nothing has been done in my favour towards the accomplishment of the Admiral's promise, since the day in which it was given, to this, the close of my life; if it had been given to me, I should have been the richest and most honoured man in the island; whereas, I am now the poorest, and have not even a house of my own to live in, but am obliged to pay rent for the roof over my head. As it would be very difficult to refund the revenues which this office has produced, I will suggest an alternative, which is this: that his lordship grant the rank of principal Alguazil of the city of San Domingo, to one of my sons, for his life, and bestow upon the other the rank of Vice-Admiral in the same city: by the grant of these two offices to my sons in the manner I have said, and by appointing some one to hold them on their behalf until they come of age, his lordship will discharge the conscience of the Admiral his father, and I shall hold myself satisfied, as duly paid for my services. I shall say nothing

---

ñora, como tutriz y curadora del Virey, mi Señor y él me son en cargo realmente y me lo deben de justicia y de foro conscientiæ, porque me fue hecha la merced de él, y no se cumplió conmigo dende el dia que se dió al Adelantado hasta el postrero de mis dias, porque si se me diera yo fuera el mas rico hombre de la isla y mas honrado; y por no se me dar soy el mas pobre della, tanto que no tengo una casa en que more sin alquiler.

Y porque haberseme de pagar lo que el oficio ha rentado seria muy dificultoso, yo quiero dar un medio y será este: que su Se-ñoría haga merced del Alguacilazgo mayor de la Cibdad de Santo Domingo á uno de mis hijos para en toda su vida, y al otro le haga merced de su Teniente de Almirante en la dicha Cibdad: y con hacer merced destos dos oficios á mis hijos de la manera que he aquí dicho, y poniéndolos en cabeza de quien los serva por ellos hasta que sean de edad, su Señoría descargará la conciencia del Almirante su padre, y yo me satisfaré de la paga que se me debe

further upon the subject, but leave it to the consciences of their lordships, and let them do whatever they think proper.

Item.   I leave as executors and administrators of my will here at the court, the bachelor Estrada and Diego de Arana, together with my lady the Vicequeen; and I beg his lordship to undertake this charge, and to direct the others to undertake it likewise.

Another clause.   Item.   I order that my executors purchase a large stone, the best that they can find, and place it upon my grave, and that they write round the edge of it these words:
" Here lies the honourable Chevalier Diego Mendez, who rendered great services to the royal crown of Spain, in the discovery and conquest of the Indies, in company with the discoverer of them, the Admiral Don Christopher Columbus, of glorious memory, and afterwards rendered other great services by himself, with his own ships, and at his own cost.   He died, etc.   He asks of your charity a Paternoster and an Ave Maria."

Item.   In the middle of the said stone let there be the representation of a canoe, which is a hollowed tree, such as the

---

de mis servicios ; y en esto no diré mas de dejallo en sus conciencias de sus Señorías, y hagan en ello lo que mejor les pareciere.

Item : Dejo por mis albaceas y ejecutores deste mi testamento, aquí en la corte, al Bachiller Estrada y á Diego de Arana, juntamente con la Vireina, mi Señora, y suplico yo á su Señoría lo acepte y les mande á ellos lo mismo.

Otra cláusula.   Item : Mando que mis albaceas compren una piedra grande, la mejor que hallaren, y se ponga sobre mi sepultura, y se escriba en derredor della estas letras : " Aquí yace el honrado caballero Diego Mendez que sirvió mucho á la Corona Real de España en el descubrimiento y conquista de las Indias con el Almirante D. Cristobal Colon, de gloriosa memoria, que las descubrió, y despues por sí con naos suyas á su costa : falleció, &c.   Pido de limosna un Pater noster y una Ave María.

Item : En medio de la dicha piedra se haga una canoa, que es un madero cavado en que los Indios navegan, porque en otra tal

Indians use for navigation; for in such a vessel did I cross three hundred leagues of sea; and let them engrave above it this word : " Canoe."

My dear and beloved sons, children of my very dear and beloved wife Doña Francisca de Ribera,—may the blessing of God Almighty, Father, Son, and Holy Ghost, descend upon you, together with my blessing, and protect you, and make you Catholic Christians, and give you grace always to love and fear Him.   I earnestly recommend you to cultivate peace and concord amongst yourselves, and that you be meek, and not haughty, but, on the contrary, be very humble and courteous towards those with whom you have to do, so that all may love you.   Serve loyally my lord the Admiral, and may his lordship grant you large recompense, considering who he is himself, and by what great services I have deserved his favours. Above all I charge you, my sons, to be very pious, and to attend devoutly to your religious duties, and in so doing, may the Lord grant you long life.   May it please Him of His infinite goodness, to make you as good as I wish you to be, and guide you always with His hand.   Amen.

---

navegó trescientas leguas, y encima pongan unas letras que digan : " Canoa."

Caros y amados hijos mios, y de mi muy cara y amada muger Doña Francisca de Ribera, la bendicion de Dios Todopoderoso, Padre y Hijo y Espíritu Santo y la mia descienda sobre vos y vos cubra y os haga catolicos cristianos, y os dé gracia que siempre le ameis y temais.   Hijos : encomiendoos mucho la paz y concordia, y que seais muy conformes y no soberbios, sino muy humildes y muy amigables á todos los que contratáredes, porque todos os tengan amor : servid lealmente al Almirante mi Señor, y su Señoría os hará muchas mercedes por quien él es, y porque mis grandes servicios lo merecen ; y sobre todo os mando, hijos mios, seais muy devotos y oyais muy devotamente los Oficios Divinos, y haciéndolo ansi Dios nuestro Señor os dará largos dias de vida.   A él plega por su infinita bondad haceros tan buenos como yo deseo que seais, y os tenga siempre de su mano.   Amen.

The books which I send you are as follows :

The Art of Well-living, by Erasmus ; a *Sermon,* of Erasmus, in Spanish ; *Josephus de Bello Judaico ;* the *Moral Philosophy,* of Aristotle ; the books called *Lingua Erasmi;* the book of *The Holy Land ; The conversations of Erasmus ; A treatise on the Complaints of Peace; A book of Contemplation of the Passion of our Redeemer ; A treatise on the Revenging of the Death of Agamemnon ;* and other small tracts.

I have already told you, my sons, that I leave you these books under the conditions described above in my will, and I wish them to be put together with my other documents, which will be found in the cedar box, at Seville, as I have already said ; I wish also the marble mortar should be placed in it, which is now in the possession of Don Ferdinand, or of his major-domo.

I, Diego Mendez, affirm that this document, contained in thirteen sheets, is my last will and testament, for I have dictated it and caused it to be written, and have signed it with my name; and by it I revoke and annul any other

---

Los libros que de acá os envio son los siguientes :

Arte de bien morir de Erasmo. Un sermon de Erasmo en romance. Josefo de Bello Judaico. La Filosofía moral de Aristóteles. Los libros que se dicen Lingua Erasmi. El libro de la Tierra santa. Los coloquios de Erasmo. Un tratado de las querellas de la Paz. Un libro de Contemplaciones de la Pasion de nuestro Redentor. Un tratado de la venganza de la muerte de Agamemnon, y otros tratadillos.

Ya dije, hijos mios, que estos libros os dejo por mayorazgo, con las condiciones que estan dichas de suso en el testamento, y quiero que vayan todos con algunas Escrituras mias, que se hallarán en el arca que está en Sevilla, que es de cedro, como ya está dicho : pongan tambien en esta el mortero de mármol que está en poder del Sr. D. Hernando, ó de su mayordomo.

Digo yo Diego Mendez que esta Escritura contenida en trece hojas es mi testamento y postrimera voluntad, porque yo lo ordené é hice escribir, y lo firmé de mi nombre, y por él revoco y doy por

will or wills whatever made by me at any other time or place, and I desire that this only be considered valid. Made in the city of Valladolid, the nineteenth day of June, in the year of our Redeemer one thousand five hundred and thirty-six.— DIEGO MENDEZ. And I, the said Garcia de Vera, scrivener and notary public, was present at all which has been herein said; and it has all been set down by me by order of the said lord-lieutenant, and by request of the said Bachelor Estrada, forming the testament in these twenty-six leaves of folio paper, as is here seen. I caused it to be written as it was presented and laid before me, and have kept the original in my possession. And to this effect I have here placed this my seal *(here was placed the seal)*, in testimony of the truth.— *(Signed)* GARCIA DE VERA.

This agrees literally with the clauses copied from a will sealed and signed by the said scrivener, Garcia de Vera, the original of which is in the archives of the most excellent the Admiral Duke of Veraguas, from which I copied it in Madrid on the twenty-eighth day of March, in the year eighteen hundred and twenty-five.—Tomas Gonzalez.

---

ningunos otros cualesquier testamentos hechos en cualesquier otros tiempos ó lugar ; y solo este quiero que valga, que es hecho en la villa de Valladolid en diez y nueve dias del mes de Junio, año de nuestro Redentor de mil quinientos treinta y seis años. Diego Mendez. E yo el dicho García de Vera, Escribano Notario público, presente fui á todo lo que dicho es, que de mi se hace mencion, é por mandado del dicho Sr. Teniente é pedimento del dicho Bachiller Estrada, este testamento en estas veinte é seis hojas de papel, pliego entero, como aquí parece, fice escrebir como ante mí se presentó é abrió, é ansi queda originalmente en mi poder. E por ende fice aquí este mi signo tal en *(está signado)* testimonio de verdad. García de Vera. *(Está firmado.)*

Concuerda literalmente con las cláusulas copiadas de un testimonio signado y firmado por el expresado Escribano García de Vera, que obra originalmente en el Archivo del Excmo. Sr. Almirante Duque de Veraguas, de donde lo copié en Madrid á veinte y cinco dias del mes de Marzo de mil ochocientos veinte y cinco años. — Tomas Gonzalez.

Note.—The other clauses of this will of Diego Mendez, refer to his funeral arrangements, and the declaration of debts, due both to him and by him, in Spain and in the island of Hispaniola, as well as other matters purely personal, and relating to his family ; but they bear no reference or allusion to the Admiral Columbus, or to his voyages and discoveries, and therefore have not been copied.

FINIS.

INDEX.

JOHN E. FAGG was born in Texas, graduated from the University of Texas, and received his Ph.D. at the University of Chicago in 1942. Contributor to the official history of the Army Air Forces and author of various studies on Spain and Latin America, he has been at New York University, where presently he is Associate Professor of History, since 1946. He is finishing a general history of Latin America, scheduled for publication in 1962.